Freedom of Information In a Post 9-11 World

Edited by

Charles H. Sides
Fitchburg State College

Baywood's Technical Communications Series
Series Editor: CHARLES H. SIDES

Baywood Publishing Company, Inc.
AMITYVILLE, NEW YORK

Baywood Publishing Company, Inc.
26 Austin Avenue
P.O. Box 337
Amityville, NY 11701
(800) 638-7819
E-mail: baywood@baywood.com
Web site: baywood.com

Library of Congress Catalog Number: 2005045202
ISBN: 0-89503-302-X (cloth)

Library of Congress Cataloging-in-Publication Data

Freedom of information in a post 9-11 world / edited by Charles H. Sides.
    p. cm. -- (Baywood's technical communications series)
  Includes bibliographical references and index.
  ISBN 0-89503-302-X (cloth)
   1. Freedom of information. 2. Freedom of speech. 3. Information policy. 4. Academic freedom. 5. Science and state. 6. Research--International cooperation. 7. Communication of technical information. I. Sides, Charles H., 1952- II. Series.

JC598.F74 2005
323.44'5--dc22

                                                                    2005045202

Table of Contents

CHAPTER 7
The Open Society and Its Enemies: A Reappraisal

CHAPTER 8
9-11 Communicative Grammar

CHAPTER 9
Accessible Information and International Business

Editor's Note

Someone is sooner or later to comment regarding what appears to be a glaring omission to this collection, particularly given its title, thesis, and the events that led to its publication: the absence of a chapter that reflects viewpoints from the perspective of faculty at an Islamic university or other experts in science, technology, or business located in that part of the world. This omission is not the result of an oversight or intended slight. Rather, during the nearly three years it took to bring the wide-ranging chapters of this collection together, I contacted faculty and administrators at approximately a dozen highly regarded universities in what we typically think of as the Islamic world, some of whom I had worked with before on other publications prior to September 11, 2001, and invited them to participate in this project. As a result of that previous experience, I knew that at many of these institutions all communications are approved by the administration; in fact, in some of those prior instances my only contact was with administrators and not with the faculty who were directly responsible for their publications.

It is not that my invitations and entreaties were considered and politely refused. Instead, not a single communication was answered. That, in itself, may say more about freedom of information in a post-9-11 world than any chapter could have.

Charles H. Sides

Preface

In science, the value of a theory is determined by its predictive ability, its ability to explain and predict observable phenomena in ways that are consistent and useful. It is not a concept often associated with the liberal arts, and perhaps even less so with technical and professional communication. Nonetheless, the thesis of this collection of essays contributed by scholars from around the world—that the perception and application of the freedom to create, deliver, and receive information may evolve in ways unforeseen prior to September 11, 2001—does have predictive value. An early draft of the introductory chapter to this collection was delivered as a presentation to a system-wide conference on engineering communication, hosted by the State University of New York at Stony Brook in November 2002. That presentation concluded, as does the current chapter, by pointing out that future court decisions may alter the standards of free speech and free access to information.

On April 7, 2003, the United States Supreme Court, deeply divided though it was in a 5–4 decision, did precisely that in reversing the earlier precepts of *Brandenburg v. Ohio* and ruling that a burning cross is not protected speech but an act of terrorism. Justice Sandra Day O'Connor succinctly described what may very well become the future of First Amendment freedoms by saying that such freedoms "are not absolute."

Time alone will tell how accurate the authors of the following chapters will have been, for predicting the future in any discipline is always a risky endeavor. But suffice it to say: this collection has passed the first test of its predictive value.

CHAPTER 1

Freedom of Information in a Post 9-11 World: Introduction

Charles H. Sides

Congress shall make no law respecting an establishment of religion, or prohibiting the free exercise thereof; or abridging the freedom of speech, or of the press; or the right of the people to peaceably assemble, and to petition the Government for a redress of grievances.
— United States Constitution, First Amendment

No State shall make or enforce any law which shall abridge the privileges or immunities of the citizens of the United States; nor shall any State deprive any person of life, liberty, or property without due process of law; nor deny to any person within its jurisdiction the equal protection of the laws.
— United States Constitution, Fourteenth Amendment

The morning of September 11, 2001, has already achieved that status in history — similar to November 22, 1963 and July 20, 1969 — that if we were present, we remember specifically what we were doing. These watershed dates permit, maybe even compel us to take stock and evaluate our personal or professional value systems or, as is often the case, that inextricable middle ground where the personal and professional meet.

Note: D. Fraleigh and J. Truman, *Freedom of Speech in the Marketplace of Ideas,* St. Martin's Press, New York, 1997, provided a significant survey of the background to this chapter when it was first conceived as a speech to the SUNY Colloquium on Technical Communication, SUNY-Stony Brook, November 2001.

On September 11, 2001, I had seen my daughter off to high school and was preparing to write my quarterly editorial for the *Journal of Technical Writing and Communication,* which I edit. At approximately 8:45, I reached to turn off my radio, which was tuned to (I admit it) the "Imus in the Morning" program, and heard Warner Wolfe, the show's New York City-based sports reporter, call in to say that a plane had just hit one of the World Trade Center towers, near where he lives in Tribeca. Don Imus asked if it was a small, private plane, and when Warner Wolfe responded that, "No, it was a huge plane and there is fire and smoke everywhere," I did turn off the radio and opted for the television, where I sat transfixed for the next several hours.

In those hours and days that followed, one event in particular stood out to me as a writer, editor, and scholar in the technical communications discipline: in two locations, flight manuals for specific jet liners had been found in abandoned automobiles and motel rooms that were traced to several of the hijackers. It is those manuals which led to my call in the editorial I eventually wrote, challenging us to examine the implications of the free access to technical information, and that leads to a question this book addresses: "Is there ever a time when information is too accurate or too available?" Ancient Greeks used the concept of *kairos* to describe a ripe or exact or critical moment in time—a moment in which many disparate events come together and crystallize to provide unique opportunities for analysis. September 11, 2001, has been a vital moment of *kairos* in the technical communication discipline. Our analysis of that date, then, should focus on whether this single event will shape new arguments over the limits of free speech and free access to information, especially technical information.

This question is disarmingly complex because it goes to the core of our profession, as well as to the core of political systems which are founded upon freedoms of speech and access to information. My goal is to put forth a rubric for examining the question, as well as to posit directions governments might entertain in attempting to regulate speech and information that heretofore were considered relatively innocuous. To do this requires a careful look at the history of free speech and access to information, as well as fundamental arguments regarding these freedoms. It also involves differentiating between the evolution of the two.

HISTORY OF FREE SPEECH

From the beginning of recorded history approximately 5000 years ago, there has been trace evidence of a growing acknowledgment of speech rights. In the Sumerian civilization, in present-day southern Iraq, approximately 2400 BCE, the first surviving reference to freedom was recorded. Even though the freedom in mind was economic freedom, this document, written in cuneiform, establishes that the concept of freedom was already being examined and debated. A surviving record from Egypt in approximately 2000 BCE describes a dissenting oration the prophet Ipuwer delivered to his king, lamenting over conditions that could have been reported in yesterday's major newspapers: disregard of the law, inadequate treasury resources, and a diminished public safety. Some time later, speech rights were defined for Egyptians in the *Maxims of Ptahhotep:* "Worthy speech is more hidden than greenstone, being found even among the slave women at the millstone" [1].

During the first millennium BCE, extraordinary evidence of free speech rights—not equaled yet in some modern countries—began to emerge in several cultures, including Israel, Athens, Rome, and China. The Hebrew Bible is replete with examples of prophets reprimanding kings over their disregard of the people's rights. Importantly, the kings rarely punished such prophets, even if their preaching was deemed a threat to the government. Additionally, there is evidence—both from the Bible and from recovered letters written in the sixth and seventh centuries BCE—that the Hebrew people were also outspoken in dealing with their kings. However, none of this should be taken as support for such modern concepts as a freedom of conscience, for ancient Israel was a theocracy, and under such a governmental system it was unlikely that a comprehensive system of free expression would evolve.

In Athens, a right to freedom of speech, *parrhesia,* was recognized for citizens; for example, the governmental assembly was founded upon the right of citizens to speak out, and debates were begun by the herald's words: "What man has good advice to give to the *polis* and wishes to make it known?" [2]. But this right did not extend to women, slaves, or men who were not citizens. Moreover, there were clear examples of laws and customs that regulated speech. One of these was the threat of ostracism, by which a citizen could be banished from Athens for ten years. Protagoras incurred this punishment, as well as the burning of his book, by stating that "concerning the gods, I am unable to know either that they exist or do not exist" [3]. And of course, the most famous case was that of Socrates who was found guilty of speech which did not recognize the state-sanctioned gods, introduced new ones, and corrupted the young. He was sentenced to death. Furthermore, since the Athenian state had no equivalent to a bill of rights, citizens could impose restrictions on speech simply by exercising the existing democratic processes. As a result of this practice, for example, verbal abuse of the dead was prohibited, while verbal abuse of the living was prohibited only if it occurred in temples, courts, official buildings, and games.

In Rome, no equivalent of *parrhesia* existed for citizens; only persons in positions of authority had a right to free speech. Roman leaders as early as 450 BCE, however, restricted speech through the Laws of the Twelve Tables, displayed prominently in the Forum. Defamation was prohibited, as was magical incantation, and the punishment for both was death. Expulsion was also used to silence objectionable speakers; it was extended to teachers whose pronouncements were considered dangerous. There are records of book burning as well. While this was the status of Roman citizens, it did not extend to political debate in the Senate where senators would attack each other and state officials "by every device of invective language, sometimes with little basis of fact" [4]. Toward the end of the Republic, political invective was often printed in verse and song, as well as on placards known as *libelli*, from whence we derive the concept of libel. During the empire, however, speech rights were seriously curtailed, with writers, critics, and philosophers often executed.

In China, while there was not even a word for "rights," there is evidence from the time of Confucius concerning a tolerance for the expression of ideas. Much of the discourse revolved around debates on government, philosophy, and the idea of virtue with respect to leaders of the state. As that state evolved more and more toward theocratic notions of a monarch, rights of free expression were effectively stamped out.

Elsewhere in the Middle East, prior to the development of Islam, leaders were often elected as "first among equals" from tribes; governmental actions were mostly informal and democratic, with a certain amount of free expression assumed. This changed dramatically with the advent of Islam and the development of the *shari'a*, a divinely ordained legal system. Under that system, the state leader became the divine representative of Allah on earth, and any criticism of the government was viewed as heresy.

In Europe, following the fall of the Roman Empire, issues of free speech lay dormant for centuries. However, in Iceland in 930 CE, the Althing, an assembly of chieftains, was formed for the purpose of making laws. While only chieftains could vote, the assembly was held outdoors and there is evidence that observers participated freely in the discussion of issues. Elsewhere in Europe, the power of the monarchy had developed to such an extent that free speech was often risky.

In England, for example, the *Magna Carta*, signed under duress by King John at Runnymede in 1215, granted free men such rights as trial by their peers, but it did not specifically grant rights to either free expression or free access to information. It did, however, set an important precedent for the development of such rights by establishing that free people can create, through law, rights that even a king may not take away. With regard to speech rights, though, this experience did not stop either kings or parliaments from trying. In 1275, Parliament outlawed "false news or tales by which discord or slander may grow between the king and his people" [5]. A century later, this statute was re-enacted, providing for punishment to be administered by the king's council, sitting in the Star Chamber. These secret proceedings established the king's prerogatives in council to use torture in order to extract confessions of wrong doing. Along these same lines, the Treason Act of 1351 includes in its definition of treason even imagining "the death of our lord the King or of our lady his Queen, or of their eldest son and heir" [6], thereby establishing, perhaps, the first recorded incidence of what we would later come to call "thought police."

Two centuries later, under the rule of Henry VIII in 1539, the "Bloody Statute" was passed by Parliament and made the denial of the doctrine of transubstantiation punishable by burning at the stake, thereby elevating this doctrine to the official faith of the Church of England. His daughter, Elizabeth I, punished Jesuits and other priests who sought converts to Catholicism with death on the grounds that their attempted conversions were equivalent to treason. She also imprisoned Peter Wentworth for having the audacity even to speak out in public, advocating free speech. When the English Bill of Rights was finally passed in 1689, it granted free speech rights only to members of Parliament.

Freedom of the press was also severely restricted in England. When printing arrived in England in 1450, new laws were soon enacted to deal with the threat of an expanding ability to communicate ideas. These laws included Henry VIII's 1529 list of prohibited books, which included books by Martin Luther and other heretics, as well as any book that reproached, rebuked, or slandered the king and his honorable council. Under the Proclamation of 1538, all books printed in England were subject to a licensing system, the prerogative of which lay solely with the king.

Given all this as a background, it probably stands to reason that English courts would establish four categories of speech that could be punished as libel. These included: seditious libel, or unfavorable speech about the government; obscene libel; blasphemy; and private libel. English rulers believed that they could not remain in power if they were subject to criticism. Chief Justice John Holt explained this in 1704:

> If people should not be called to account for possessing the people with an ill opinion of the government, no government can subsist. For it is very necessary for all governments that people should have a good opinion of it [7].

This law was so broad that any speech which brought the government into disrepute could be punished, even if the criticism of the government was justified. Truth only made the libel worse. Moreover, penalties for violating the laws against seditious libel were particularly severe. William Twyn published a book in 1663 that endorsed the right to revolution; for that expression of speech he was hanged, emasculated, disemboweled, quartered, and beheaded [8]. In 1793, illustrating an increasingly benefi-cent approach to punishment, John Frost was only disbarred, pilloried, and jailed for stating that he "supported equality, no king, and a better constitution" [9].

Obscene libel, interestingly enough, was not punished by the British government early on, so bawdy books were printed with impunity. In 1727, this changed when Chief Justice Robert Raymond ruled that obscenity could be punished as a criminal offense, agreeing with the argument that "it tends to corrupt the morals of the King's subjects, and is thus against the peace of the King" [10]. British treatment of obscenity established precedent in the laws of England and the United States for hundreds of years, with obscenity generally defined as the following:

> . . . the test of obscenity is this, whether the tendency of the matter charged is to deprave and corrupt those whose minds are open to such immoral influences, and into whose hands a publication of this sort might fall [11].

Because Christian doctrine had been protected by British Common Law for over 250 years, it is only natural that blasphemy would become a category of criminal libel. Speech denying God's existence, reproaching Jesus Christ, or bringing any doctrine of Christian religion into disbelief or ridicule was forbidden. As a result, the publisher of Thomas Paine's *The Age of Reason* was convicted of blasphemy because the book contained a passage which maintained that the savage conduct of persons in the Old Testament had brutalized and corrupted mankind. Statements of this sort were seen not only as offenses against God but crimes against the laws of the land, because they broke the bonds that bound a civil society together.

The final category of prohibited speech, private libel, included speech that attacked the reputation of another person. This was an ancient concept, as 1000 years ago Anglo-Saxon law provided that any person who insulted another person could have his tongue cut out.

As British subjects colonized America, they brought with them their ideas and experiences regarding freedoms of speech and access to infor-mation. The development of those freedoms over the past 400 years has been neither easy nor straight-forward. For example, one scholar describes Colonial America as "an open society dotted with closed enclaves [into which] one could settle with his co-believers in safety and comfort and exercise the right of oppression" [12]. Interestingly enough, the early settlers of the Northeast found rudimentary aspects of free expression which must have seemed as exotic to them, given their own history, as did the aboriginal inhabitants who exercised those freedoms. The Kaianerekowa, or Great Law of Peace, had established the Iroquois Confederation by achieving peace among the Seneca, Onondaga, Oneida, Mohawk, and Cayuga tribes; it also required chiefs to tolerate the criticism of their people:

> The chiefs of the League of Five Nations shall be mentors of the people for all time. The thickness of their skins shall be seven spans, which is to say that they shall be proof against anger, offensive action, and criticism [13].

By contrast, early English settlers brought with them much less tolerant traditions. Governor Dale's Code, established in Virginia in 1610, imposed the death penalty for speaking against the articles of the Christian faith and called for severe punishment of persons convicted of taking the Lord's name in vain [14]. Persons who spoke out against the governor were often subjected to equally severe punishments, including having their arms broken and having an awl driven through their tongues.

The Puritans of New England, seeking to recreate the City of God through religion, hard work, and poverty, published and adopted the *Body of Liberties* in 1641, which included the right to be executed for adultery, along with surprisingly progressive rights as well, such as a prohibition against wife-beating [15]. Among these liberties was the right to choose magistrates; however, the thus-elected government retained powers more akin to those of ancient sacred monarchs. John Winthrop, founder of the Massachusetts Bay Colony, recorded in his journal that a petition to have a magisterial order repealed "savors of resisting an order of God" [16, p. 64]. The journal also records examples of speech suppression. Philip Ratcliff was whipped, had his ears cut off, and was banished from the colony for uttering "most foul, scandalous invectives against churches and government" [16, p. 67]. Henry Linne was whipped and banished for writing letters to England that slandered colonial administration [16, p. 144].

But there were glimmers of an emerging concept of free expression, even in the earliest colonial settlements, particularly in Rhode Island, Maryland, and among the Quakers. The Rhode Island charter, in 1663, provided that persons in the colony could not be punished for differences of opinion in religious matters, unless those differences disturbed the civil peace. It is probably not surprising, therefore, that many of the persons banished from Massachusetts eventually found themselves as colonial leaders in Rhode Island. The Maryland Act of Toleration, passed in 1649, gave rights to Christians by ensuring that anyone who professed a belief in Jesus Christ should not be troubled because of his or her religion or the "free exercise thereof" [17]. But perhaps most significantly, in terms of serving as a harbinger for future free expression developments, was the Quaker's creative use of symbolic speech to protest what they saw as Puritan abuses. This included appearing naked in public streets and in Puritan churches to symbolize the spiritual nakedness of the Congregationalist church, expressions for which the protestors were often hanged.

While religious speech was not truly free in America's colonies in the seventeenth century, one clear trend was developing—a greater tolerance for criticism of the government [18].

Nonetheless, sedition and governmental action against what was perceived as seditious speech remained a threat to the growth of free speech rights—particularly with respect to the printed word. The trial of John Peter Zenger was telling in the attempts of colonists to assert their rights to freedom of expression. Zenger, publisher of the *New York Weekly Journal*, was jailed for printing seditious libels that purportedly inculcated in the minds of the people a contempt for the king's governance, especially as it was administered by Governor William Cosby. Zenger, in his trial, was defended by 80-year-old Andrew Hamilton of Philadelphia, one of the most respected lawyers in the colonies, who argued that Zenger's claims were among those that any free subject of the crown had a right to make. Zenger's defense rested on Hamilton's argument that the jury could find Zenger guilty only if the information he had published could be proven to be false. At the time, truth was not an accepted defense against charges of seditious speech. The jury found Zenger not guilty; the citizens in the crowded courtroom responded with three loud huzzas; and all treated Hamilton to a dinner at the Black Horse Tavern. Yet, no legal precedent had been established in this case; the jury simply chose to ignore the law.

Colonial legislatures also participated in attempts to regulate expression, claiming this prerogative based on its existence in British Parliament. In Boston, James Franklin ran afoul of this practice by printing in his *New England Courant* in 1722 that the colonial government of Massachusetts would pursue a band of pirates "sometime this Month, if the Wind and Weather permit" [19]. As a result he was imprisoned, but during his imprisonment the paper continued to be printed by his 16-year-old brother, Benjamin, who avoided directly criticizing the government, but who nonetheless published the following which would become ever more important as a point of discussion as the century unfolded:

> In those wretched countries where a man cannot call his tongue
> his own, he can scarce call anything his own. Whoever would over-
> throw the liberty of a nation must begin by subduing the freedom
> of speech [20].

Years later, following the success of the American Revolution, the citizens found themselves in 1787 discussing precisely these and other matters as they set about establishing the form of self-government for which they had fought. Interestingly enough, however, the United States Constitution, as first drafted, contained no bill of rights; rather, it was a document that prescribed the operation and maintenance of the new country. In fact, Pennsylvania delegate James Wilson is recorded as observing that many of his colleagues never gave thought to the need for such specific guarantees of rights and freedoms [21]. George Mason, however, was troubled by the omission and volunteered to compose a bill of rights that would be appended to the constitution. His attempts to have this passed by the convention failed on two separate occasions. As a result, the constitution was sent to the states for ratification without any specific guarantees of individual freedoms, leading to the well-documented debates between federalist and anti-federalist camps over the issue of whether the national government or state governments would predominate; in other words, whether the newly formed country would be a confederacy of sovereign states founded on a respect for individual rights or a union of states under an over-arching and powerful national government. Finally, two years later, in 1789, the constitution was ratified, with the promise that a bill of rights would be added. In the House of Representatives, James Madison maintained that freedom of expression was the most valuable of the amendments being debated; it was finally included fourth in a list of 17, in the following form:

> The freedom of speech, and of the press, and the right of the people to
> assemble, and consult for the common good, and to apply to the
> government for redress of grievances, shall not be infringed [22].

The Senate, in considering the House version and in taking into account opponents of the Constitution who believed that it placed too many limits upon states, changed the language to read: "Congress shall make no law abridging the freedom of speech, or of the press, . . ." [22, p. 19]. As a result, for well over 100 years and through a civil war fought over such issues, nothing stood in the way of states' attempts to abridge freedoms of expression—with grave consequences for speakers of unpopular views—until the passage of the Fourteenth Amendment, guaranteeing equal protection under the law. Despite this, scholars have consistently suggested that:

> The First Amendment was written by men who intended to wipe out the common law of sedition, and make further prosecution for criticism of the government, without incitement to law-breaking, forever impossible in the United States of America [23, p. 21].

This good will that emanated from freedoms newly won did not last. In 1798, less than ten years after the ratification of the Constitution and the Bill of Rights, in a response to the growing split among Americans regarding whom to support in a developing war between Britain and France, Congress passed the Sedition Act, which in part read:

> If any person shall write, print, utter, or publish . . . any false, scandalous, and malicious writing or writings against the government of the United States, or either house of Congress of the United States, or the President of the United States, with intent to defame . . . or to bring them . . . into contempt or disrepute; or to excite against them . . . the hatred of the good people of the United States, or to stir up sedition within the United States . . . then such person . . . shall be punished by a fine not exceeding two thousand dollars, and by imprisonment not exceeding two years [24, pp. 596-597].

On the face of it, this law should have been prohibited by the First Amendment, and in fact, Republicans in Congress made this argument against the Federalists who supported it with the argument that the federal government possesses an incumbent right to protect itself. The Supreme Court never ruled on the act's constitutionality, although lower courts did uphold it. The Federalists arrested at least 25 people for violating the Act, and 10 were convicted, including Benjamin Franklin's grandson, who had portrayed the Federalists as warmongers in his paper, the *Aurora* [25].

The Sedition Act was a major issue in the election of 1800, which emerged in an Electoral College tie between Aaron Burr and Thomas Jefferson, requiring the House of Representatives to elect the President. Matthew Lyon, who was imprisoned as a result of the act and re-elected to Congress while yet in jail, cast the deciding vote for Jefferson. The Sedition Act expired on March 3, 1801 — the date of the presidential inauguration; Jefferson pardoned all defendants who had been convicted under the act; and Congress paid most of their remaining fines. Jefferson considered the act to be a test of the American people, to see how far they would be willing to see their Constitution subverted; and the American people clearly demonstrated that restrictions on their elemental rights to criticize their government would not be tolerated. But the battle for free expression was far from over, as the sedition matter would be replaced by other attempts to abridge free speech.

While the modern judiciary has consistently interpreted the Constitution to protect speech rights, nineteenth century courts were at times considerably less forceful in their protection of the First Amendment. For example, in 1833 the Supreme Court ruled that the Bill of Rights limited only the authority of Congress (as it seemed originally to have been intended with statements such as "Congress shall make no law . . .") and instructed that these amendments did not protect individuals from the actions of states to encroach upon their rights. This ruling was consistent with the prevailing attitudes of society at the time, as a limited judicial construction of the Constitution was perfectly acceptable to persons, who, though they desired to protect individuals' rights to criticize their government, were not as likely to support open expression of ideas on controversial subjects nor by members of oppressed segments of society. The idea, therefore, that free speech would extend to slaves or to women or that it would include such topics as obscenity, birth control, and unionization, was far beyond the values of most people of that time. Thus, there arose a significantly long period in the United States in which free speech matters did not make their way to judicial decisions. Following World War I and during the Supreme Court of Oliver Wendell Holmes and Louis Brandeis, all this changed dramatically.

Twentieth century judicial decisions regarding freedoms of expression (and by extension a concept that developed throughout that century, free access to information) have sought to balance the "inevitable tension between protecting freedom of speech and reducing the risk that speech will inspire others to break the law" [26, p. 89]. That balance has often been constructed by applying what has been called the "clear and present danger test." This test was firmly established in rulings regarding The Espionage Act of 1917, which in part read:

> . . . whoever, when the United States is at war, shall willfully utter, print, write, or publish any disloyal, profane, scurrilous, or abusive language about the form of government of the United States, or the Constitution of the United States, or the military or naval forces of the United States, or the uniform of the Army or Navy of the United States in contempt, scorn, contumely, or disrepute, . . . or shall willfully by utterance, writing, printing, publication, or language spoken, urge, incite or advocate any curtailment of production in this prosecution of the war in which the United States may be engaged, with intent by such curtailment to cripple or hinder the United States in the prosecution of the war . . . shall be punished by a fine of not more than $10,000 or imprisonment for not more than twenty years, or both [27, pp. 553-554].

Although the establishment of a clear and present danger test was at best evolutionary, Justice Holmes defined it by rendering the following decision in a 1919 Supreme Court Case involving speech and the distribution of leaflets in a protest against armed forces recruitment during World War I:

> The most stringent protection of free speech would not protect a man in falsely shouting fire in a theatre, and causing a panic. . . . The question in every case is whether the words used are used in such circumstances and are of such a nature as to create a clear and present danger that they will bring about substantive evils that Congress has a right to prevent [28].

The Supreme Court decided this case unanimously in favor of the government, holding that the defendant Schenk's speech and actions could be punished because they were intended to obstruct the recruiting service, thereby creating a clear and present danger to military operations. Two other similar cases were also unanimously decided and could have made any opposition to future war hazardous, because they established precedent that the First Amendment did not protect speech that could impair military recruitment. However, in the 1920s, Justices Holmes and Brandeis began to disagree with the Court's majority, insisting that First Amendment protections should be set aside only if the danger presented by speech is truly clear and truly present. In a now famous ruling, Brandeis established this concept firmly in 1927:

> If there be time to expose through discussion the falsehood and fallacies, to avert the evil by the processes of education, the remedy to be applied is more speech, not enforced silence. . . . Such must be the rule if authority is to be reconciled with freedom. Such, in my opinion, is the command of the Constitution [29].

This ruling led to a growing protection of freedom of speech over the next 20 years, including the protection of Communist speech in the late 1940s and early 1950s. In the late 1960s, it even led to the protection of Ku Klux Klan generated hate speech in *Brandenburg v. Ohio* [30]. As a result, it was established that the government cannot punish speech because it has a tendency, or even a reasonable possibility, of inciting illegal conduct. Before the government can punish speech on the grounds that it is incitement, a three-part criterion must be passed. First, the speech must be directed to inciting lawless action. Second, the advocacy must be calling for imminent lawbreaking, rather than illegal conduct at some future time. Finally, the advocacy must be likely to produce such conduct [26, p. 115]. Clearly, the long and often tortuous history of an evolving right to free expression can be summarized by considering now-established fundamentals of free speech.

FREE SPEECH FUNDAMENTALS

Traditionally, four reasons have been put forth to justify a freedom of speech: such freedom is valuable to systems of self-government; it promotes the discovery of truth; it promotes dignity and self-worth among individuals; and attempts to control it would be unworkable and deleterious [26]. In democratic societies from Classical Greece forward, the ultimate power of control over government resides in the people — even if how "the people" have been defined has varied greatly over the centuries. In order to exercise that control, citizens must have access to all ideas regarding government policy, as well as the ability to freely discuss those ideas. In many, if not most instances through history, exercise of this freedom with regard to this particular justification has taken the form of exposing government wrong doing. Consequently, whether it has had to do with Watergate or the Bay of Pigs, the teaching of Socrates or the conquests of Caesar (and notice that I intentionally selected matters of state that were resolved in drastically different ways), the citizenry has had the opportunity to evaluate and debate each of these to their different resolutions.

Free speech and free access to information — in each of these cases and countless others — promoted the discovery of truth, even if from political standpoints we might ask "Whose truth?" The idea that truth will emerge from open discussion dates at least back to Aristotle who writes: "the true and the just are by nature stronger that their opposites" [31]. John Milton makes a similar argument in *Areopagitica,* an argument against Parliament's Licensing Order of 1643, in which parliament subsumed control over what was printed in England:

> And though all the windes of doctrin were let loose to play upon the earth, so Truth be in the field, we do injuriously by licensing and prohibiting to misdoubt her strength. Let her and Falsehood grapple; who ever knew Truth put to the wors, in a free and open encounter [32].

Throughout history, however, attempts to curtail free speech have been used by states and other agencies of power to suppress ideas which later proved true. Nowhere was this case more notorious than the Catholic Church's censorship and forced recantation of Galileo's support for the Copernican theory of the universe [33].

Freedom of speech, as it has evolved from the Renaissance on, has increasingly come to be associated with individual autonomy and self-worth. The extent of that concept is best put, also, by Milton, who suggested that suppression of books denies the writer's essential humanity and, since ideas outlive the person responsible for them, "slays an immortality" [32, p. 72]. John Stuart Mill concurs by suggesting that suppressing the expression of a single person is illegitimate:

> If all mankind minus one were of one opinion, and only one person were of the contrary opinion, mankind would be no more justified in silencing that one person, than he, if he had the power, would be justified in silencing mankind [34].

More recently, California Chief Justice Rose Bird established that

> Free speech is also guaranteed because of our fundamental respect for individual development and self-realization. The right to self-expression is inherent in any political system which respects individual dignity [35].

Finally, it has been consistently argued that, even for speech which is injurious to society, attempts to regulate it will do more harm than good. Consistently cited modern cases involve World Wide Web filters that, in an attempt to screen pornography, also screen legitimate and valuable medical sites.

To be fair, arguments supporting the curtailment of free speech rights have also consistently been promulgated throughout history. There have been at least three categories within which such arguments have taken place. Some have maintained that individual rights should not supercede the rights of society, community, or groups. This communitarian argument has varied between those who would hold that group rights have a higher standing than individual rights to those who would hold that individual and group rights are equivalent in importance and that resolving issues in which these rights compete requires careful analysis. For example, Amitai Etzioni, of George Washington University, argues:

> The individual and the community have the same basic primary moral standing. . . . One cannot use the needs of society — or individual rights — to shut out other considerations, as for instance, do First Amendment absolutists [36].

Others frame the argument for limiting speech freedoms in terms of what individuals owe society. For example, Molefi Kete Asante, in maintaining that at the least individuals owe society civility, suggests that such civility requires a commitment to courtesy, safety, and common sense. Courtesy involves self-expression from the perspective of recognizing the humanity of others, even in disagreement. Since democratic political systems, the supporters of this argument would say, are founded on principles of equality, uncivil or denigrating speech denies the equality of those who are targets of it. The principle of safety would hold that speech should not be used to incur circumstances in which physical harm might result. Demagoguery that results in violence would fall into this category, as would speech that jeopardizes national security. Common sense suggests that some speech is inappropriate in a decent society. Moralistic arguments, mostly concerning various forms of media from books to music videos, are founded on attempts to define what is decent and what is obscene.

Another category of argument used to limit free speech centers around the claim that speech rights should not supersede other individual rights. Those who would hold to these arguments have suggested that there should be more balance between the rights granted in the First Amendment and those granted in the Fourteenth, which provides for equal protection under the law. Catherine MacKinnon, of the University of Michigan, for example, challenges First Amendment protection of the speech rights for such groups as Neo-Nazis, Ku Klux Klan, and pornographers as forms of injury to the equality of individuals [37].

A third argument has held that speech rights do not guarantee effective freedom. This argument is based on the distinction between formal freedoms and effective freedoms. Formal freedoms are those specifically guaranteed, for example, by the First Amendment's proscription against governmental abridgement of speech. If the Constitution guarantees all people this right, then there is a formal guarantee to free speech. Effective freedom views speech in a broader context, maintaining that if some segments of society do not have the economic means to exercise their rights through, for example, access to mass media and the audiences they command, then there is not effective freedom. While such new technologies as the World Wide Web have ameliorated these concerns to some degree, there is still an economic component involved in participating in the World Wide Web marketplace of ideas.

This concept of a marketplace of ideas was also first developed by Supreme Court justices Oliver Wendell Holmes and Louis Brandeis in the early twentieth century and is based on regarding the source of a message as the seller who is allowed to express ideas to anyone who is willing to listen. The receiver, then, is analogous to a buyer who may decide whether or not to accept or disagree with the message. Holmes argued, in dissent by the way, in a 1919 Supreme Court decision limiting speech that encouraged persons to resist participating in World War I. In his dissent, he stated that "the ultimate good desired is better reached by free trade in ideas, and that the best test of truth is the power of the thought to get itself accepted in the competition of the market" [38]. The implication of Holmes's and later Brandeis's views has been that free speech rights protect speech we despise. Holmes, again in dissent, expresses this eloquently in 1927:

> If there is any principle of the Constitution that more imperatively calls for attachment than any other it is the principle of free thought — not free thought for those who agree with us but freedom for the thought we hate [39].

Along those same lines, Brandeis suggested that the First Amendment protects the rights of Communist Party members, even when engaged in speech supporting the overthrow of the United States government. Rather than suppression of disagreeable speech, he argued that "the fitting remedy for evil counsels is good ones" [40]. In other words, we are called by our commitments to individual freedoms to combat bad ideas with more and better speech.

MODERN DOCTRINES OF FREE SPEECH

Several competing doctrines regarding free speech arose in the late twentieth century. One that seems most frequently to gain attention, in political arenas and ubiquitous talk media programs, is an absolutist position that claims all speech is protected by the First Amendment. Supporters of this position point out that the Constitution states "no law" (emphasis mine) may be created that abridges freedom of speech. They maintain that when the framers debated the wording of the Constitution they considered the costs and benefits of protecting all speech and decided not to create any exceptions. The difficulty with maintaining this position, however, is that almost all legal authorities as well as almost all citizens acknowledge a need for curbing some forms of speech. Historically, that has made the absolutist position difficult to defend.

By comparison, others have maintained that there is a hierarchy of speech; it includes high value speech, intermediate value speech, and low value speech. Political speech, including discussing all issues that relate to self-government in a free society, has consistently been awarded the greatest degree of First Amendment protection, with the Supreme Court requiring a strong showing of need before it will sustain a curtailment of such speech. Academic freedom, primarily as it applies to institutions of higher education, has also consistently benefitted from First Amendment protections. Freedom of speech in university environments maintains the truth-seeking function of the First Amendment as students and faculty should be able to (again, emphasis mine) put forth any opinion without fear of retribution. However, the fact that political speech and academic debate have historically been placed in the highest class of speech has not protected either from incursions against free exercise of their rights.

A second class of speech, what we might call intermediate value speech, has received fewer protections. This category of speech includes such communications as advertising, which is protected when proven to be true but not when proven to be false, as well as virtually all of the communication disseminated in business and industry. Other expressions at the lower end of this intermediate category, such as nude dancing, for example, and speech carried over limited communication channels such as radio and television, have historically received less protection than speech delivered through presentations or written in books.

Finally, low value speech—often called categorical exceptions to the First Amendment—has historically been regulated. These types of speech, consistently viewed as without social value, include defamation, obscenity, and fighting words. Recently, including racial and gendered forms of hate speech has been advocated. The basis of support for this doctrine has been a prevailing interest in order and morality, as well as a conviction that the First Amendment was derived to protect speech which facilitates the discovery of truth [26, pp. 21-22].

Throughout the history of the United States, and in fact derived from its ancestry among tenets of English Common Law, a variety of tests have arisen that can be used to evaluate government restrictions upon speech. Speech has been successfully regulated if it can be proven that such speech may cause illegal action. Other successful regulations of speech have been founded on the issue of balance between the interests of the state and those of the individual. If there is a proven, significant, and compelling government interest in restricting narrowly defined forms of speech, such restriction may pass legal challenges. In 1938, Supreme Court Justice Harlan Stone introduced what has come to be called the "preferred position," when he wrote in a decision that "there may be a narrower scope for operation of the presumption of constitutionality when legislation appears on its face to be within a specific presumption of the Constitution, such as those of the first ten Amendments" [41]. This doctrine shifted the emphasis toward constitutionally guaranteed rights by requiring the government to justify its restrictions upon speech, as well as upon other freedoms granted by the Bill of Rights. Finally, the Supreme Court has also given a deference to legislative judgments that a regulation on expression is necessary, but such deference has historically been limited to low value speech and expression. More recently, doctrines involving vagueness and overbreadth have arisen to protect freedom of speech. These have been the primary reasons why laws attempting to regulate such expressions as "obscene art" have consistently been found to be unconstitutional, even though obscenity would reasonably fall under the category of low value speech. A chilling effect has been the by-product of attempts to promulgate vague restrictions upon speech and expression. Individuals may be unwilling to exercise their freedoms if such vague laws create in them the fear that there may be retribution for doing so, thereby nullifying their First Amendment rights.

PROBING THE FUTURE OF FREE SPEECH IN A POST-9-11 WORLD

But what if the incitement to illegal conduct threatens the very existence of a free society? Is free speech inconsistent with issues of national security? It is these concerns, many of which have developed over the last 40 years, that have also led to an evolving definition of free access to information and upon which some of the considerations regarding future free speech controversies may be explored. For example, should military secrets be kept out of the public arena on the grounds that without national security, a foreign power could destroy a free country as well as that country's freedoms? By extension, should certain types of technical information (i.e., flight manuals, technical specifications, procedures, etc.) be kept out of the public arena on the same grounds? In other words, are there forms of speech, particularly in high technology industries, which today would pass the clear and present danger test? In order to answer these questions, one must resolve the conflict between freedom of expression (including the public's implied right of access to information) with the need for national security. The First Amendment assumes that a free society can remain so best by exploring such issues in what Holmes described as an "unrestrained marketplace of ideas" [38].

In the United States, the controversy of a president's right to censor materials claiming the prerogative of national security was tested in the 1971 Pentagon Papers case. Most national security cases involve governmental attempts to impose a prior restraint on the communication of information; having learned of secret information that is about to be published, the government seeks a judicial injunction to prohibit such publication. The doctrine of prior restraint dates from the 1920s and subsequent rulings evolving out of the Schenk case, which limited certain expressions during times of war. This exception to constitutional guarantees of free speech did not become an issue in either World War II or the Korean War, but it did during the Vietnam War, when two newspapers planned to publish information—classified information that detailed the history of America's involvement in the war—that the government alleged would impair national security [42]. By a 6–3 margin, the case was decided in favor of the defendant, thereby allowing publication and establishing a strong presumption against the use of prior restraint. The opinions written by justices in this case lay out examples of arguments regarding the use of prior restraint in matters of national security. The most important of these are:

- Burden of proof, in which it was agreed that the government must meet a stringent standard of proof before prior restraint is justified;
- Clash of values, in which the importance of a free flow of information about a government's foreign policy must be weighed against the right of a president, who traditionally conducts that policy in ways that may require keeping some policy information secret—particularly as it might be expected by other nations; and
- Pragmatic considerations, in which the benefits of publishing certain types of information are weighed against the potential risks to society of doing so.

Justices Black and Douglas summed these issues up succinctly:

> Madison and the other Framers of the First Amendment, able men that they were, wrote in language they earnestly believed could never be misunderstood: "Congress shall make no law . . . abridging the freedom . . . of the press. . . . " Both the history and language of the First Amendment support the view that the press must be left free to publish news, whatever the source, without censorship, injunctions, or prior restraint. . . . To find that the [government] has inherent power to halt the publication of news by resort to the courts would wipe out the First Amendment and destroy the fundamental liberty and security of the very people the Government hopes to make secure [42].

Justices White and Stewart, while agreeing however, point out that:

> The Criminal Code contains numerous provisions potentially relevant to these cases [including making it] a criminal act for any unauthorized possessor of a document relating to the national defense either (1) willfully to communicate or cause to be communicated that document to any person not entitled to receive it or (2) willfully to retain the document and fail to deliver it to an officer of the United States entitled to receive it [42].

These are important distinctions and form the crux of the matter under consideration in this chapter. For example, prior restraints have been deemed justifiable in the case of government or former government employees disclosing secret information [43]. Similarly, prior restraints on nuclear bomb concepts have been deemed justifiable:

> This Court concludes that publication of the technical information on the hydrogen bomb . . . is analogous to publication of troop movements or locations in time of war and falls within the extremely narrow exception to the rule against prior restraint [44].

In addition, prior restraints have been found permissible regarding limits on the rights of access to information about the Central Intelligence Agency:

> The public interest lies in a proper accommodation that will preserve the intelligence mission of the Agency while not abridging the free flow of unclassified information [45].

Consequently, while the Supreme Court decision with regard to the Pentagon Papers established that a doctrine of prior restraint could not be justified, other ways in which the press or other communicators could be punished based on alleged threats to national security have evolved. The key distinctions upon which they have evolved have been the concepts of "clear and present danger" and "pragmatic considerations," both of which can lead to increased designations that some information requires classification.

A free society is always precariously balanced between the competing desires for freedom and security. Based on the events of 9-11 and the discovery of certain types of technical information used in preparation for the attack on the World Trade Center towers, as well as the open access to training in the use of that technical information, certain predictions may be entertained. Future governments may conclude that much more of what we write about technology has national security interests, that it passes the requisite tests of "clear and present danger," "pragmatic considerations," and "prior restraint." Future governments may therefore argue to classify and prohibit the general publication of far greater ranges of information out of a concern that non-governmental organizations might develop ways to use it in acts of war or terror against the United States and its citizens. Future court decisions may create entire new categories of restricted speech, as *Virginia v. Black* recently did in linking cross-burning with terrorism, citing in the words of Sandra Day O'Connor that First Amendment freedoms "are not absolute," and effectively overturning the spirit of First Amendment protections afforded by *Brandenburg v. Ohio* [46]. Future court decisions may, as a result, forge a new balance between security and freedom, and as the pendulum swings back toward security—as it clearly has in the past—the high water marks of free speech and free access to information may have already been reached.

REFERENCES

1. *Maxims of Ptahhotep.* (www.hetkaptah.com/maxims.htm)
2. M. I. Finley, *Politics in the Ancient World,* Cambridge University Press, Cambridge, 1983.
3. D. M. MacDowell, *The Law in Classical Athens,* Cornell University Press, Ithaca, New York, 1978.
4. L. Robinson, *Freedom of Speech in the Roman Republic,* Ph.D. dissertation, Johns Hopkins University, 1940.
5. L. W. Levy, *Freedom of Speech and Press in Early American History: Legacy of Suppression,* Harper Row, New York, 1963.
6. A. Wharam, *The Treason Trials, 1794,* Leicester University Press, Leicester, United Kingdom, 1992.
7. *Rex v. Tutchin,* 14 Howell's State Trials 1095, 1118, 1704.
8. *Rex v. Twyn,* 6 Howell's State Trials 513, 536, 1663.
9. *Rex v. Frost,* 22 Howell's State Trials 471, 1793.
10. L. Birket, *To Deprave and Corrupt . . . Original Studies in the Nature of Obscenity,* Association Press, London, 1962.
11. W. B. Lockhart and R. C. McClure, Why Obscene? in *To Deprave and Corrupt . . . Original Studies in the Nature of Obscenity,* Association Press, London, 1962.
12. J. P. Roche, American Liberty: An Examination of the Tradition of Freedom, in *Aspects of Liberty,* Cornell University Press, Ithaca, New York, 1958.
13. B. E. Johansen, *Forgotten Founders,* Gambit, New York, 1982.
14. L. W. Levy, *Blasphemy,* Knopf, New York, 1993.
15. J. Adair, *Founding Fathers, The Puritans in England and America,* Dent, London, 1982.
16. J. Hosmer (ed.), *Winthrop's Journal* (Vol. I), Scribner's, New York, 1908.
17. *American State Papers on Freedom in Religion,* Religious Liberty Association, Chicago, 1949.
18. L. D. Eldridge, *A Distant Heritage: The Growth of Free Speech in America,* New York University Press, New York, 1994.
19. J. Franklin, *New England Courant,* Boston, 1722.
20. B. Franklin, *New England Courant,* Boston, 1722.
21. B. Schwartz, *The Bill of Rights: A Documentary History,* Chelsea House, New York, 1971.
22. C. R. Smith, *To Form a More Perfect Union: The Ratification of the Constitution and the Bill of Rights, 1787-1791,* New York University Press, New York, 1993.
23. Z. Chafee, Jr., *Free Speech in the United States,* Harvard University Press, Cambridge, Massachusetts, 1948.
24. *United States at Large,* 1798.
25. B. F. Bache, *Aurora,* 1799.
26. D. Fraleigh and J. Tuman, *Freedom of Speech in the Marketplace of Ideas,* St. Martins Press, New York, 1997.
27. *40 U.S. Statutes at Large,* 1918.
28. *Schenk v. United States,* 249 U.S. 47 (1919).
29. *Whitney v. California,* 274 U.S., 357, 372 (1927).
30. *Brandenburg v. Ohio,* 395 U.S. 444 (1969).

31. G. Kennedy, *Aristotle on Rhetoric: A Theory of Civic Discourse,* Oxford University Press, Oxford, 1991.
32. J. M. Patrick, *The Prose of John Milton,* New York University Press, New York, 1968.
33. A. Einstein, *Introduction to Dialogue Concerning the Two Chief World Systems, Ptolemaic and Copernican,* University of California Press, Los Angeles, 1953.
34. J. S. Mill, *On Liberty: Annotated Text Sources and Background Criticism,* D. Spritz (ed.), Norton Press, New York, 1975.
35. *Gugliemi v. Spelling-Goldberg Productions,* 25 Cal.3d 860, 866 (1979).
36. A. Etzioni, *A Responsive Society,* Jossey-Bass, New York, 1991.
37. C. A. MacKinnon, *Only Words,* Harvard University Press, Cambridge, Massachusetts, 1993.
38. *Abrams v. United States,* 250 U.S. 616, 630, 1919.
39. *United States v. Schwimmer,* 279 U.S. 644, 645-655, 1927.
40. *Whitney v. California,* 274 U.S. 357, 375, 1927.
41. *United States v. Carolene Products,* 304 U.S. 144, 1938.
42. *United States v. Washington Post Co.,* 446 F. 2d 1327 (1971).
43. *United States v. Marchetti,* 409 U.S. 1063, 1972.
44. *United States v. The Progressive,* 467 F. Supp. 990, 1979.
45. *Snepp v. United States,* 444 U.S. 507, 1980.
46. *Virginia v. Black,* 01-1107, 2003.

CHAPTER 2

Information Law since September 11: The USA PATRIOT Act and Other Government Limitations of Expression Rights

George F. Bohrer, Jr.

In the days and weeks following the September 11 terrorist attacks, it quickly became a cliché to say that American society would be undergoing deep and significant changes—that, as with the aftermath of the Pearl Harbor bombing in 1941, how we lived our lives would be altered for a long period. However, as Bill Maher points out in *When You Ride Alone You Ride with Bin Laden: What the Government Should Be Telling Us to Help Fight the War on Terrorism*, we accommodated that day's events within our lives in a remarkably short time [1]. True, we are more conscious today of our security, and we have learned to accept more than cursory checks at airports and other travel terminals. However, in many other ways, particularly in how we consume, our experience may feel much as it did before September 11.

In several essential ways, though, substantial change has occurred. One of the most significant areas of change has been in the body of law relating to information—our rights to express and to receive ideas. From the 1960s until the 1990s, beginning with the passage of the 1966 Freedom of Information Act (FOIA), Congressional legislation consistently expanded our rights to express ourselves, to maintain information privately, and to have access to the information stored by the government. This legislation was in many ways a response to an opposing body of law written from around the time of the First World War through the early years of the Cold War, including the Espionage and Seditions Acts of 1917 and 1918 and the Smith Act of 1940. Laws such as these allowed the government complete privilege to secretly maintain information of any kind and to gather information at will. In the 1960s, public disenchantment with such laws prompted Congress to enact legislation such as the FOIA, the Privacy Protection Act, the Sunshine Act, and the Federal Privacy Act. These laws assured the privacy rights of individuals, afforded protection from government scrutiny, and allowed public access to governmental records and meetings. Despite Reagan administration attempts to reverse this trend during the 1980s, Congress maintained the movement into the new millennium.

This trend was dramatically and substantially reversed with the legislation enacted since the September 11 attacks. Beginning with the USA PATRIOT Act (2001) and followed by the Homeland Security Act (2002), the government's relationship with the public and its power to control and gather information have been significantly altered. An administration proposal for an extension of the first Patriot act, USA PATRIOT II, also known as the Domestic Security Enhancement Act of 2003, would make even more remarkable changes to the laws concerning rights to information. These legislative measures and certain actions by the executive and judicial branches of the government are effectively combining to bring about deep and consistent changes in the government's powers concerning public and private information.

On October 26, 2001, President George W. Bush signed into law the USA PATRIOT Act of 2001. He described the law as an ". . . essential step in defeating terrorism, while protecting the constitutional rights of all Americans" [2]. The act's title is an acronym for Uniting and Strengthening America by Providing Appropriate Tools Required to Intercept and Obstruct Terrorism. The law is actually a compendium of several elements of law. Largely these amend previously existing law, thus changing the meanings of and protections provided under these laws.

It should be noted that when the act was passed by Congress on October 24, 2001, a majority in the House and Senate had not had the completed law with sufficient time to read the bill. Some did not receive the complete text until after voting for the law [3, p. 1]. While it is not unusual for members of Congress to vote on a bill without having read it, they usually do so only after members of their staff have read the bill and recommended action. The fact that so few members of Congress· voted with actually having information about the completed text is an indication of the pressure placed on the legislature to take responsive action to the September 11 attacks.

While the law itself runs over 300 pages, and affects a wide array of civil liberties ranging from fair trial rights through search and seizure guarantees, the elements of the law that address information issues may be summarized in a few pages.

A crucial part of the USA PATRIOT ACT, Section 215, grants the government, specifically the FBI, the power to order any person or entity to turn over "any tangible things" as long as the agency asserts that the order serves an authorized investigation related to terrorism [4]. The language of the bill is sufficiently nonspecific to allow the government access to material ordinarily protected under privacy and First Amendment rights. A study conducted by the University of Illinois determined that by December 2001, only two months after the passage of the USA PATRIOT Act, the FBI had already approached 85 libraries out of 1,500 queried for the study. In essence, the law permits the government to investigate people based on the content of their library use or Internet visits.

While traditionally the government has had the power to conduct such investigations, it has only had such power when granted a court order, following Fourth Amendment dictum to establish probable cause. In contrast, Section 215 requires only that the government specify that a search is necessary in order to "protect against international terrorism or clandestine intelligence activities." Thus, the government is able to act without a full review of that action by the court, as guaranteed under the Fourth Amendment.

In addition to these elements of the law, the USA PATRIOT Act also prohibits those contacted for information, a librarian for example, from informing the subject of the search. Clearly, this is intended to keep potential terrorists from being forewarned about an investigation. However, it also has the effect of limiting the freedom of speech.

This power to solicit information without court approval is related to permission for "roving" surveillance granted under the law [5, p. 14]. Under roving surveillance, a court grants a blanket search order that omits identification of particular institutions, facilities, instruments, or places where the surveillance is to occur. The purpose of this change in the system of court control of police investigation is to prohibit terrorist agents from using the government's responsibilities to publish information in order to provide those terrorists warning. The law also disallows individuals approached for information from making that fact public.

The law also extends the government's powers concerning pen registers and trap and trace devices. The purpose of these devices is to collect information about outgoing calls (pen register) and incoming calls (trace and trap). Title III of the 1968 Omnibus Crime Control and Safe Streets Act initially granted the government the power to use these devices as a means of eavesdropping on telephone communications when the court was satisfied that the conversations are related to "serious criminal cases" [5, pp. 3-4]. These devices permit a kind of remote "Caller ID" so that agents are able to determine both whom an individual is calling and whom that individual is receiving calls from. The USA PATRIOT Act both grants the government power to conduct such investigations without traditional Fourth Amendment court approval and extends that power to cover other electronic means of communication. The result is that, in addition to observing the calls made and received by individuals, the government may also track an individual's e-mail and general Internet use. Again, this may be done both without specific court approval and without any requirement to inform the subject. And the law specifically allows agencies of the government to hide such activity from surveillance subjects.

The required level of court scrutiny is at issue here. The Electronic Communications Privacy Act, which had previously granted the government similar powers for surveillance of Internet use, required that a judge be satisfied by "specific and articulable facts that the information sought is relevant and material to an ongoing investigation" [6]. The USA PATRIOT Act allows similar investigation but *without* the same level of court scrutiny.

The USA PATRIOT Act also essentially amends the Foreign Intelligence Surveillance Act (FISA) to limit the legal distinction between foreign citizens and U.S. citizens — again, this distinction is a crucial one. Congress passed FISA in the 1970s to grant the government power to scrutinize foreign citizens as a means of protecting the U.S. citizenry from foreign agents. FISA made a clear distinction between a foreign citizen and one from the United States. While FISA granted the government greater powers to conduct surveillance on foreign nationals, it very specifically left intact restrictions on surveillance of U.S. citizens. Under USA PATRIOT, the government has the power to conduct surveillance not only on foreign nationals but also on U.S. citizens who are suspected of having information relating to national defense and security and to the conducting of the foreign affairs of the United States [6, p. 2]. This inclusion of U.S. citizens in the government's extensive foreign surveillance powers is reminiscent of the Smith Act, which essentially made it a crime to in any way support a seditious organization. (The Smith Act served as the legal basis for the actions of the House Un-American Activities Committee in the 1940s and 1950s. While the blacklisting that ensued was extralegal, it took place in a political climate that the Smith Act helped engender.)

One result of these changes to the law is the simple fact that professional communicators, who rely on the very channels surveilled by the government, must realize that their communications may be scrutinized. In its analysis of the law, the Electronic Frontier Foundation identifies three general areas of concern raised by the USA PATRIOT Act:

- The law provides expanded surveillance powers with reduced checks and balances.
- The law is overboad, lacking focus on the terrorism it is nominally intended to address.
- The law allows Americans to be more easily spied upon by foreign intelligence agencies such as the CIA and the FBI [3, pp. 3-5].

Ultimately, those using the channels of communication the government is now empowered to overview — which essentially means all professional communicators — must keep the fact of this surveillance in mind when they conduct their work. It also might be suggested that those concerned about the impact of these changes to the law be alert to further Congressional action in regard to USA PATRIOT Act. In general, the law has a built-in sunset provision requiring legislation to be passed for the complete law to be maintained beyond December 31, 2005. However, there are two concerns about the sunset provision.

First, several sections of the law will remain in place after 2005 *without* Congressional action. Most important, the following provisions of the law will be maintained unless Congress specifically acts to remove them:

- The government's power to obtain e-mail routing information.
- "Sneak and peak" powers to delay notification of warrant execution.
- Modifications of rules governing the use of pen registers and trap and trace devices.

Second, since the USA PATRIOT Act provides no requirement that the executive branch report to Congress on any actions taken through the provisions of the law or the effectiveness of those actions, Congress will have to make decisions about whether to continue all provisions of that law without full information. Thus, Congress ultimately will have to make decisions based on anecdotal information and media reports rather than a thorough accounting from the agencies affected by the law.

The USA PATRIOT Act is not the only law passed by Congress in response to the 2001 terrorist attacks that has implications for communication professionals. The Homeland Security Act, passed in the last days of the 107th Congress, ordered the largest reorganization of the federal government since the conclusion of the Second World War. The law is huge—nearly 200 pages longer than the over 300-page USA PATRIOT Act. Included within this legislation is an open-government exemption that Senator Patrick Leahy termed ". . . the most severe weakening of the Freedom of Information Act in its 36-year history" [7, p. 1]. This section of the Homeland Security Act is titled the Critical Infrastructure Information Act of 2002. The proposed law was challenged by several right-to-know organizations. Senator Leahy, along with Senators Carl Levin and Robert Bennett, worked to produce a bipartisan compromise on the law that would have made the Department of Homeland Security more responsible for information access, but the effort was apparently undone by the legislators' intent to complete the bill prior to the end of the congressional session.

The Critical Infrastructure Information Act as passed essentially exempts the Homeland Security Department from the access requirements of both the Freedom of Information Act and the Federal Open Meeting Law/Sunshine Act, an exemption seen by many as the most damaging element of the new law. Both the FOIA and the Sunshine Act were created with a series of exemptions that allow the government to maintain information secretly under specified circumstances. For example, information related to individuals' privacy is exempted, as are law enforcement records of ongoing investigations. The first category within both laws is that of material classified to protect national security. Under the law, it is the responsibility of the president to establish criteria for the classification of such material. The Critical Infrastructure Information Act establishes the new criterion of "sensitive" information. The law instructs the president to "identify and safeguard homeland security information that is sensitive but unclassified." However, the law neither defines the term "sensitive" nor requires the president to do so.

When the FOIA was first passed, the first exemption, excepting information posing a threat to national security, was similarly undefined. Any agency could label any record as "classified" and no mechanism was established to evaluate such labeling. Given the Nixon administration's penchant for secrecy, it is not surprising that this exemption was used to such an extent that Congress amended the law. Following the 1974 amendment to the FOIA, the law obligated presidents to establish criteria for classification of information as a threat to national security. Courts could (and can) then review information thus classified to determine whether it actually satisfies the criteria.

The Critical Infrastructure Information Act essentially establishes this same kind of "catch-all" exemption to the FOIA and the Sunshine Act. This new change to the law again allows the government to close access to information and official meetings for any reason. Ultimately, the courts will almost certainly provide a definition for the term or Congress will require the executive branch to do so. However, under the current climate, this is not likely to occur in the near future.

One particularly alarming aspect of this change in the law is the fact that these new limitations on the public's right to know went through the legislative process with almost no public discussion. Gary Bass, executive director of OMB (Office of Budget Management) Watch, a government watchdog organization, says, "People didn't know soon enough about this issue [because] press coverage focused on the larger bill creating the department" [7, p. 2]. Perhaps because such watchdog groups realized after the fact the implications of the law just passed, the executive branch has found its most recent proposal for post-9/11 security law to be treated with far more scrutiny.

In the spring of 2003, the Justice Department proposed a bill titled The Domestic Security Enhancement Act; however, even before its formal presentation to Congress, it became known as Patriot Act II. As its proper name suggests, the administration intends this bill to be a necessary enhancement to the powers granted the government under the USA PATRIOT Act. However, unlike the limited public response to both that law and the Homeland Security Act, Patriot Act II has generated an intense response from many groups interested in the protection of civil liberties, ranging from the American Civil Liberties Union and the American Bar Association to the National Council of Churches and the Consumer Alert National Consumer Coalition [8, p. 1]. The American Civil Liberties Union, in its fact sheet on PATRIOT Act II, outlines several specific concerns the proposed legislation is raising:

- The government would have no obligation to reveal the identity of anyone, even U.S. citizens, detained in connection with an investigation related to terrorism until criminal charges are filed.
- Court limitations on local police surveillance would be removed.
- The government would be free to obtain credit records, library records and similar documents without a court's warrant.
- The government could conduct wiretaps for 15 days without court approval.
- Information related to public safety that could be used by terrorists (such as chemical plant hazards) would be restricted.

Perhaps the most serious concern raised regarding the proposed legislation is the fact that it broadens the definition of terrorism radically. In effect this broadened definition would mean that many acts now considered criminal and which could thus lead to investigations and trials conducted under Fourth, Fifth, and Sixth Amendment restrictions, would be considered, under the terms of Patriot Act II, as terrorist acts — meaning that the government would be able to handle such infractions *outside of* constitutional restrictions [9, p. 1].

As of January 2005, the Domestic Security Enhancement Act has not come before either house of Congress for a vote. Given the amount of public concern over the proposed law, it is possible the administration will not press for action until after the 2004 elections. Given the results of the 2004 election, it seems likely that the bill will resurface.

It is not the actions of the legislature alone that raise concerns about the future of information law. Both the executive branch and the judiciary have taken actions in the last few years that have important implications for information rights. The executive branch is given considerable power under USA PATRIOT, and it has taken advantage of those powers. In addition, it has taken action to further control information flow by taking the most restrictive approach to the Freedom of Information Act since the Nixon administration. Under the FOIA, as amended in 1974, the President has the obligation to establish criteria for the classification of information as a threat to national security. Like the previous two Republican presidents, George W. Bush has determined that information may be so classified if an agency asserts that the publication of the information could lead to a threat to national security. The agency is not obligated to detail the nature of the threat. Further, once classified, an agency is under no obligation to review its decision at any future date. Only upon challenge and court review must an agency defend its decision.

During the first months of the current Bush administration, the executive branch had already begun declining requests for information at a substantially greater rate than had been true of the Clinton administration. However, in the year following the 9/11 attacks, requests under the Freedom of Information Act were declined at an even greater rate than in the first eight months of the current administration [10, p. 1].

The Bush administration's decision to conduct military tribunals in trying some terrorist suspects gave the administration even greater powers of secrecy. The administration has refused to make public the names of dozens of detainees held, in some cases since the fall of 2001. In July of 2003, it announced its intention to proceed with military tribunals of six suspects. Military tribunals do not carry the constitutional requirement of a public trial, and the administration's decision to hold the trials in Guantanamo Bay naval base in Cuba makes them essentially inaccessible to the media. While many detainees were released in 2004, the number of remaining detainees and their identities remain undisclosed as of January 2005.

With the actions of both the legislative and the executive branches serving to curtail information freedoms, many have looked to the federal court system to place a check on these changes in the law. It is the role of the judiciary to supply a check and balance on the legislative and executive branches. However, historically, in periods of war the court has allowed the government to place limitations on civil rights.

Chief Justice William Rehnquist has made clear his belief that the court should give the government considerable leeway during times of threats to national security [12, p. 2]. Justice Antonin Scalia goes further in his public statements concerning civil rights. In a speech before John Carroll University in March of 2003, he expressed his belief that the role of the Constitution is simply to "set minimums" for basic rights. "Most of the rights that you enjoy today go way beyond what the Constitution requires" [13, p. 15A]. Thus, at least these two members of the court seem to feel that the government would be acting within its authority to curtail civil liberties during times of national threat.

Apparently, the court as a whole is in agreement. The Supreme Court has rejected challenges to the government's expanded surveillance powers under the USA PATRIOT Act, turned away an appeal over the Guantanamo Bay detention of hundreds suspected of having information related to terrorist acts, and rejected a challenge to closed deportation hearings, all within the spring of 2003 [14, p. B-7]. In June 2003, a federal appeals court ruled that the government acted properly by withholding names and other information about hundreds of detainees following the September 11 attacks, as revealing this information could give terrorists insight into the government's investigations.

A major Supreme Court decision from the spring of 2003 indicates that the court not only is in support of the government's actions related to its investigations into terrorism, but that the Supreme Court itself is changing the way the law is to be understood and upheld. *Virginia v. Black* is, on its surface, a victory for those opposed to racial hatred. It deals with two cases that came before the courts in Virginia related to that state's law that makes burning crosses a crime when the act is conducted with the intention to intimidate. In 1992, the Supreme Court, via *R.A.V. v. City of St. Paul,* determined that cross burning, like flag burning, is protected speech under the Constitution.

What reason does the court have for protecting such vile "speech?" This protection actually serves at least three purposes. First, the court has long held that any constraints on speech must be content-neutral. Thus, the law cannot differentiate between approved ideas and disapproved ideas. Since all ideas are protected under the Constitution, the government cannot bar any ideas. All are free to express ideas, even those that most abhor, so that any idea may be expressed. We are all free to receive and evaluate any idea.

This leads to a second purpose of this protection. The First Amendment is a very libertarian document. It suggests the government has no business limiting speech (*Congress shall make no law...*). Thus, following the libertarian model, all speech—all ideas—are free to compete in the "marketplace of ideas." By having access to all ideas, we can determine which ideas should be used in addressing the problems we face. The government avoids stagnancy by being constantly refreshed by new ideas—even those that challenge the existing government.

Finally, the protection of abhorrent ideas serves a warning function. If the government can close the discussion of hatred, as a society we will be ignorant of the problem that hatred poses. Only by knowing that some in society want to harm others or to destroy our social systems can we act to stop such action. In other words, by allowing hateful speech, we can stop hateful action.

In *Virginia v. Black,* however, the Court upheld the Virginia law criminalizing cross burning, effectively overturning the Court's earlier decision in *R.A.V. v. City of St. Paul.* What reason did the court have for seemingly changing its mind over this issue? In writing the majority opinion, Justice Sandra Day O'Connor noted that the St. Paul ordinance struck down as unconstitutional in *R.A.V. v. City of St. Paul* was overboad, in that it found any instance of cross burning a criminal act. As such, the law identified the act of cross burning itself as a crime. Whether it was used as a threat or not, the act was still a crime. The Virginia law, on the other hand, specifies that cross burning is a crime when it serves to intimidate. This distinction, in the court's opinion, keeps the Virginia law from crossing the line of banning the act of cross burning as a form of speech. Only cross burning that intimidates is affected by the law.

This distinction is both confusing and a matter of concern for free expression rights. It is confusing in that it is difficult to imagine a cross burning that is not also an act of intimidation. Ironically, O'Connor acknowledged this aspect of the act when writing the opinion. "The history of cross burnings in this country shows that cross burning is often intimidating, intended to create a pervasive fear in victims that they are a target of violence" [15, p. 7]. So, while the argument has shifted between 1992 and 2003, the effect has changed substantially. Cross burning is no longer protected speech as long as it serves to intimidate, to "create pervasive fear." That it did so in 1992 as well as in 2003 is immaterial, since intimidation did not serve as the basis for the St. Paul law.

Ultimately, the concern raised by this decision is that the court offers a more limited form of free expression protection than it did previously. It may be inferred from the court's language that the decision in *Virginia v.*

Black is related to the government's overall response to terrorism. By its very nature, terrorism intimidates, creates pervasive fear, and threatens even greater violence. Could the Court's decision here serve as a precedent so that terrorist speech receives no protection under the constitution? (Not criminal and violent action but the expression of hatred and intimidation that is commonly associated with terrorist rhetoric.) And, most importantly, do those who raise questions about the historical underpinnings of terrorist attacks find that their speech has lost protection because it serves to or seems to serve to provide support for terrorist expression and action?

Whether the Court would allow law to go that far in limiting speech is uncertain. What is certain is that expression, albeit vile expression, is less protected today than before this decision, and that this decision comes in the wake of governmental response to the terrorist attacks of September 2001.

The behavior of the government following the 9/11 attacks has had the effect of placing increasing limitations on civil liberties, including those related to information freedoms. This behavior has been enacted by all three government branches, the legislative in making laws like the USA PATRIOT Act, the executive for both taking full advantage of the new legislation and by changing its application to existing law, such as the F.O.I.A., and the judiciary, by upholding these laws and actions.

The administration of George W. Bush has argued that while concern has been raised about the potential for abridgements of expression rights, the administration has taken little advantage of that potential. In essence, they encourage a view that the government needs the ability to take the actions discussed here, but that the public should understand that such actions would only be taken when essential for the protection of national security.

While this may be true, a current administration cannot speak for future administrations. The fact is that when the government had the power to intrude into people's communications in the past, it did so. This is most obvious when examining the actions of the government during the first decades of the Cold War. The government used its powers to investigate the actions and communications of private individuals, most noticeably in the entertainment industry. The actions of the late 1940s House Committee on Un-American Activities (HUAC) and the investigations and pronouncements of Senator Joseph McCarthy in the 1950s are only the most obvious aspects of the manner in which the government used its ability to gather information to intrude into the private lives of individuals. Today, it could be argued that this nation is entering into a period, which, like the early Cold War years, is highly prone to a government's defensive posture. The changes of the last few years to information law have returned to the government the freedom to gather information, essentially at will, about American citizens and other private individuals. Indeed, as discussed, these changes actually grant the government more power than it has ever had before.

The concern raised by this is increased by the fact that the government has far more ability to gather private information than during the early Cold War years. The changes in technology over the last half century require that almost all of us are constantly leaving an electronic trail of our activities and communications. Today a single investigator, without leaving a desk, can gather more information about an individual's political associations and interest in weaponry, as a few examples, in an hour than a team of agents could over a period of weeks in the 1950s.

All of this means that communication professionals must be aware that every communication they have via telephone lines or over the Internet is open to government scrutiny. Our purchasing history is easy to follow whenever we use plastic (even debit cards) instead of cash. Our use of libraries and even of book stores is open to scrutiny, and we must not forget this. For individuals involved in international communication, it is increasingly likely that government agents will be attending. Whenever those communications are with individuals from "suspect" areas, an investigation is more than a possibility. For individuals researching and writing about technology that could be considered a potential danger or a matter of national defense, likewise they should anticipate government scrutiny. A screen-writer who researches weaponry or infiltration methods may well find that simply the act of gathering that information has brought on government attention.

Where would this government scrutiny lead? It is, of course, impossible to answer this with certainty. But we can see that in the past it has led to both official and unofficial censure. While relatively few were actually imprisoned during the 1940s and 1950s for their political affiliations — or suspected affiliations — many more were cast out of the communications industry on the mere hint of "disloyalty." *Red Channels* [16] was not a governmental publication, but it had the effect of ruining the professions and lives of hundreds, perhaps thousands, of individuals.

Is such a comparison between the tensions and actions of the 1950s and the new millennium unreasonably dire? Perhaps. However, it is only through the concern and surveillance of an alert public today that such a repetition can be best avoided. The recently proposed and enacted legislation discussed above has drawn the attention and the ire of civil rights advocates, librarians, booksellers and governmental bodies ranging from town councils to Congress. The erstwhile guardian of civil liberties, the American Civil Liberties Union (ACLU), has determined that Section 215 violates the First, Fourth, and Fifth Amendments and is considering a legal challenge to have it declared unconstitutional.

On July 3, 2003, the ACLU published a special report entitled: *Independence Day 2003: Main Street America Fights the Federal Government's Insatiable Appetite for New Power in the Post 9/11 Era* [17]. The report highlights the ways in which over 130 communities, encompassing more than 16 million people in 26 states, have passed resolutions opposing the USA PATRIOTS Act.

Some of these resolutions contain strong legal language directing local police to, among other things, refrain from engaging in racial profiling, enforcing immigration laws, or participating in federal investigations that violate civil liberties. Communities adopting such resolutions include the states of Alaska, Hawaii, and Vermont as well as traditionally conservative locales, such as Oklahoma City, Tucson, and Flagstaff, along with Detroit, Philadelphia, Minneapolis, Oakland, and Broward County, Florida (which includes Fort Lauderdale).

Denver was the second city to pass such a resolution, after Ann Arbor, Michigan. That resolution, among other things, states that the Denver police should not gather information on the individual's First Amendment activities unless the information relates to criminal activity and the subject is suspected of criminal activity [17, p. 9].

In Congress, Representative Bernie Sanders (I-VT) has introduced the Freedom to Read Protection Act (H.R.1157), which would exempt libraries and bookstores from Section 215 of the USA PATRIOT Act. As of the date of this report's release, the bill has 122 co-sponsors, including many Republicans. Under the bill, federal agents could still seek bookstore and library records, but only with a criminal subpoena or search warrant based upon probable cause. The two largest booksellers in the United States—Barnes and Noble and Borders—have backed the proposed law and California's Democratic Senator Barbara Boxer (D-CA) has introduced a companion bill in the Senate [17, p. 14].

On January 29, 2003, the American Library Association Council adopted the "Resolution on the USA Patriot Act and Related Measures That Infringe on the Rights of Library Users." It reads in part: "The ALA urges all libraries to adopt and implement patron privacy and record retention policies that affirm that the collection of personally identifiable information should be a matter of routine or policy when necessary for the fulfillment of the mission of the library."

The resolution also notes that it considers certain sections of the USA PATRIOT Act "a present danger to the constitutional rights and privacy rights of library users and urges the US Congress to . . . hold hearings to determine the extent of the surveillance on library users and their communities and . . . amend or change the sections of these laws and the guidelines that threaten or abridge the rights of inquiry and free expression. . . ."

One more example of the citizenry's response to the germane proposed or enacted laws since 9/11 is a Website created by graduate students at the Massachusetts Institute of Technology (Web address: opengov.media.mit.edu). Named "Government Information Awareness," it is intended to serve as a scope into the actions of the government, similar to the way the government is using the Internet to examine the interests and actions of citizens. Its primary founder, Ryan McKinley, explains that he hopes the site will become a kind of "Google of government," a clearinghouse of information to help individuals track the actions of their leaders and government [18, p. 1].

The changes to the laws that govern and protect information rights as described here provide a challenge to all Americans, particularly those who work as professionals in the communication field. At minimum, one must be aware of potential government scrutiny today in a manner that hasn't been necessary since the first two decades of the Cold War. Journalists and others who need access to government information must be prepared for a much more determined effort, and must be prepared for more common government refusals. And, ultimately, we must all be alert and aware of the government's next steps in addressing information issues in this post-9/11 environment.

REFERENCES

1. B. Maher, *When You Ride Alone You Ride with Bin Laden: What the Government Should Be Telling Us to Help Fight the War on Terrorism*, New Millennium Press, New York, 2002.
2. Weekly Compilation of Presidential Documents, Remarks on Signing the USA PATRIOT Act of 2001, 2001. Available online at:
   http://frwebgate.access.gpo.gov/cgibin/getdoc.cgi?dbname=2001_presidential_documents&docid=pd29oc01_txt.-26
3. Electronic Frontier Foundation, EFF Analysis of the Provisions of the USA PATRIOT Act, October 2001. Available online at:
   www.eff.org/Privacy/Surveillance/Terrorism/20011031_eff_usa_patriot_analysis.html
4. American Civil Liberties Union, Section 215 FAQ, April 2002. Available online at: http://www.aclu.org/Privacy/Privacy.cfm?ID=11054&c=130
5. C. Doyle, *The USA PATRIOT Act: A Legal Analysis*, Congressional Research Service/The Library of Congress, Washington, D.C., 2001.
6. J. Podesta, USA Patriot Act: The Good, the Bad, and the Sunset, *ABA Network*/American Bar Association [Electronic Journal], Winter 2002. Available online at: http://www.abanet.org/irr/hr/winter02/podesta.html

7. P. McMasters, *Homeland Security Law Blasts Hole in FOI*, American Society of Newspaper Editors, March 2003. Available online at: http://www.asne.org/index.cfm?id=4384
8. R. M. Schmidt, Jr. and K. M. Goldberg, *ASNE Memo on the Patriot Act II*, American Society of Newspaper Editors, 2003. Available online at: http://www.asne.org/index.cfm?id=4348
9. American Civil Liberties Union, *ACLU Fact Sheet on PATRIOT Act II*, March 2003. Available online at: http://www.aclu.org/SafeandFree/SafeandFree.cfm?ID=12234&c=206
10. B. Berkowitz, *Freedom of Information Act on the Ropes*, The Freedom of Information Center, October 2002. Available online at: http://208.34.222.235/bin/rdas.dll/RDAS_SVR=www.altavista.com/...
11. R. Schlesinger, Bush Designates 6 as "Enemy Combatants," *The Boston Globe*, July 4, 2003. Available online at: http://208.34.222.235/bin/rdas.dll/RDAS_SVR=www.newslibrary.c...
12. W. Mears, *Court Opens New Session with Terrorism, Campaign Finance on Agenda*, CNN.com/Law Center, October 2002. Available online at: http://www.cnn.com/2002/LAW/10/07/scotus.preview/
13. C. Page, Defending Our Privacy Rights Against All-Out Assault, *The Baltimore Sun*, p. 15A, April 25, 2003.
14. J. Perkins, Democratic Duplicity on the Patriot Act, *The San Diego Union-Tribune*, p. B-7, May 30, 2003.
15. *Virginia v. Black*, Barry E. et al./01-1107, as obtained via On the Docket-Medill School of Journalism, April 7, 2003. Available online at: http://journalism.medill.northwestern.ed...et%2fdetail.srch&-recordID=33075&-search
16. G. Mast and B. F. Kawin, *A Short History of the Movies* (6th Edition), Allyn and Bacon, Boston, p. 298, 1996.
17. American Civil Liberties Union, *Independence Day 2003: Main Street America Fights the Federal Government's Insatiable Appetite for New Power in the Post 9/11 Era*, July 3, 2003. Available online at: http://www.aclu.org/SafeandFree/SafeandFree.cfm?ID=13060&c=207
18. MIT Project Aims to Give Citizens a Google for their Government, *USAToday*, p. 1, July 3, 2003.

CHAPTER 3

Freedom in Internet Mediated Communication (IMC): Does This Foster True or Untrue Relationships?

James Poon Teng Fatt

Internet-mediated communication (IMC) may be seen as lacking in face-to-face interaction but it is gaining popularity with the new found freedom people now have on the Internet. However, the relationships formed online may be questioned on their genuineness. If we are indeed concerned as to whether face-to-face communication or IMC is preferred in developing and maintaining friendships, then we should ask people about their preferred IMC usage patterns compared to face-to-face communication. That was what I mainly did for 200 students in Singapore. However, in order to compare the responses of working adults in a business world and that of students to see how relationships differ between the two groups, I also surveyed some 130 working adults. Then, by examining their online relationships using Aristotle's notions of friendships and the dimensions of relationship development (namely interdependence, breadth, depth, understanding and predictability, and commitment), I found that, in spite of the freedom of communication on the Internet, the students preferred face-to-face interaction rather than IMC in forming and developing friendships. Moreover, their online friendships did not have the specific dimensions of relationship development, indicating that their relationships were superficial rather than the true friendships as defined by Aristotle. This study also found that the working adults did not view frequency of communication as an important attribute in making friends, use ICQ less often than do students, and rarely interact with strangers online to consider them as friends or even to meet them in real-life.

THE INTERNET AND COMPUTER-MEDIATED COMMUNICATION (CMC) IN ONLINE RELATIONSHIPS

Welcome to communication in a high-tech world. To get terms right, CMC refers to the form of communication requiring the use of large, computer-based networks or meta-networks like organizational Intranets and the Internet. Forms of CMC can be synchronous and asynchronous. Synchronous CMC allows for "real time" exchanges between parties, while asynchronous CMC is non-instantaneous. The Internet is a joint form of synchronous and asynchronous CMC as it facilitates both real time communication (e.g., chat rooms) and non-instantaneous communication (e.g., e-mail).

Advancements in information technology have led to an exponential growth in the use of CMC, especially for the Internet. It is estimated that 529 million people worldwide have gone online, and the number is expected to increase [1]. Such widespread popularity and usage of the Internet has dramatically changed the ways we communicate and relate to one another. With it, we can transcend international boundaries to interact with one another of similar interests. Internet-mediated communication (IMC) has created new opportunities that supposedly foster personal relationships, with similarity in interests and attitudes as the basis for such social linkages.

As IMC is mostly text-based, it lacks face-to-face communication in relationship formation. Can we then question the genuineness of relationships formed online in virtual communities?

DEFINITIONS OF FRIENDSHIP

Webster's dictionary definition of friendship as "a relationship of mutual regard" reveals little on what actually constitutes friendship. A deeper understanding of the meaning of friendship comes from Aristotle's notions on three different kinds of friendship: friendships of utility, friendships of pleasure, and friendships of virtue.

Friendships of utility are based on the usefulness of friends to one another insofar as providing for each other. As such friendships are only motivated by one's need for something that others can provide, they do not last. Friendships of pleasure are friendships formed primarily for the enjoyment they bring to the individuals involved. Finally, friendships of virtue are motivated by the concern for each other's well being through sharing of similar virtues and merits, and having one another's interest in mind. Because of this intimate nature, they can only be on a one-to-one basis.

Aristotle's Hierarchy of Friendships

In Aristotle's Hierarchy of Relationships, each subsequent level inherits features from the levels below. Friendships of utility or *filios* are at the lowest level, while friendships of virtue or *agape* are at the highest level (see Figure 1). As the friendship level progresses to the next higher level, the degree of relationship development in terms of the five dimensions also increases such that the degree of sincerity and commitment increases. At the highest level, ideal friendships of virtue exhibit all five dimensions, where individuals share the same values, depend on each other deeply, and are highly motivated to form long-lasting relationships. Conversely, friendships of utility show few or none of the elements since individuals only engage in the relationships to gain personal benefits rather than the desire to have a true friend. Thus, there is little encouragement to continue these functional relationships once individuals have obtained what they had wanted. Friendships of pleasure or *eros* are motivated by the enjoyment individuals derive from one another's company. This level of friendship shows a stronger desire to maintain and develop the relationship than friendships of utility because at this level the individuals may desire to continue the pleasure derived by furthering the relationships through knowing each other better or widening their scope of activities. However, such friendships of pleasure still fall short of being virtuous because they are primarily motivated by personal welfare.

THE CONCERN OF IMC IN ONLINE RELATIONSHIPS

Our concern of IMC in online relationships is whether face-to-face interaction is necessary for the formation and development of friendships in terms of the role of IMC in maintaining existing friendships, and in forming and maintaining new friendships. How genuine are online friendships from their degree of development in terms of interdependence, breadth, depth, understanding and predictability, and commitment? Are online friendships a prelude to real-life face-to-face friendship?

Today, rapid advancements in information technology are changing the nature of the Internet as a freely accessible communication medium. Developments to improve its interactivity, such as video-conferencing and telephony, are constantly underway. If we examine only text-based IMC in order to isolate the effects of the absence of face-to-face elements

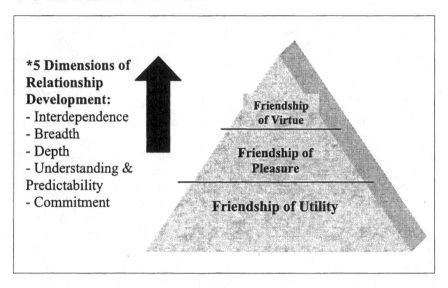

Figure 1. Aristotle's friendship paradigm.

in IMC settings in the formation and development of relationships, can we expect friendship, being a most popular and common type of interpersonal relationship, to be formed online?

Our primary concern on CMC relationships is the absence of face-to-face interaction in their formation and development. Online relationships are typically formed in a text-based environment that is devoid of face-to-face elements like body language and eye contact. This lack of face-to-face interaction makes us skeptical about the substance and authenticity of social relationships formed through the Internet. In this respect, there are two opposing views — traditional and contemporary — on CMC relationships that have emerged.

TRADITIONAL VIEWS ON CMC RELATIONSHIPS

The classical perspective that CMC relationships are impersonal and superficial arose from the design and analysis studies involving comparisons of groups communicating through computers with those interacting face-to-face [2]. Participants were typically engaged in ad hoc problem-solving tasks that provided little opportunity for social communication and linkages to be formed and the results were often analyzed and explained using theories of relational development, which emphasize the importance and need for face-to-face interaction in relationship formation and development. Examples of such theories are the Social Presence Theory, the Social Cues Approach [3], the Uncertainty Reduction Theory [4], and the Social Penetration Theory [5].

Social Presence Theory

The Social Presence Theory was widely used in the past. The social presence of a communication medium is its capacity to convey a communicator's presence to another party. The better able the medium is in transmitting information about the communicator's tone, facial expression, posture, and other verbal and non-verbal cues, the greater will be the communicator's social presence. The way individuals interact with one another is influenced by the degree of the medium's social presence. It was thought that when the medium projects lower social presence, the other parties will become less aware of the communicator's presence and consequently pay less attention to him or her, thereby making the communication process impersonal and less interactive.

This theory implies that CMC, which lacks both verbal and non-verbal cues, has very low social presence, and therefore makes it cold, impersonal, and unsuitable for establishing relationships. Consequently, this model led many to conclude that positive personal relationships could not occur frequently with CMC [6].

Social Cues Approach

It has been observed that CMC groups tend to engage in verbal aggression, blunt disclosure, and nonconforming behavior more often than do face-to-face groups [7, 8]. While such behavior could be due to the anonymity of CMC [9], it could also be explained using the Social Cues Approach. For example, Culnan and Markus observed that social cues, such as vocal qualities and facial expressions, were filtered out in online settings [10]. Consequently, the participants found it difficult to relate to one another. In addition, with the impact of social norms reduced, hostile behavior called "flaming" resulted. Sproull and Kiesler echoed this sentiment with their Social Context Cues Approach by theorizing that the lack of social cues and the need to focus on written text in CMC settings made the participants less sensitive to and aware of one another, thereby making the communication process cold and impersonal [3]. Consequently, positive relationships were less likely to foster.

Uncertainty Reduction and
Social Penetration Theories

The Uncertainty Reduction Theory postulates that the development of relationships is driven by a reduction in an individuals' uncertainty towards another. In a similar way, the Social Penetration Theory proposes that interpersonal relationships develop as interactions between parties become more intimate [4, 5]. For CMC and IMC, however, the lack of face-to-face elements like physical proximity and verbal cues limit the amount of information individuals can gather about one another. As this was thought to discourage intimate disclosures and hinder the uncertainty reduction process, many early researchers predicted that online relationships would unlikely develop into meaningful ones [6, 11].

In summary, the traditional views on CMC relationships are limited. Theories of relational development typically assume physical proximity and frequent interaction between individuals in establishing interpersonal relationships and they emphasize other aspects of face-to-face communication like physical appearance and physical attraction [5, 12]. But none of these theories can conclusively prove that face-to-face elements are prerequisites for the formation and development of personal relationships [13].

We must look beyond early CMC on online friendships in today's society. The fact that the majority of early researches were not set in a social context but rather in task-oriented laboratory sessions where participants were given limited periods of time to solve structured problems, these studies did not provide participants any opportunity to form interpersonal relationships with one another. Also, field studies commonly report that individuals were able to socialize, develop, and maintain relationships in CMC settings [14]. Lastly, the conclusion that personal relationships in a computer-mediated environment were either superficial or could not be established was made well before the Internet became a popular and dominant form of communication media as we are aware of today.

CONTEMPORARY VIEWS ON CMC
RELATIONSHIPS

Although online relationships are generally thought of as impersonal, hostile, unreal, and lacking in social orientation, contemporary field studies suggest otherwise — that online relationships are in fact becoming more common and meaningful.

We can criticize the *Social Presence Theory* on its rationale, which is not well supported. Early studies based on the Social Presence Theory were incomplete as they only considered the medium of communication itself. For a more comprehensive view of communication in a computer-mediated environment, it is important to consider both medium charac-teristics and user perceptions [15], especially when people nowadays are likely to view CMC more positively in view of the Internet's popularity and usage. Furthermore, the Social Presence Theory was originally devised for studying new telecommunications media such as audio and video teleconferencing, which do not have the same characteristics as CMC. It is therefore inappropriate to use this theory when we discuss CMC.

The *Social Cues Approach* has the following failings:

1. The absence of physical and nonverbal cues does not necessarily mean that CMC is impersonal or devoid of social cues, or that the transmitted cues lack the subtlety of those communicated face-to-face [16]. There can be degrees of socio-emotional content in CMC. Studies have found that CMC users not only sought information but also com-panionship, social support, and a sense of belonging [17]. Moreover, CMC users have also been observed using textual cues to develop rapport and to overcome the lack of verbal and non-verbal cues [15, 18, 19]. According to Walther [15], people would adapt non-verbally expressed social information into online communication. As we are aware, "smileys" are often used to imitate facial expressions and paralinguistic features of conversation. Words are also embedded in the text to express emotion and meta-communicative intent. Hence, it is not that CMC is unable to convey relational and personal information, but rather it just needs a longer time to do so [13].

2. Flaming, mainly a result of the lack of social cues, can be chal-lenged. Walther and others found that socio-emotional content was greater when interaction time was unrestricted [18]. It was observed that hostile responses did not arise simply because the medium was the computer. Instead, they arose as a result of participants responding too slowly. This suggests that the negative effects attributed to CMC as a communication tool might be due to the stringent time restrictions placed on the interaction process [13]. Furthermore, McCormick and McCormick noted that many of the hostile messages studied came from college computer centers where such exchanges were common and meant as pranks [20]. Although participants called one another names, the mocking only seemed to strengthen their relationships. Thus, viewed more positively, flaming could be a sign of affection and trust rather than detest or offense. This implies that flaming in CMC does not always indicate a hostile impersonal atmosphere, nor does it necessarily hinder the formation or development of relationships such as friendships.

The *Uncertainty Reduction and Social Penetration Theories* have the following failings:

1. They assume that the lack of face-to-face elements discourages self-disclosure and impedes the uncertainty reduction process, thereby hampering the development of interpersonal relationships. However, physical proximity and visual information alone do not automatically encourage self-disclosure or facilitate uncertainty reduction [13]. A person's degree of uncertainty or familiarity toward another hinges on how much information the other party is willing to divulge. Hence, uncertainty reduction and the intimacy of a relationship are both dependent on the individuals' personalities and their willingness to disclose information about themselves. "Heavy" Internet users are more likely to use CMC to interact with others and initiate new relationships than "light" users who tend to prefer building relationships with the traditional face-to-face approach.

2. Walther reasoned with his social information processing theory that the uncertainty reduction process is slower for CMC because people take longer to get used to the medium [15]. Parks and Floyd found that the lack of proximity and visual information could be overcome by meeting one another or by exchanging photographs [13]. Thus, the uncertainty, lack of intimacy, and other limitations attributable to CMC can be overcome by simply supplementing it with additional channels of communication like telephone conversations and face-to-face meetings. Therefore, it should not be presumed that the absence of face-to-face elements in CMC would definitely obstruct the development of genuine personal relationships.

What I have so far presented are two very distinct views on online relationships. One view is that online relationships are infrequent and shallow while the other view perceives them as genuine and common. Because many studies done on CMC generally involve asynchronous CMC like newsgroups, I would like to extend the knowledge of the appropriateness of CMC to users of chat-rooms, ICQ, and the Inter-relay chat (IRC), all of which are synchronous forms of CMC. It would also be interesting to explore whether differences in culture might influence the preference of using IMC to initiate and maintain relationships.

Past researches primarily focused on the reasons for the formation of online relationships and ways in which CMC and IMC could overcome the lack of face-to-face elements. They did not specifically examine the nature and genuineness of the relationships formed. Hence, it would be interesting to further examine the characteristics of online friendships and compare this with Aristotle's definition of friendship. Such a comparison can help us in understanding the motivation behind the formation of online relationships and their genuineness.

THE STUDY

In this study, I asked 200 respondents from secondary schools, colleges, and educational institutions such as technical institute, polytechnics, and universities in Singapore to compare online communication with face-to-face communication by rating some Likert-type statements in a questionnaire (see Appendix). I also examined their usage patterns for the different types of online communication mode. The survey was conducted at 10 randomly chosen areas in Singapore (five from Mass Rapid Transit stations, three from shopping malls, and two from bus exchange terminals), with the number of respondents for each age group about equal in the 10 areas. Finally, in order to compare the relationships between working adults and students, I also gave the same questionnaire to some 130 working adults.

Specifically, I wished to find answers to the following questions:

- Do people prefer to develop new friendships through the Internet or face-to-face communication?
- Do people prefer to maintain friendships through the Internet or face-to face communication?
- Is it easier to express one's thoughts and feelings through the Internet or face-to-face communication?
- Does the use of the Internet or face-to-face communication enable one to know more about his/her friends?
- Does the use of Internet or face-to-face communication improve relationship with friends?
- How are online relationships developed in terms of interdependence, breadth, depth, predictability and understanding of one another, and commitment?

FINDINGS

The student sample (200) comprises 53% females and 47% males from educational institutions, which include secondary school (13%), technical institute (10.5%), polytechnic (25.5%), junior college (8%), and university (43%). The working adult sample (130) comprises equal numbers of males and females from fields of accounting (15%), education (50%), human resources (5%), and sales and marketing (30%).

Attributes Necessary in Friendships

The respondents consider positive response, frequency of communication, similarities, and humor important when making and maintaining friendships. The unimportant attributes are physical attractiveness and indifference (see Tables 1 and 2).

Table 1. Important Attributes in Making Friends

	Very important (%)		Not important (%)	
	Students	Adults	Students	Adults
Physical attractiveness	17.5	23.1	82.5	76.9
Positive response	76.5	69.2	23.5	30.8
Frequency of communication	76.0	57.6	24.0	42.4
Similarity	68.0	65.4	32.0	34.6
Indifference	38.0	25.0	62.0	75.0
Humor	55.0	50.0	45.0	50.0
Tendency for other party to disclose information	47.0	52.0	53.0	48.0

Table 2. Important Attributes in Maintaining Friendships

	Very important (%)		Not important (%)	
	Students	Adults	Students	Adults
Physical attractiveness	9.0	0	91.0	100.0
Positive response	78.0	73.1	22.0	26.9
Frequency of communication	84.0	69.2	16.0	30.8
Similarity	72.0	69.2	28.0	30.8
Humor	56.5	42.3	43.5	57.7
Tendency for other party to disclose information	65.5	56.0	34.5	44.0

Physical attractiveness is an attribute that is absent in an online environment and may be thought to affect an individual's preference for using IMC. However, the respondents did not perceive IMC as being inferior to face-to-face interaction in forming and maintaining friendships.

The respondents also did not think indifference is important perhaps because they would not mind a little indifference when they are unfamiliar initially with one another but, as the friendship develops, this perception would change.

There is no clear difference among the working adults concerning the importance of attribute in making friends. This is a contrast to the many students (76%) who viewed frequency of communication as very important.

There is also no clear inference on the importance of the tendency to disclose information. The Uncertainty Reduction Theory emphasizes the importance of disclosures in reducing the uncertainty caused by IMC's anonymous nature and in facilitating the development of friendship. However, anonymity to individuals means that they can disclose any information they choose in order to project a desirable image without fear of being exposed. Hence, individuals who are unlikely to believe them totally do not expect frank disclosures of personal information. Thus, the respondents did not view disclosures as helpful or necessary but significant in the maintenance phrase (see Table 2) perhaps because they felt that at this stage they would need more information to understand one another better and gain intimacy.

Usage Patterns

The respondents' usage patterns such as their usage frequency may indicate their development and maintenance of online friendships. E-mail is the most commonly used (>95%) IMC channel with IRC and discussion group being less popular. The students used ICQ more often (66.5%) than did the working adults (37.5%). Also, the channels were used rather infrequently compared to e-mail, with greater than 55% daily usage rate (see Figures 2 and 3, and Table 3).

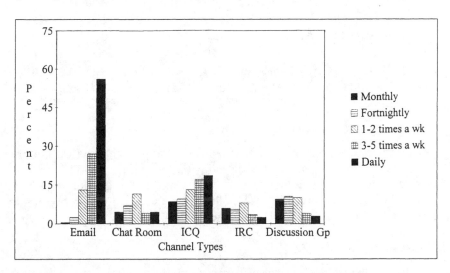

Figure 2. Usage frequency (students).

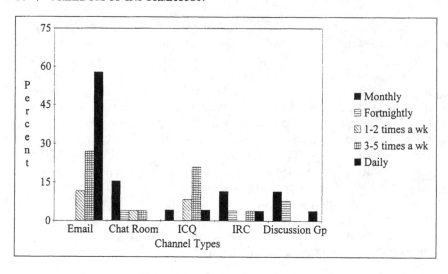

Figure 3. Usage frequency (adults).

Table 3. Usage Frequency Data

	Students (%)					Adults (%)				
	E-mail	Chat room	ICQ	IRC	Dis-cussion	E-mail	Chat room	ICQ	IRC	Dis-cussion
Monthly	0.5	4.5	8.5	6.0	9.5	0	15.4	4.2	11.5	11.5
Fortnightly	2.5	7.0	9.5	5.5	10.5	0	3.9	0	3.9	7.7
1-2 times a week	13.0	11.5	13.0	8.0	10.0	11.5	3.9	8.3	0	0
3-5 times a week	27.0	4.0	17.0	3.5	4.0	26.9	3.9	20.8	3.9	0
Daily	56.0	4.5	18.5	2.5	3.0	57.7	0	4.2	3.9	3.9
Total	99.0	31.5	66.5	25.5	37.0	96.1	27.1	37.5	23.2	23.1

The majority of users spent less than an hour on each channel. Although e-mail is the most popular channel with ICQ second, only 32% or less of e-mail users spent more than an hour using it. Except for ICQ, the rest of the channels saw 20% or less of their users exceeding the one-hour usage duration (see Figures 4 and 5 and Table 4).

Reasons for Using IMC

Individuals use IMC for various reasons, mainly to keep in touch with friends (>80%) and share news about oneself, friends, or people whom

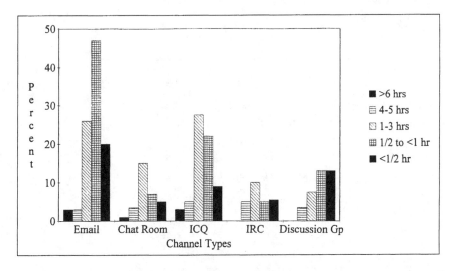

Figure 4. Usage length (students).

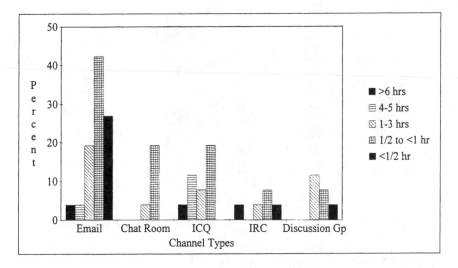

Figure 5. Usage length (adults).

one knows, share something interesting or funny, and make plans to get together. Using the Internet to look for "long lost" friends is the least common (32.5% or less), suggesting that the respondents prefer face-to-face communication for activities of high emotional content (see Figure 6 and Table 5).

Table 4. Usage Length Data

	Students (%)					Adults (%)				
	E-mail	Chat room	ICQ	IRC	Dis-cussion	E-mail	Chat room	ICQ	IRC	Dis-cussion
More than 6 hours	3.0	1.0	3.0	0	0	3.9	0	3.9	3.9	0
4-5 hours	3.0	3.5	5.0	5.0	3.5	3.9	0	11.5	0	0
1-3 hours	26.0	15.0	27.5	10.0	7.5	19.2	3.9	7.7	3.9	11.5
_ to <1 hour	47.0	7.0	22.0	5.0	13.0	42.3	19.2	19.2	7.7	7.7
<_ hr	20.0	5.0	9.0	5.5	13.0	26.9	0	0	3.9	3.9
Total	99.0	31.5	66.5	25.5	37.0	96.2	23.1	42.3	19.4	23.1

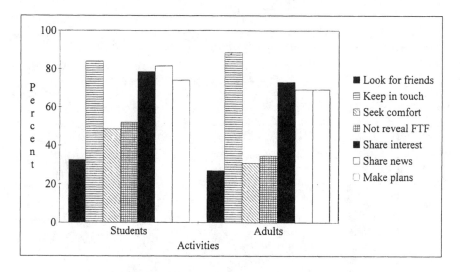

Figure 6. Activities on the Internet.

IMC v. Face-to-Face Interactions

A comparison of IMC and face-to-face interactions reveals the following.

Making Friends

The respondents prefer to develop new friendships through face-to-face communication than the Internet. The explanation could be that the respondents disclose too little personal information on the Internet, which

Table 5. Activities on the Internet Data

	Students (%)	Adults (%)
Look for "long-lost" friends.	32.5	26.9
Keep in touch with friends whom one seldom meets.	84.0	88.5
Seek comfort and/or advice.	48.5	30.8
Write something that one wouldn't want to say or reveal face-to-face.	52.0	34.6
Share something interesting or funny.	78.5	73.1
Share news about oneself and people whom one knows.	81.5	69.2
Make plans about getting together.	74.0	69.2

impedes the development of online friendships that require more in-depth knowledge of one another. It could also be that the respondents have negative perceptions of IMC from online media reports on the abuse of personal information, which add to their unwillingness and insecurity in revealing personal information and making friends online. Furthermore, the decline of the IMC fad may have reduced motivation to use the Internet to make friends.

Maintaining Friendships

The respondents prefer face-to-face communication than the Internet to maintain friendships. Perhaps this is because existing friends meet frequently offline, which reduces the need to contact one another online. Moreover, the low usage of IMC channels suggests that the respondents do not need to depend on IMC to keep in touch with one another. Also, the high Internet usage required to make plans to meet may have caused the respondents to opt for meeting offline instead.

Ability to Express Thoughts and Feelings

The respondents find it easier to express their thoughts and feelings through face-to-face communication rather than the Internet. As mentioned earlier, most respondents do not use IMC to seek comfort or reveal things that are difficult to express offline, so it could be that they are not comfortable using the Internet to express their thoughts and feelings. Moreover, they may not wish to disclose sensitive information, regardless of the communication medium.

Internet and Closeness

The use of the Internet does not enable the respondents to know more about one another as compared to face-to-face communication. This could be that the respondents do not maintain friendships online, so they are unable to learn more about one another through IMC. Besides, the respondents do not prefer to use IMC to convey sensitive personal information. As a result, they cannot understand their friends better through IMC, which is further worsened by their infrequent use of IMC.

Internet and Relationship Improvement

The use of the Internet does not improve relationships with friends as compared to face-to-face communication. As mentioned earlier, the infrequent and short usage spans and the uneasiness of revealing one's thoughts and feelings online hinder the maintenance of friendship through IMC. Consequently, friendships are not enhanced online.

Interaction With Strangers

About 69.6% of the students often and even all the time used IMC (see Figure 7), compared to 11.7% of working adults (see Figure 8) to interact with strangers (see also Table 6). According to the Social Information Processing Theory, IMC is not inferior to face-to-face interaction in reducing uncertainty; it merely takes longer. Therefore, increased IMC usage frequency would help to speed up the uncertainty reduction process and facilitate the fostering of online friendships. Thus, understanding the usage behavior of the respondents in their online conversations with strangers is necessary.

About 20.3% of students used discussion groups to interact with strangers and e-mail has the least usage (7.6%). Although more than 50% of the students have interacted with strangers online, the frequency of such interaction is low, which suggests that most of these online meetings are just one-time, non-recurring events (see Figure 7). For working adults, the interaction with strangers is very rare (see Figure 8).

The Degree of Friendship Development

Interdependence — There is no interdependence between the respondents in online relationships. Without frequent interaction and disclosures of personal information, individuals could not be familiar with one another. Hence, they would not confide in other parties for advice or help.

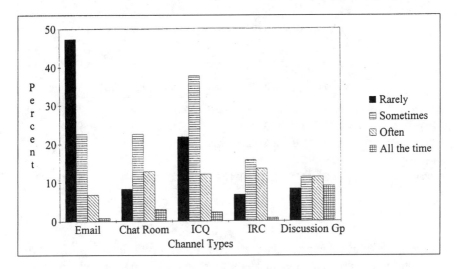

Figure 7. Interacting with strangers (students).

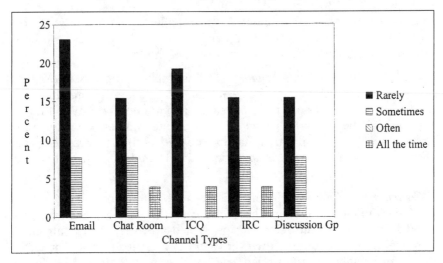

Figure 8. Interacting with strangers (adult).

Breadth—Communication topics vary widely in online relationships, suggesting that the respondents do not wish to engage in in-depth discussions for fear of divulging too much information or changing the topic when the conversations become too personal. Also, as the respondents do not contact one another offline, they probably just interact out of novelty rather than with desire to develop the friendship further.

Table 6. Frequency of Interacting with Strangers Data

	Students (%)					Adults (%)			
	E-mail	Chat room	ICQ	IRC	Dis-cussion	E-mail	Chat room	ICQ	IRC	Dis-cussion
Rarely	47.4	8.3	21.8	6.8	8.3	23.1	15.4	19.2	15.4	15.4
Sometimes	22.6	22.6	37.6	15.8	11.3	7.7	7.7	0	7.7	7.7
Often	6.8	12.8	12.0	13.5	11.3	0	0	0	0	0
All the time	0.8	3.0	2.3	0.8	9.0	0	3.9	3.9	3.9	0
Total	77.6	46.7	73.7	36.9	39.9	30.8	27.0	23.1	27.0	23.1

Depth—Online friendships lack depth. As mentioned earlier, the respondents seem reluctant to reveal personal information, which makes their online interactions superficial. The respondents are uncomfortable with using IMC to express their thoughts and feelings, supported by findings of this study that online friendships lack interdependence and individuals cover wide topics to prevent in-depth discussions. All these add to preventing online friendships from becoming in-depth.

Predictability and Understanding—Online relationships lack predictability and understanding. The lack of interdependence, breadth, and depth in online relationships impedes the respondents' ability to understand each other better. The lack of trust in one another, the reluctance to let other parties know them better, coupled with the infrequent and short interactions, provide little upon which to build predictability and understanding in online friendships.

Commitment—Online relationships lack commitment. Commitment toward maintaining relationships requires that the respondents be interested in continuing the relationships, which arises from how attached they feel for one another. However, without interdependence, breadth, depth, predictability, and understanding, this interest cannot be developed. Besides, most people interact online to pass time rather than search for true friends. Added to these is the decline of the IMC fad, which could have reduced the respondents' motivation to continue with such activities. Consequently, the respondents view online relationships as short-lived and are therefore not committed to them.

While 86.5% of the students compared with only 15.4% working adults continued to correspond with people they had met online, only 73.7% students and 15.4% working adults continued to interact with some of these strangers. Such a selective communication behavior implies that only a few relationships are being developed through IMC, especially for working adults.

About 69.9% of students and 23.1% working adults viewed strangers as friends. However, as it has been shown earlier that there are no elements of relationship development, this anomaly can be better understood if we combine Aristotle's definition of friendship with the specific dimensions of interdependence, breadth, depth, understanding, and predictability, and commitment to arrive at a friendship paradigm.

APPLICATION OF ARISTOTLE'S
FRIENDSHIP PARADIGM

Applying Aristotle's Friendship Paradigm, we can see that initially people interact with one another online because of personal needs. For instance, people use IMC to gain knowledge on a particular subject or matter of interest. However, there is little development of friendship in terms of interdependence, breadth, depth, understanding and predictability, and commitment. Once the need has been satisfied, individuals are unlikely to continue the relationship until a similar need arises again. This kind of behavior is in line with friendships of utility.

Likewise, many people turn to IMC to seek enjoyment (friendships of pleasure). For example, many people participate in discussion groups and chat rooms in their leisure time to be entertained by others. Individuals may wish to continue corresponding with those strangers they take delight in chatting with by interacting more frequently and exchanging information through e-mail. Nonetheless, such relationships seldom develop further because individuals will turn to something else after some time when they get bored. Also, the unwillingness to disclose personal information to strangers adds to the uncertainty caused by IMC's anonymous nature. Besides, many individuals also perceive the Internet environment as unreal, which makes them even less inclined to take online relationships seriously.

People, however, do communicate with one another to provide support or encouragement. Such behavior results in friendships of virtue found in online virtual communities. However, the fostering of such relationships requires time, effort, and commitment. Few respondents in my study had such behavior, perhaps because of their low usage frequency and short interaction spans. Furthermore, most individuals interact online out of need or to seek enjoyment, so they are not really serious about the relationships. There is also the lack of trust and understanding that are the distinguishing elements of friendships of virtue. Consequently, true forms of online friendship are rather uncommon.

About 62% of the students compared with only 11.5% working adults would consider online strangers as friends and want to meet them in real-life, which may indicate that online relationship can be a starting point for friendship development for students but not for working adults. Those who indicated they do not want to meet their online friends could be harboring lack of trust and insecurity or they might be afraid that the meeting would spoil their impression of one another and thereby ruin their "virtual" relationship.

IMPLICATIONS AND CONCLUSION

Thus far, I have shown that e-mail is preferred over synchronous channels like chat rooms and ICQ, and that the occurrence of real online friendships is low, especially for the generally busy working adults who probably need to spend more time at work than at communicating online for friendship purposes. This may imply that asynchronous IMC alone is insufficient in encouraging online friendships, which needs a greater usage of synchronous channels for speedier responses.

One reason why genuine online friendships are found uncommon in this study, unlike the results from studies done in the West, is perhaps the reluctance of Asians to disclose personal information by virtue of being more reserved and less comfortable in expressing themselves to strangers. In an online setting that lacks face-to-face elements, this behavior becomes even more pronounced. Therefore, this marked difference between the East and the West with regard to the willingness to disclose implies that culture can be an influencing factor in the development of online friendships.

For example, people of individualistic cultures tend to use low-context communication (LC) more than do people of collectivist cultures (as in the East). By definition, in individualistic culture (as in the West), individual goals are emphasized over collectivist goals (as in the East) and vice versa. If we consider the global nature of the Internet, cultures may be changed by communication in cyberspace. In order to determine these changes, we need to examine more closely how the low context communication style inherent in the Internet or Internet-mediated communication may differ from the cultural norms of its users. In this respect, Gudykunst and others have laid the framework for determining HC and LC traits [21].

I have also shown that most online relationships are not true friendships. Individuals may think that they have established online friendships when in reality what they have instead are friendships of utility and pleasure. This implies that even though the Internet can approximate certain aspects of conventional interaction, face-to-face elements are still important. In this regard, we may wish to consider communicator context as an important aspect of one's communication style. Edward Hall refers to context as what is being said, when, where, and how [22]. According to Hall, the communication process comprises five categories: the subject or activity, the situation, status, prior experience, and culture. If the context is high (HC), then it is more dependent on the five categories than the low context (LC). This can be a problem in Internet-mediated communication, which exists as a low context communication due to fewer situational aspects available to the online communicator than in real life. Those who communicate in a HC manner tend to rely on insinuation, analogy, and the environment to convey meaning without much explicit explanation in the form of informational content. LC communicators, who are more reliant on informational content and less on situation, may then mis-understand HC communicators.

Furthermore, as it was found from this study that the respondents use e-mail more frequently and for a longer time than other IMC channels combined, this may indicate that communication via an LC medium such as IMC is not as frequent for collectivist culture. For the indi-vidualistic culture, high frequency of use and long usage length may result in consequences when the users log off the LC environment and return to real life to communication in a HC environment.

Therefore, in order for us to develop greater trust and commitment in fostering friendships of virtue, online settings should be made more conducive. To enhance IMC's role in developing genuine friendships, more ways of enabling individuals to see and hear one another over the Internet should be devised. Text-based IMC can be supplemented with audio and video features like video-conferencing, which will increase the face-to-face components. Besides, educating the public on the Internet can help increase the public's confidence in using IMC to establish and maintain friendships.

Questions that remain to be answered are:

1. Why is there little fostering of online friendship through IMC even though it has most of the attributes needed for friendship development?
2. Although physical appearance is absent in an online environment and this study has shown that appearance is unimportant in friendship development and maintenance, does this suggest that the development and intimacy of friendships are more dependent on culture and personality?

With the Internet's growing popularity and freedom on the net, there is increasing interest in the role of IMC in fostering relationships like friendships and in the nature of such online relationships. As IMC is found to be inferior to conventional face-to-face interaction in fostering friendship, the implication is that people prefer face-to-face interaction in forming and developing friendships. Also shown in this study is that online relationships are at most friendships of pleasure rather than the true friendships defined by Aristotle. Perhaps the cultural differences between the East and the West can influence the preference of using IMC to initiate and maintain relationships, which can thereby affect friendship development and maintenance. Interestingly, this study has found that online friendships are a prelude to real-life face-to-face friendships, indicating that online relationship might be a starting point for developing new friendships.

APPENDIX:
The Questionnaire on Internet and Friendship

This survey is on how the Internet affects personal relationships, particularly friendship. Please fill out this survey. Your reply will be kept confidential. Thank you very much for your participation.

Instructions: Please circle your choice.

Section 1:

1. In making friends, how important are the following factors to you?

	Very important	Important	Neutral	Not so important	Not important at all
• Physical attractiveness	1	2	3	4	5
• Positive responses (e.g., attentiveness, complements)	1	2	3	4	5
• Frequency of communication with each other	1	2	3	4	5
• Similarity (e.g., interest, attitudes, sex, race)	1	2	3	4	5
• Indifference (e.g., initial dislike, inattentiveness)	1	2	3	4	5
• Humor	1	2	3	4	5
• Tendency of the other party in disclosing personal information	1	2	3	4	5

2. In maintaining friendships, how important are the following factors to you?

	Very important	Important	Neutral	Not so important	Not important at all
• Physical attractiveness	1	2	3	4	5
• Positive responses (e.g., attentiveness, complements)	1	2	3	4	5
• Frequency of communication with each other	1	2	3	4	5
• Similarity (e.g., interest, attitudes, sex, race)	1	2	3	4	5
• Humor	1	2	3	4	5
• Tendency of the other party in disclosing personal information	1	2	3	4	5

Section 2:

3. How often do you use the following Internet channels?

	Daily	3.5 times a week	1-2 times a week	Fort-nightly	Monthly	Don't use
• Send or read e-mail to/from friends	1	2	3	4	5	6
• Go to a chat room	1	2	3	4	5	6
• Chat using ICQ	1	2	3	4	5	6
• Chat using inter-relay chat (IRC)	1	2	3	4	5	6
• Discussion groups	1	2	3	4	5	6

4. For each session, how long do you usually use them?

	≥ 6 hours	4.5 hours	1-3 hours	½ – <1 hour	<1/2 hour	Don't use
• Send or read e-mail to/from friends	1	2	3	4	5	6
• Go to a chat room	1	2	3	4	5	6
• Chat using ICQ	1	2	3	4	5	6
• Chat using inter-relay chat (IRC)	1	2	3	4	5	6
• Discussion groups	1	2	3	4	5	6

5. What do you use the Internet channels (mentioned in **Q3**) for? (You may tick more than one option.)

Make plans about getting together for dinner, a movie, or some social activity.	
Share some news about yourself, friends, or people that you know.	
Share something interesting or funny.	
Write something that you would not want to say or reveal face-to-face.	
Seek comfort and/or advice on something you are upset or worried about.	
Keep in touch with friends whom you seldom meet.	
Look for friends whom you have lost contact with.	

Others:

_____

_____

6. Have you ever engaged in a conversation with a stranger(s) online? Yes/No
   If yes, go to section 3. If no, go to section 4.

Section 3:

7. How often do you use the following Internet channels to interact with a stranger(s)?

	Rarely	Sometimes	Often	All the time	Don't use
• Send or read e-mail	1	2	3	4	5
• Go to a chat room	1	2	3	4	5
• Chat using ICQ	1	2	3	4	5
• Chat using inter-relay chat (IRC)	1	2	3	4	5
• Discussion groups	1	2	3	4	5

8. Please rate the following statements regarding your online interactions with the people you have met through the Internet.

	Strongly disagree	Disagree	Neutral	Agree	Strongly agree
• There are times when we waited for one another's opinions before deciding what to do.	1	2	3	4	5
• We set aside time to communicate with one another.	1	2	3	4	5
• We often influence one another's feelings toward issues we encounter.	1	2	3	4	5
• Our communication topics vary widely.	1	2	3	4	5
• We move easily from one topic to another.	1	2	3	4	5
• We contact one another in ways besides the Internet.	1	2	3	4	5
• I usually tell this person exactly how I feel even if our opinions differ.	1	2	3	4	5
• I feel quite close to this person.					
• I have told this person what I like about him/her.	1	2	3	4	5
• I could confide in this person about almost anything.	1	2	3	4	5

	Strongly disagree	Disagree	Neutral	Agree	Strongly agree
• Our communication is not just superficial.	1	2	3	4	5
• We have developed the ability to "read between the lines" of one another's message to figure out what is really on the other's mind.	1	2	3	4	5
• I can get an idea across to this person with a much shorter message than I would have to use with most people.	1	2	3	4	5
• I am very certain about what this person is really like.	1	2	3	4	5
• I can accurately predict how this person will respond to me in most situations.	1	2	3	4	5
• I can usually tell what this person is feeling inside.	1	2	3	4	5
• I am very committed to maintaining this relationship.	1	2	3	4	5
• This relationship is very important to me.	1	2	3	4	5
• I would make great efforts to maintain my relationship with this person.	1	2	3	4	5
• I expect this relationship to be long lasting.	1	2	3	4	5

9. For how many of the stranger(s) you have met do you continue to communication with using the Internet?

    (A) None of them
    (B) Some of them
    (C) Most of them
    (D) All of them

10. If you have continued to communicate, would you think of the stranger(s) as being your friend(s)?
    Yes/No
    If yes, continue. If no, go to section 4.

11. Do you want to meet your online friend(s) and develop the friendship in real life?
    Yes/No
    Please go to section 4.

Section 4:

12. In comparison to face-to-face communication, how would you rate following students?

	Strongly disagree	Disagree	Neutral	Agree	Strongly agree
• Communicating online enables me to make new friends more easily.	1	2	3	4	5
• I communicate with my friends more often now using the Internet.	1	2	3	4	5
• The use of the Internet has brought me closer to my friends.	1	2	3	4	5
• It is easier for me to express my thoughts and feelings through the use of the Internet.	1	2	3	4	5
• I have learned more about my friends through the use of the Internet.	1	2	3	4	5
• I would prefer to use the Internet to make new friends.	1	2	3	4	5
• I would prefer to use the Internet to keep in contact with my friends.	1	2	3	4	5
• Overall, the use of the Internet has improved my relationship with my friends.	1	2	3	4	5

General Information:

Name: _____

Contact Number: _____ (H) _____ (O)

(a) Gender: (1) Male   (2) Female

(b) Age: (1) 15-20   (2) 21-30   (3) 31-40   (4) 41-50   (5) 51-60

(c) Education Level: (1) None
                    (2) Primary
                    (3) Secondary
                    (4) ITE
                    (5) Polytechnic
                    (6) Junior College
                    (7) Undergraduate
                    (8) Graduate/Post graduate
                    (9) Others (please specify): _____

(d) Occupation: _____

(e) Monthly Income Level: (1) < $1000
                         (2) $1000 to less than $2000
                         (3) $2000 to less than $3000
                         (4) $3000 to less than $4000
                         (5) $4000 to less than $5000
                         (6) $5000 to less than $10,000
                         (7) > $10,000

(f) Housing Type: (1) 1-2 Room
                  (2) 3 Room
                  (3) 4 Room
                  (4) 5 Room
                  (5) Executive Apartment
                  (6) Private Apartment
                  (7) Condominium
                  (8) Landed Property

REFERENCES

1. Global Reach, 2001. Available online at:
   http://www.global-reach.biz/globalstats/index.php3
2. L. Garton and B. Wellman, Social Impacts of Electronic Mail in Organizations: A Review of the Research Literature, in *Communication Yearbook* (Vol. 18), B. Burleson (Ed.), Sage, Newbury Park, California, pp. 434-453, 2001.
3. L. Sproull and S. Kiesler, Reducing Social Context Cues: Electronic Mail in Organizational Communication, *Management Science, 32*, pp. 1492-1512, 1986.
4. C. R. Berger and R. J. Calabrese, Some Explorations in Initial Interaction and Beyond: Toward a Developmental Theory of Interpersonal Communication, *Human Communication Research, 1*, pp. 99-112, 1975.
5. I. Altman and D. Taylor, *Social Penetration: The Development of Interpersonal Relationships*, Holt, Rinehart, & Winston, New York, 1973.
6. R. E. Rice and G. Love, Electronic Emotion: Socioemotional Content in a Computer Mediated Communication Network, *Communication Research, 14*, pp. 85-108, 1987.
7. V. J. Dubrovsky, S. B. Kiesler, and B. N. Sethna, The Equalizion Phenomenon: Status Effects in Computer-Mediated and Face-to-Face Decision-Making Groups, *Human-Computer Interaction, 6*, pp. 119-146, 1991.
8. S. B. Kiesler, J. Siegal, and T. W. McGuire, Social Psychological Aspects of Computer-Mediated Communication, *American Psychologist, 39*, pp. 1123-1134, 1984.
9. M. Lea, T. O'Shea, P. Fung, and R. Spears, "Flaming" in Computer-Mediated Communication: Observations, Explanations and Implications, in *Contexts of Computer-Mediated Communication*, M. Lea (ed.), Harvester-Wheatsheaf, London, pp. 89-112, 1992.
10. M. J. Culnan and M. L. Markus, Information Technologies, in *Handbook of Organizational Communication: An Interdisciplinary Perspective*, F. M. Jablin et al. (eds.), Sage, Newbury Park, California, pp. 420-443, 1987.
11. J. B. Walther and J. K. Burgoon, Relational Communication in Computer-Mediated Interaction, *Human Communication Research, 19*, pp. 50-88, 1992.
12. T. L. Huston and R. L. Burgess, Social Exchange in Developing Relationships: An Overview, in *Social Exchange in Developing Relationships*, R. L. Burgess and T. L. Huston (eds.), Academic, New York, pp. 3-28, 1979.
13. M. R. Parks and K. Floyd, Making Friends in Cyberspace, *Journal of Communication, 46*, pp. 80-97, 1996.
14. C. Haythornthwaite, B. Wellman, and M. Mantei, Media Use and Work Relationships in a Research Group, in *Proceedings of the 27th Hawaii International Conference on Systems Science*, J. Nunamaker, Jr. and R. Sprague, Jr. (eds.), IEEE Press, Washington, D.C., pp. 94-103, 1994.
15. J. B. Walther, Interpersonal Effects in Computer-Mediated Interaction: A Relational Perspective, *Communication Research, 19*, pp. 52-90, 1992.
16. M. Lea and R. Spears, Love at First Byte? Building Personal Relationships Over Computer Networks, in *Understudied relationships: Off the Beaten Track*, J. T. Wood and S. Duck (eds.), Sage, Newbury Park, California, pp. 197-233, 1995.

17. B. Wellman and M. Gulia, *Net Surfers Don't Ride Alone: Virtual Communities as Communities*, 1995. Available online at: http://www.sscnet.ucla.edu/soc/csoc/cinc/wellman.htm
18. J. B. Walther, J. F. Anderson, and D. W. Park, Interpersonal Effects in Computer-Mediated Interaction: A Meta-Analysis of Social and Antisocial Communication, *Communication Research, 21*, pp. 460-487, 1994.
19. J. B. Walther, Impression Development in Computer-Mediated Interaction, *Western Journal of Communication, 57*, pp. 381-398, 1993.
20. N. B. McCormick and J. W. McCormick, Computer Friends and Foes: Content of Undergraduates' Electronic Mail, *Computers in Human Behavior, 8*, pp. 379-405, 1992.
21. W. Gudykunst, Y. Matsumoto, S. Ting-Toomey, T. Nishida, K. Kim, and S. Heyman, The Influence of Individualism-Collectivism, Self-Construals, and Individualistic Values on Communication Styles Across Cultures, *Human Communications Research, 22*:4, pp. 510-543, 1996.
22. E. T. Hall, Context and Meaning, in *Beyond Culture*, Anchor Press, New York, 1976.

CHAPTER 4

The New Challenges for Intercultural Encounters Post 9/11

John Chetro-Szivos

Those living on the East Coast of the United States may recall the beautiful late summer day of September 11, 2001. Not long after most people began their day, horror and confusion shattered the dream like brilliance of the morning. Hijacked aircraft crashed into landmark buildings leaving behind devastation and a profound sense of loss for a nation of people. The feelings that ensued were a sharp contrast to the everyday experiences of people going about their lives on a beautiful morning. This flood of emotions served as a catalyst for deliberation and a warning sign of the challenges that lie ahead. The goal of this chapter is not to comment or offer solutions to the political aspects of terrorism, or international relationships on a macro scale. Instead, this chapter explores the new challenges post September 11 for intercultural encounters between U.S. Americans and others. Communication across cultures has always faced a number of obstacles, but these challenges are amplified by this tragic event. Here the practical issue of developing productive relationships with people from other cultures is addressed. Given the depth of the emotions associated with the events of September 11, the role emotion plays in communication and intercultural encounters is explored. Whether it is the fear and suspicion of more terrorist attacks, or a sense of confusion about what to feel when interacting with people of other backgrounds, the everyday world demands that we find productive ways to interact with others. The intent of this chapter is to offer points for consideration and hopefully insights that may lead to ways to ameliorate or lessen differences between people in situated interaction.

The focus of the chapter is on two key areas. The first is the central role of communication in our lives and the role emotion plays in our communication with others. Second, the chapter explores intercultural encounters and the how the events of September 11 have presented new challenges to intercultural communication. The chapter begins by introducing the reader to a theory of communication called "Coordinated Management of Meaning" (CMM). I refer the reader to the work of Pearce and Cronen [1], Cronen [2, 3], and Cronen and Chetro-Szivos [4]. CMM offers an alternative to traditional perspectives of communication and ways to make sense of intercultural encounters. Most importantly, CMM is a communication theory that can account for the ambiguous nature of communication especially present in intercultural encounters, and the significant role emotion plays in human interaction. The chapter offers practical considerations of culture through the CMM lens, and a discussion of the dimensions of communication that can facilitate intercultural communication. The chapter will conclude with a discussion of finding ways to go on with others in productive and meaningful exchanges.

THE COMMUNICATION PROCESS AND THE COORDINATED MANAGEMENT OF MEANING (CMM)

Many approaches regard communication as an information exchange where words are instruments that send a message from sender to receiver. This traditional view contends that people use communication to express their inner purposes, attitudes, and feelings. This perspective regards communication as a tool to describe the events, objects, and ideas. It is believed that effective communication is achieved only when it can accurately express inner feelings, or external realities, and this is measured by the ability to produce an understanding between a speaker and the audience. Critics of this point of view have felt that this is too simplistic of an explanation for the complex act of communication. This may be even more apparent when we enter into an intercultural exchange because of the many meanings a word or object can take on to members of another culture. Mutual understanding is much more difficult to attain with people from other cultures because of the differences that meanings, words, and actions have across cultural groups.

CMM offers an alternative perspective of communication that contends people live in communication as opposed to merely use it. At its foundation, CMM may be traced to theories of American pragmatism, most notably William James, George Herbert Mead, and John Dewey. CMM has also been influenced by Gregory Bateson's ideas of human systems. These two traditions share a common commitment to evolutionary biology, which promotes the idea that forms of institutional life, identity, relationship, and culture emerge in the process of social action and cannot be sufficiently explained by the principles external to the patterns of activity [4, pp. 31-33]. CMM also calls upon the Wittgenstein's later philosophy of language with particular attention to the idea of grammar and language games to interpret interaction.

CMM regards communication as having a central role in our lives. Communication is not merely message transmission, it is coordinated action that is co-constructed by people in specific episodes. It is the way that social phenomena are created when we act with others, or what CMM theorists refer to as conjoint action. All human action is conjoint action, which is to say that what we and others do is influenced by the interests, desires, and the actions of both persons in an episode of interaction. We are affected by the action of people, objects, and events in our environment and we in turn influence those people and things found there. In the intercultural context, CMM would regard people in various cultures as not simply communicating differently, but they are experiencing different ways of being human because they communicate differently. There is a shared way others understand and interpret the world with members of their culture. The importance is not their choice of symbols; the importance lies in the meaning they place on objects, events, and ideas. Human beings become persons by acquiring a sense of self that can only occur in a social setting and their interaction with others in that setting. Within social settings, there are certain ways people learn to relate to one another. This begins when members of our primary social unit, which may be the family or for some others the tribe, interact with us and reinforce the rules of interaction. Vygotsky recognized that infants become persons as their biological resources are synthesized into a coherent and unified structure [5, pp. 80-84]. He felt this is done through the acquisition of both symbolic and practical skills through relationship with competent caregivers. Mead pointed out that from the first weeks of life a child is engaged in a process of coordination with others in order to ensure their survival, and later in relations with others they develop a competence that is necessary to succeed in the world they live within [6, pp. 317-318]. It was Dewey who indicated that social transmission is only possible by and in communication [7, p. 4]. By and in represents an interesting use of prepositions that helps us see that it is not a simple transmission of symbols that makes social life possible. How language is structured, what actions are deemed coherent as a common way of living within a group, and the shared ideas or rules for living are the product of a group of people. A society exists by transmitting its ways of acting, thinking, and feeling from older members to younger members and by such transactions a society is made. A society also exists in a community where people share common ideas through the process of communication. For these theorists the process of communication plays a crucial role in shaping society and the identity of its members.

Communication is not a simple tool that we call upon to express and describe the world we live in. Philipsen and Albrecht described communication as a primary social process because of its capacity to maintain a society, and create moments of shared identity through forms of ritual, myth, and social drama [8, pp. 10-15]. To say that communication is the primary social process is to say that persons, relations, and institutions are the outcomes of communication. It is in the interaction between people that creates, sustains, and changes the world in which they live.

If we were to think of an ordinary day, we would find that it is made up of many interactions of different kinds. It may have included conversations with friends or family, a simple exchange at a local shop, a discussion in a meeting, or a direction given or received at work. These are just a few examples of how prevalent the communication process is in our everyday life, and how these interactions comprise our world. Communication is necessary for human association, and our lives become the sum total of these conversations and exchanges with others. We achieve understanding when we have the ability to act with others and know the meaning of objects, events, and actions. A plausible starting point to make sense of culture lies in exploring the everyday practices of people and the meaning they assign to the world in which they live. Evidence of this is found in words and phrases that explain or direct how one should act in many cultural settings. Philipsen talked about the significance of the statement "being a man" in his study of Teamsterville [9], and I found the Acadian-Americans[1] saying they live their lives in order to "make a difference" [10]. These key phrases are more than just words as they become forces for living one's life as a member of a specific community. The phrases carry with them specific rules for action in living one's life. Acting like a man, or making a difference carry shared meanings of ways of acting, feeling, and thinking as a person should as a member of a group. An outsider may recognize these words, but understanding their significance is contingent upon knowing the meaning in that particular setting. These key phrases show us that there is more to communication than words, and that meanings are made among people who share a common culture.

---

[1] Acadian-Americans refer to a group of people who immigrated in large numbers to the United States during the late 1800s through the mid-1900s from Eastern Canada. This was a French speaking group with a unique history. The reader is directed to *The Acadians of the Maritimes: Thematic Studies*. This work was produced by the Center for Acadian Studies at the University of Moncton (1981) and it provides a detailed history of this culture.

Harre stated that it is nature that provides the can, but it is culture and language that provide the may or may not [11, p. 21]. This memorable statement directs us to view culture not as a mere physical occurrence, but as a world of meanings and rules that come about through the social process. In fact, Harre stressed that we use diverse communication skills to create and maintain human social relations. Within social relations each person is equipped with a dual identity and recognized by others as such. We are both an individual and a member of a social group. We exist as social beings only in relation to the networks of relations we share with others. The ability to exist simultaneously as a member of a social group and as an individual is an achievement of the greatest magnitude and one that is often taken for granted.

Wittgenstein provided the critical idea that our lives are composed of clusters of language games in which meaning is derived from social rules [12, p. 19]. To know a language is simply not enough, as we often find in an intercultural context. Wittgenstein showed that social actions have an impending rationality, or what he called a grammar. Grammar refers to more than the syntax people use, it also includes the feelings, behavior, and actions that accompany an utterance. Acting like a man or making a difference are examples of specific grammars used by speakers of those cultural groups. A proficient speaker needs to know the meaning and rules for action in order to be understood. The rules that govern a language are much like the rules of a game. Knowing the words and syntax of another language is not enough in order to interact fully with others; a speaker must know what rules to follow in order to be understood.

A student from Holland related a story that demonstrates the limitations of relying on words alone. This student spoke fluent English and her accent was nearly imperceptible, but she described that she would find herself in awkward moments when she arrived in the United States. On one of her first nights at college her roommate said to her, *"Hey let me see your pen."* She dutifully held up her pen in full view and smiled. The roommate restated the command and once again the student held up the pen. Angrily her roommate said to her, *"You just don't get it. Give me the stupid thing! What is wrong with you?"* The command "let me see your pen" is not a simple set of words or symbols that has one exact meaning. Among U.S. American speakers, the request to "see" something signals the action of give the object to me. Knowing how to go on with others requires that we move beyond the words or symbols they use. We must know the rules implicit in their language games. It requires the ability to see multiple meanings exist, and it requires an ability to interpret social action within a particular context.

Theorists who have been identified as social constructionists adopted the view that communication is a constitutive force, a force that shapes our view of reality and a force that shapes our identity. Communication is not seen as an epiphenomenon that has a banal and benign nature to it. Berger and Luckman coined the term social constructionism and offered a practical idea about knowledge [13]. Social Constructionism contends that commonsense knowledge constitutes the fabric of meanings without which no society could exist. Most importantly this commonsense knowledge comes about through interaction among the members of a culture. Within this view, communication is no longer limited to expressing and describing the world or thoughts. Communication creates the experience itself. Events and objects of the social world are more than what they appear to be. We can take an event such as a family dinner and see how it is the product of social action and shared meaning. Its meaning, structure, and continued existence are dependent upon the pattern of practices people have adopted as part of an episode of a family life and family dining [14, pp. 89-105]. Numerous events in our social world have led us to adopt new behaviors and expectations of family dinners. Within the U.S. American culture we have constructed new meanings, expectations, and actions for families sharing, or in many cases not sharing, meals together.

CMM is not the only theory that claims our knowledge of reality is mediated by language, or even that the way we use language shapes our perceptions, relationships, and the organizations where we work and live. However, CMM differs from other theories in its claim that there is a reciprocal relationship between communication and ways of being human. The significance of this for this discussion is to see that communication and culture are not things, but a series of actions that are organized in a way that makes sense to the participants there. People become who they are because of the cultural group they interact with and the communication they use. The process of learning a language, or the rules for action reveal how significant cultural influences are. Learning how to communicate is embedded within years of parents or caregivers instructing by more than just naming objects. Children do not learn only the names of things, but they also learn how to enact certain types of interaction, what to think about objects, events, and later on how to enact concepts that are more abstract such as honesty, deceit, love, or hatred.

We see these social rules and social expectations for action all around us. In a work setting we find rules for action that may be specific to that place. At each work setting there are actions and meanings that are unlike those at any other setting. In fact, there are likely to be different conversations, and different meanings assigned to the things talked about at different organizations. Communication is inclusive of all human action, and our challenge is to see it as more than an auxiliary of human activity. CMM's perspective of communication helps us to understand the aspects of living that are so much more than a physical event. The birth of a child, the death of a family member, or the loss of life at the proportions witnessed on September 11 are not simple events. They are filled with moral significance and emotional experience far beyond the mere definition of the word birth, death, or terrorism. The significance of these events is developed by people who share a common understanding of these events and what they mean to them. September 11 has impacted what it means to be a member of the U.S. American culture. People do not act impulsively outside of the context of their culture. Personal relationships, social roles, and our autobiographies are constructed within the framework of a culture, and culture exerts a force on what we talk about, do, and expect of our self and others. The magnitude of the events of September 11 has changed the context in which U.S. Americans live, the ways they talk about certain ideas, and what they expect of self and people from other cultures.

THE ROLE OF EMOTION AND THE IMPACT OF SEPTEMBER 11

CMM regards emotion as an important aspect of experience and one that should not be discounted when considering human communication. Understanding the emotional aspect of experience is critical when explaining the meaning of events and actions in a person's life. It is through emotions that we feel a unity with experience as emotional states are attached to objects and events. Emotions are usually thought of as an individual event, but their coherence is developed within a culture. Averill described emotions as emerging in coherent ways in patterns of social action and roles that are socially defined [15, pp. 307-312]. These socially defined roles are important in telling a person how to act in particular contexts where they experience emotions. There are numerous examples of how affection, sorrow, or joy are demonstrated within different cultures. What may be expected or appropriate in one culture may not be appropriate in another. Emotional states are not permanent states that people live in for long periods of time. They are transitory and socially constructed. A culture defines the appropriate length of time and how a person should express emotional states. A public display of grief or elation cannot and would not be displayed for extended periods in the same way without the person appearing to be inappropriate or even pathological. In coming to understand emotions, it is important to note that emotions do not occur independently. Feeling an emotion is always a result about or from something. Emotions are the result of something going on in the environment and emotions take an object. We do not simply feel rage; our rage is the result of an event that upset us. Emotional experiences provide a qualitative immediacy that goes beyond what can be observed. When we consider the importance of emotion, we discover a different way to think and talk about events that go on in a person's world.

When an event as momentous as September 11 occurs, most people are likely to feel overwhelmed or confused. At the time of such an event, or in the days that followed, it was unlikely that people knew how to clearly express their feelings. Immediately following September 11, there were public displays of sentiment as evident in the number of American flags that appeared in many places. In the months that followed, countless people visited Ground Zero where they described a deep feeling of loss and/or reverence while visiting the site. In time, the expression of grief and ways of talking about the tragedy developed a grammar with its own rules and ways to organize feelings and action. People of the U.S. American culture have constructed a range of behaviors and feelings that are associated with this event. It is doubtful that the event took on the same level of meaning or significance for people of other cultures. The meanings and emotions attached to September 11 sets U.S. Americans apart from other cultures. This difference presents another potential barrier in the ability to go on with others.

The events of September 11 tell us that people do more than perceive the world. People learn how to form joy, disappointment, happiness, or fear from their actions and events in the world. Most U.S. Americans had a profound emotional experience and they had to find ways to express this experience. It may be argued that many U.S. Americans are still seeking a way to express or make sense of the event and the changes it has brought to notions of security and vulnerability. Recently I conducted a discussion group with U.S. American managers where we explored the impact of September 11 on their work and travel. These managers reported feeling what they referred to as a "twinge." They feel a twinge when they first encounter a person of a different culture, particularly members of specific cultures or parts of the world. They described the grammar of a twinge as a feeling of discomfort. This discomfort leads them to be more vigilant when they are among people of other cultures and defensive when talking about their nation or September 11. While the majority of the managers stated they experienced discomfort, vigilance, and defensiveness, they all talked about feelings of guilt for being mistrustful of others. This ambivalence and uncertainty indicates the complexity and unfinished nature of the experience and the number of challenges that exist for them when they interact with people of other cultures.

Dewey made an important distinction between an act of expression and an act of discharge. An act of discharge has as its intent to rid of or dismiss an emotional state [16, pp. 58-65]. For example, an outburst can serve as a channel to vent inward rage. However, on its own an outburst is not capable of carrying the moment forward in order to give it meaning or help to make sense of an event. An act of expression differs in its ability to develop or extend meaning. Expression represents thoughtful reflection and bringing together many aspects of an experience to say something meaningful about an event or an idea. Unlike discharge, expression is more than ridding the self of emotion. Expression has a way of clarifying emotional events. It can transform events into a new level of meaning and it represents the actions of responsible and thoughtful people. There is a range of choices and responses people can make to an event such as September 11. Some of these may be described as discharge while others may be classified as transformative and expressive. There were many instances where we witnessed public statements or acts that were a discharge of emotions, and given the circumstances this is understandable in some cases. Many of these statements and acts could be classified as a discharge of anger. These included the political rhetoric of some government leaders, public slogans, and acts of violence against innocent people as retaliation. While the range of acts differ greatly in terms of their moral significance, many of these were fueled by the emotions of anger or rage. September 11 will not be forgotten, but the need exists to move beyond discharging emotions and instead find ways to express what has been experienced. There is a moral responsibility to take stock of how the event has influenced interaction with people of other cultures. U.S. Americans may begin by asking questions such as: How does the emotional weight of this event influence my interaction with members of other cultures? When interacting with people of other cultures is my communication and my actions a discharge of emotion or are they indicative of fair and balanced expressions? These questions are only a few among many that could assist in developing relationships with people of other cultures that are more productive.

A CMM VIEW OF CULTURE

Like communication, we can see that culture is everywhere, found in all things around us, and is impossible to extricate from communication itself. Culture will determine the conditions under which people may/may not or can/cannot speak, or how exchanges can be interpreted. A starting point in defining culture is to see it as an ongoing process where people engage in continual social interaction. Within these interactions we find people who communicate with symbols, and share a world that is not as much bounded by geography as it is held together by the ways they communicate. Our repertoire of actions relies on the culture we have been raised in, and how the actors take each other's acts into account and decide on what actions follow. Within a culture, features of living and acting have to be coherent in order for us to be understood. Common understanding comes about when people share a basis of agreement about what their acts and events mean to them. The language games that occur within a culture are the product of collective meanings that cultural members share. A shared perspective is necessary in order to sense one's place in the interaction, and it makes communication possible. Simply put, culture is the everyday practices of people, their agreements, shared understanding of rules that govern their interaction, and the knowledge they share for living a life. Many theories of culture provide descriptions of class, gender, and ethnicity. These are important, but they cannot alone substitute for the detail necessary to understand and interact effectively with others.

The view of culture offered by Cronen, Chen, and Pearce through the lens of CMM makes valuable contributions to understanding what culture is and what it is not [17, pp. 89-95]. First, CMM regards culture as patterns of co-evolving structures and actions that guide peoples' interactions. What this means is that culture resides in the everyday activities of people and what they do with others. Instead of relying on generalizations and a listing of traits attributed to ethnic heritage, CMM develops an understanding of another type by treating culture as the dynamic interaction of people that we can observe as well as participate in. Many approaches to intercultural communication rely on listing the features of a culture with the intent of building a degree of competence. The lists may say people of Arab nations act this way, or Germans will act that way. There is little doubt that the lists have served as starting points, but they cannot account for the uniqueness of each person in a culture, and what meaning is informing the actions people take. When we rely on fixed conceptions of culture we may neglect the richness of intercultural encounters. The ambiguity or confusion we feel about another culture can be a source of productive coordination and understanding when we recognize that cultures represent others' ways of living that can advance our understanding of diversity. The study of other cultures can offer us more than finding an underlying unity among them. It can provide us with a range of possibilities for being human in productive ways. CMM contends that the dynamic social world is better treated as a highly complex pattern of evolving practices. Reducing a culture to a listing of variables along lines of differences leads us to artificial essentialism. The negative consequences of this include the inability to grasp the detail and nuance of life as lived by people who are engaged in a process of conjoint action.

Second, a CMM view of culture contends that cultures are polyphonic, borrowing a metaphor from the world of music. Music is made up of many sounds or voices. Instead of parts simply proceeding together, the parts move independently but fit together harmonically. Consider how instruments come together in a symphony or a jazz composition even though different notes or rhythms are being played. The same can be said about culture. Within a culture there are a variety of resources that include traditions, forms of leisure, and patterns of relationships to mention a few. Each culture has a number of ways a person can choose to live. Consider the range of choices U.S. Americans have in terms of recreation. Some people may enjoy watching sporting events while others may be interested in outdoor activities. Although there are differences among people, they still maintain group membership as a part of their culture. The range of possibilities also applies to selfhood. Each culture has within it different forms of selfhood. Members of a culture often experience interests, ways of talking, and appreciations for events and objects in ways that vary from other cultural members. Within a culture individual interpretations arise, and no two persons are likely to call upon the same exact actions in a given context. The critical element to take from this is that there are a range of choices that people exercise in living their daily life. It is likely we may find members of a culture who are unlike other members. In spite of these differences, people remain a member of that culture. Our reliance on generalizations about a culture will not adequately explain the different forms of self that emerge in a group of people.

Third, CMM argues that a social theory designed to help us understand cultural differences should be able to identify the practices that sustain and produce certain forms of selfhood. Our understanding of culture is contingent on our ability to see what practices people use when interacting with others. It is in the interaction and exchanges between people that we can come to know a culture, and see how an individual must act. It should be clear that selfhood and social practices are not the same in all places. This is one of the contributing factors that makes the ability to speak a language not enough to know what it means to be a person in a specific cultural context.

In order to understand human communication, CMM brings two major issues to the forefront that are beneficial in making sense of people in interaction. First, the social world is inherently unfinished. People are engaged in a world that requires their participation and adaptation. This tells us that social patterns may be stable, but they are not static or stuck, and over time we do witness changes in cultures. Our own culture has witnessed changes in family life, participation in religious life, or membership in community organizations. These changes may be attributed to economic or complex social events and they have altered how we live. We now have different kinds of relationships with others and engage in different actions as a result of these changes. A contemporary description of U.S. American life will differ in many ways from a description a decade or two ago.

Second, words alone do not have meaning. Words are tools and instruments used for making meanings, and meanings are not fixed. The words we use are inherently imperfect. The imperfection of communication is seen in the ability of symbols to extend beyond their current definitions. This imperfection is not raised pejoratively, because it is this imperfection that makes new understanding and expression possible. People are capable of creating and changing their world because of the possibilities to see and express self in different ways.

We are active participants in making a social world that is dynamic and filled with ambiguity, ambivalence, contradiction, and conflict. Therefore, we need a position to view an unpredictable and dynamic world that may render it coherent. CMM does offer a position that considers these features of our world and can enhance our understanding.

LEARNING TO GO ON WITH OTHERS

Perhaps one of the greatest challenges we face in the intercultural encounter resides in the fact that we erroneously assume others are like us and we are familiar with the meanings in their world. However, in making sense of others we draw on meanings found within our own cultural framework. This leads us to treat others as if they are interpreting, evaluating, and responding to events and objects in the world as we do. This may have come about because we regard communication as a simple process where each symbol has only one fixed meaning. In order to go on with others we need to develop a perspective that allows us to first recognize that cultural differences means people experience different ways of being human, and second to find a way to achieve productive communication with people of other cultures.

Barnett Pearce, a co-founder of CMM, made the distinction between a cosmopolitan and ethnocentric viewpoint. This distinction can be helpful in intercultural encounters. In episodes of communication, an ethnocentric point of view may be simply understood as people viewing the world from their perspective and the patterns for living that they call upon. These patterns of feeling, thinking, acting, and talking become the way they do things as a member of a cultural group. Their ways of acting becomes so ingrained that people may find it difficult to act any other way or understand others who act differently. An ethnocentric view is using our culture's meaning system to view other cultures. It leads a person to feel their group is superior to other groups whose way of doing things are not valid or as good as how their group does things. Communication from the ethnocentric view means we use our understanding of ways of acting to engage others and make sense of their actions. The challenge in an intercultural encounter is to understand each other's motives, reasons, and meanings. The cosmopolitan view begins by recognizing there are multiple ways people make sense and act into the world. It recognizes that each culture has developed its own definition of truth or how a person should live derived from its own historical tradition. A cosmopolitan perspective is concerned with discovering the process of how groups of people construct their own stories of how to live a life. Pearce thought we can make sense of the everyday practices of people when we take our beliefs and the beliefs of others seriously. In other words, to find respect and appreciation for different ideas, stories, and practices others use. We live in a world of multiple and valid ideas of ways to live. Whatever beliefs a person may adopt, a cosmopolitan communicator is likely to know we live in a world of differences, and each group has a unique way of defining the world. Respecting the beliefs of a culture does not mean we have to like all of the practices of all cultures. Different cultures have found different ideas to believe in, actions they must take or not take, and ways of living. Some ways of living may represent better connections in living than others do. We are not obligated to adopt ways of living that conflict with our morals and beliefs, but we cannot discount that these are valid to members of a particular culture.

The task of knowing how to go on in episodes of intercultural communication is not an easy one. It demands that we learn to coordinate interactions between divergent systems, and we do so by being observant, finding the meaning behind actions, and recognizing our ethnocentric tendencies. Within an ever-changing social world, there is a need to learn to go on with others. This has always been a challenge in the intercultural context because of the wide variations in meaning systems. It is even more pronounced after the events of September 11. This tragic event is likely to influence the way that many U.S. Americans perceive and relate to people from other nations and cultures. On several levels, September 11 brought many U.S. Americans together. However, in coming together, U.S. Americans need to be cautious of how feeling a stronger national sense can lead to more ethnocentric bias toward others.

Yet, still another challenge confronts people in learning how to form productive relationships with others. Learning to go on in an intercultural encounter begins with a tolerance for ambiguity and an ability to be flexible. This requires people to suspend their need for certainty in a time when ideas about security or what is dangerous are changing. Some of the difficulty of entering a new culture may occur because patterns and beliefs we rely on may no longer be valid. Successful intercultural communication is more likely to happen when people act inquisitively as opposed to search for certitude, and when they learn to feel wonderment instead of hostility, frustration, or withdrawal. This can begin by recognizing communication is unpredictable, but capable of revealing aspects of a culture. In addition, intercultural communicators should ask how fear, hyper-vigilance, isolation, and defensiveness affect the openness needed in intercultural encounters.

The process of interacting with members of another culture is a process of inquiry. Inquiry allows us as adaptive beings to act intelligently by connecting a moment of action with other moments. In the process of inquiry, ideas come together, are tested by action, and through thinking and acting our ideas and experiences are adapted and adjusted in order to make sense of what we find in the world. If intercultural exchanges were approached as inquiry, it is likely that ideas and understandings will emerge that are richer than a simple listing of the traits of a culture. Managing intercultural encounters is inquiry because it calls upon our ability to observe, listen to stories, and use ways of thinking and feeling to know what is going on in a particular setting. These can be valuable skills when we are interacting with members of another culture.

A while ago, I watched a skilled craftsman apply plaster onto a ceiling. It looked quite easy. There was a rhythm and flow to his movements. Over time he must have developed a feel for the movement of the trowel, the consistency of the plaster, and a relationship of the stroke of the trowel to the shape and boundaries of the ceiling. I am reminded that this kind of knowing applies to the process of coming to know how to act and think as a member of a culture. We learn how to listen and observe emotional cues, make connections between words and actions, and reflect on what we see and hear. Like the craftsman, we have a feel for how things should be done and how things make sense. We can enter into another culture when we are aware that each culture has its own grammar and we learn how to listen to it. In the process of listening, we become better observers of actions, emotions, and key terms. When we understand these we will find ways to participate and join with others.

A visit by eight students from France to a graduate class that I was teaching in the United States provides an illustration of the power of entering into the grammar of another culture. The assignment was for the U.S. American students and the French students to discuss the role of wine in their culture. The French began by describing the importance of wine while the U.S. American students listened. At first, the conversation was blocked. The U.S. American students tried to understand wine by using their own experiences and framework. The U.S. American students kept making comparisons with what they knew about wine. They kept stating, *"well it sounds sort of like coffee, or chocolate in our culture."* The French students responded by saying, *"no we have coffee and chocolate and they are important to us but they are different than wine."* After awhile I asked the U.S. American students to try listening without making comparisons, and observe how important wine was to the French. I suggested that maybe the word wine has a different meaning in the French culture, and to discover this they should try to suspend and challenge their current definition of wine. An interesting change came about in the conversation. The U.S. American students began to realize that the French understanding of wine was not commensurate to a U.S. American conception of wine. Cronen, Chen, and Pearce defined the importance between commensurate and comparable in the intercultural encounter [17]. Commensurate would mean things are of the same exact size, extent, or duration, while comparable sees similarities but recognizes that differences exist. In an intercultural encounter, we are prone to regard words that describe objects, events, and abstractions as commensurable, and this disregards what is different. The students were able to learn that their American notion of wine was not helpful in terms of developing an understanding of what wine meant to the French. The real progress came when the Americans began to ask questions about wine such as: *When do you use it? How do you use it? How did you learn about it? What would life be like without it? Do you feel the same about wines from other countries?* The French students seemed to relax as they were engaged in a different kind of discourse. What also became clear is that human communication has an ineffable dimension to it and spoken words are only one part of communication. The feelings and emotions the French students were showing became important elements in discussing wine. The French students could answer the specific questions about time and use, but communicating their appreciation for wine or the degree of appreciation were expressed in utterances that were not words in either language. Statements accompanied by movement of their body or the tone used such as *"it is just mmm, (pause) like (pause) . . . umm (pause) it just is WONDERFUL,"* or *"it is so (pause) social,"* became critical parts of the communication and keys to developing an understanding about what they were saying. People do not merely use language, they feel language. In talking with others, we can become excited or experience moments of awkwardness. What a person feels is an important part of communicating with others, and recognizing this dimension of communication is an important part of coming to know what others are saying. What became clear in this transaction was that there was more to understanding wine for the French students than what could be found in the simple symbol or word wine. Communicating the meaning of this symbol could not be adequately expressed through the word alone. Eventually a U.S. American student stated, "*I think I understand now.*" He sat back and said, "*Gee, I am envious there is nothing like that in my life and I wish there was.*"

Weeks later, several U.S. American students reported that after drinking wine they thought its meaning had changed for them. Two students said they developed a respect for wine now they did not feel before. It was clear that the American students were able to enter into the grammar of the term. They could see that an important aspect of coming to know what wine meant in the French culture was achieved by observing peoples' feel for it and how people organize their experiences around this object. When they became better observers and participants in an interaction with the French students, they could organize information for analysis and action. They found that the term wine took on a particular configuration and meaning within a moment of conversation, as well as moments of living. Here they saw the unique details of lived experience for someone of French culture. Their understanding was expanded when they surrounded its definition with stories, listened to examples, and heard how a person comes to experience wine in that culture.

STORIES AND IMPROVISATION

Several times the idea of stories has been mentioned, and CMM contends that stories play a critical role in how people come to know their world. People tell stories about who they are, would like to be, and how episodes of action should go. Stories do not have a logical order, but they do fit together in a way that makes sense in a cultural frame. When we listen to life stories we find reasons why people act in certain ways, explanations of what a person should do in a specific context, and what is important to a community of people. Listening for stories is easily accessible for most of us. Over time, we have developed skills in listening to the stories of others, and even call upon this as a form of entertainment. Stories can contribute in at least two ways in learning how to go on with others after September 11. First, we can use our ability to listen to stories to develop understanding of other cultures. In the intercultural context, we can call upon our ability to listen to life stories and learn a lot about people in a culture. Part of coming to know a culture is finding how the stories fit together. For example, long lunch breaks from work may be part of a larger story about the quality of life and what position the quality of life has in a culture. The relationship of one story to another may help make sense of how things have come to be in a culture. However, we should be careful when we are listening to stories. Listening from our ethnocentric point of view is unlikely to lead us to make useful interpretations of stories and cultures. Second, stories can help us make sense of September 11 and what consequences we would like to see. There are a number of stories about September 11 that people may tell, and it is important to see how these stories may be related to other stories of the right thing to do, to be American, or stories of trust and willingness to interact with other cultures. When a person recognizes that they live through stories, they may find that they have the ability to tell other kinds of stories or better stories. The stories they tell about their lives and the stories they live can be changed to make better stories. U.S. Americans may want to tell a better story about interacting with others from other cultures. When they can imagine what that better story is, they can take the steps to make this story reality. A story about the tragedy of September 11 has the capacity to become a better story about the importance of unity among cultures or a story of new avenues of understanding if people can find ways to imagine and live that story. Not all stories about September 11 are tragedy stories. There were many stories about heroic firefighters, pubic servants, and passengers on the hijacked aircraft. These stories are helpful in developing abilities to see the importance of kinship and altruism, and they could become part of better stories. The ability people have to tell better stories about our lives and their interactions can lead them to live more productively with others.

In the intercultural encounter it may also be helpful to recognize that interaction has an improvisational nature. When a person interacts with another person, conditions are never fully under their control. No one can predict a person's response, or what will follow. People act into a future, imagining the consequences for action and not fully knowing what will happen next. Interaction may be better thought of as an improvisational act instead of one that is certain and predictable. Thinking of communication as improvisational requires the ability to sharpen powers of observation to see, listen, and feel in sensitive ways. Better observation leads us to see how things have a relation to one another, and then we can grasp the value and meaning of what is present. Everyday actions are often based on habit or routine, which is a disadvantage when we find ourselves within a new context. When we are improvising, we first make sense of a situation, then develop a course of action, implement the course of action, adapt by watching the other person, and lastly adjust or expand our thinking by reflecting on what has occurred. Improvising is the ability to assume an open position that makes us more receptive and open to making discoveries about self and others. In the unfolding of an unexpected situation we call upon a degree of ingenuity that can lead us to new insights into the situation we find ourselves in. There is no doubt that interaction within a new culture causes a degree of discomfort, and this may be attributed to the fact that it forces us to abandon a social role or script we usually enact. Taking an improvisational stance may lessen that discomfort as we learn to direct our emotions and fully respond to a world of complexity and abstractions.

Knowing what to do relies more on improvisation guided by social rules or language games than it does on one way of doing things. Like an improvisational actor, we' develop a feel for the rules or the language games that people call on within a culture, in time we come to recognize that when certain signs are present there are a range of appropriate actions available to us.

CONCLUSIONS

The memory of September 11 has become part of the U.S. American culture. While it presents new challenges, it should not be viewed as an event that renders intercultural communication and relationships impossible. We cannot lose sight of the fact that this was an act of terrorism. The goal of a terrorist is to create reactions by the attacked that further the cause of the terrorist. Fear, suspicion, and isolation from others may be what the terrorists had intended to achieve. The terrorists do succeed in remaining nearly invisible, but we cannot regard all people of other cultures as the enemy or potential enemy. People face the challenge of going on with others in spite of the reality of terrorism, but they can make a far better world through understanding than they can through fear, suspicion, and isolation.

At the outset of the chapter, a goal was established of finding ways of developing productive relationships with people from other cultures. The discussion focused mostly on the theoretical aspects of communication, and more specifically intercultural communication. However, theory should never be far from practice and it has a duty to serve as a way of understanding what we experience at work and all other places in our social world. The theoretical dimensions of intercultural communication were presented here for consideration so that we can act into the world more intelligently. There are several practical ideas that emerge from theory about intercultural communication that can assist us in our dealings with others.

A beginning point for improving intercultural communication is to understand and embrace differences. It seems the default position of being human is to feel threatened when we encounter differences. Historically, when people encounter differences the approach has been to make others like them. There is evidence of this in efforts by the West to colonize people of other places. Said reported on centuries of colonialism where the West imposed its political order, economic systems, and religious beliefs on others [18, pp. 3-9]. When this was met with resistance, the colonized would face retribution. A Western notion of addressing difference is to maintain power and control over others. Changing and controlling others is a detriment to developing productive relationships. The challenge lies in our ability to see that people are different because they have constructed different ways of living. Avoiding these differences or minimizing their existence only sustains the barriers to going on with others. When we regard others as being the same as us we are defining what that sameness is. There are similarities, but there are also differences and both must be appreciated. Appreciation is a far different experience than tolerating or respecting others. Appreciation is recognizing what is different and approaching it with curiosity, amazement, and often admiration. The appreciation of other cultures can make our world much richer and thus expand abilities to see what the world offers. There is a world of meaning informing the action of others and this is what causes differences. Meaning is not fixed and not the same for all people. Each culture has developed its own meaning and ways to see the world. Our goal should be to discover and appreciate what those meanings are. When we encounter people of other cultures, our starting point should not be to critique or compare what they are doing to our ways of acting. Instead, our challenge is to discover and understand the meaning behind their actions. This begins by learning to observe and actively listen to what people do and what they say. Often good communication is regarded as the ability to speak effectively. Effective speaking is a valuable accomplishment, but good communication should be dialogic, that is when we can listen and speak effectively. Communication is most effective when people are able to understand one another and coordinate their actions. This is only possible when people can observe and listen to what the other person is saying and doing. In the intercultural episode this may be even more important because we can seldom rely on our ways of doing that are culturally based. The quality of our intercultural communication will rely on the quality of our ability to observe and listen to others.

U.S. Americans cannot and should not deny or avoid the depth of what they have experienced. However, they can channel what they feel into constructive acts of expression or better stories of their world. There are no guarantees that shifting to a cosmopolitan perspective and approaching others will make encounters with people of other cultures better because we cannot be certain that they will do the same. Yet, someone must initiate action that is morally good and recognizes the importance of sharing this world in productive ways. All around us, there are more opportunities for interaction with other cultures. The workplace and the classroom are but two examples of locations we share with people of many cultures. This creates a need to learn about others, and to promote international understanding and effective relationships more than any other time before. The promising news is that knowing how to go on in an intercultural context should not really be that difficult because people have developed skills of interpreting the world they live in. This can be less challenging when they recognize that making sense of the world relies on finding the meanings behind actions and calling on our interpretation skills. Perhaps the biggest obstacle to overcome in the intercultural context is the need for certainty. Communication itself is not based on accuracy as much as it is on consensus, and even consensus changes across contexts. Entering another culture requires an ability to see that symbols and words can have more than one meaning, and that language is only one dimension of communication. People also express satisfaction or disappointment through tone and other nonverbal features. The ability to go on with others is possible when we recognize that we can enter into meaning systems by observing and participating in the grammar of others. The inherently imperfect features of communication provide us with opportunities to see the world in new and interesting ways.

Professionals and others who interact with members of other cultures will benefit from observation and listening; however, they also have the ability to ask questions in a spirit of cooperation and wanting to know more about other cultures. Some of the best moments in intercultural encounters occur when people ask others about their culture with a deep level of interest, respect, and appreciation for the other's culture. Once again, the workplace and the classroom offer many chances to engage in constructive dialogue where people can explore their cultural differences and find ways to go on. If we commit to the idea that people live in communication rather than just use it, communication itself is raised to a primary position in living a life. Recognizing the importance of peoples' communication and how it shapes their view of reality is a central point of finding ways to go on with others. Entering into their world is contingent upon our abilities to enter into their grammar. Once we enter into a grammar, we find ways to interact effectively because we know the meaning of ideas, objects, and events. We will also come to see how certain actions make sense to the people and how they attach emotional significance to certain experiences. It is here that people can develop the ability go on with others collaboratively. U.S. Americans have been changed by September 11, but the potential to make this profound experience the beginning of a story of hope and possibility exists.

REFERENCES

1. W. B. Pearce and V. Cronen, *Communication, Action and Meaning, The Creation of Social Realities*, Praeger, New York, 1980.

2. V. Cronen, Coordinated Management of Meaning: The Consequentiality of Communication and the Recapturing of Experience, in *The Consequentiality of Communication*, S. J. Sigman (ed.), Erlbaum, Hillsdale, New Jersey, pp. 17-65, 1995.

3. V. Cronen, Coordinated Management of Meaning: Practical Theory and the Tasks Ahead for Social Approaches to Communication, in *Social Approaches to Communication*, W. Leeds-Hurwitz (ed.), Guilford Press, New York, pp. 183-207, 1995.

4. V. Cronen and J. Chetro-Szivos, Pragmatism as a Way of Inquiring with Special Reference to a Theory of Communication and the General Form of Pragmatic Social Theory, in *Pragmatism and Communication Research*, D. Perry, Erlbaum, Highland, Maryland, pp. 27-65, 2001.

5. L. Vygotsky, *Thought and Language*, The MIT Press, Cambridge, Massachusetts, 1986.

6. G. H. Mead, *Mind, Self and Society from the Standpoint of a Social Behaviorist*, The University of Chicago Press, Chicago, Illinois, 1934.

7. J. Dewey, *Democracy and Education: An Introduction to the Philosophy of Education*. The Free Press, New York, 1916.

8. G. Philipsen and T. Albrecht, *Developing Communication Theories*, State University of New York Press, New York, 1997.

9. G. Philipsen, *Speaking Culturally: Explorations in Social Communication*, State University of New York Press, New York, 1992.

10. J. Chetro-Szivos, *Acadian-American Voices: Work, Communication, and Self-Hood*. University Press of America, Lanham, Maryland, in press.

11. R. Harre, *Social Being*, Blackwell, Oxford, United Kingdom and Cambridge, Massachusetts, 1993.

12. L. Wittgenstein, *Philosophical Investigations*, Oxford, United Kingdom, 1958.

13. P. Berger and T. Luckman, *The Social Construction of Reality: A Treatise in the Sociology of Knowledge*, Doubleday, Garden City, New York, 1966.

14. W. B. Pearce, *Communication and the Human Condition*, Southern Illinois University Press, Carbondale, Illinois, 1989.

15. J. Averill, A Constructivist View of Emotion, in *Theories of Emotion*, H. Plutchik (ed.), Academic Press, New York, pp. 305-337, 1980.

16. J. Dewey, *Art as Experience*, Minton Balch and Company, New York, 1934.

17. V. Cronen, V. Chen, and W. B. Pearce, Coordinated Management of Meaning: A Critical Theory, in *Theories in Intercultural Communication*, W. Gudykunst and K. Y. Gudykunst (eds.), Sage, Beverly Hills, California, pp. 66-98, 1988.

18. E. Said, *Orientalism*, Vintage Books, New York, 1979.

CHAPTER 5

What Should We Teach to Our Students in the Age of the Internet?

Fumiko Yoshimura

INTRODUCTION

We live in the age of free access to various information and easy communication. In addition to mass media such as TV, radio, and movies which have dominated our lives for decades, the recent advancement of information technology has brought about various computer programs, CD-ROM products, the Internet, and so on. Nowadays information presentation is more dynamic and flexible. Communication is more interactive.

Especially, the emergence of the Internet has been changing our lives significantly. We can now find and gather information on the World Wide Web (also called the WWW or the Web) without physically visiting different places or manipulating materials. We can purchase commercial products at virtual malls there. We can easily and cheaply communicate with friends living in distant places by e-mail. There is no physical boundary on the Internet. Even between countries which have little or no cultural exchange, information can be exchanged freely on the Internet. The other day, a freshman from South Korea sang a Japanese popular song at a welcome party. I asked him if he had the Japanese artist's CD. Then he answered that it was still prohibited to import Japanese goods such as CDs or journals to South Korea. But when he heard the song on the Internet, he liked it very much and he downloaded it onto his computer and practiced singing the song. This demonstrates how powerful the Internet is as a tool to access information from all over the world. This digital networked technology was expected to solve many inconveniences and problems of the world and many were excited to think that it could lead to more learning experiences and more business opportunities. However, high-tech crimes remind us of the danger of free access to information and communication. I sometimes receive e-mails to my address posted on my Web site from total strangers inviting me to join their business proposals. These are notorious global fraud schemes reported in IFCC 2002 Internet Fraud Report [1]. Information could be used for good and bad intentions. Information on the Internet is not always credible and not always worth believing. We are learning that being able to get unlimited access to information is not always favorable to us and does not necessarily expand our knowledge or result in deeper learning. We have started to realize the importance of evaluating the capability and implications more objectively.

In this chapter, I would like to study text processing on the Internet. Especially, I will focus on the text processing on the World Wide Web of the Internet. The World Wide Web is growing rapidly and has many revolutionary characteristics. It is changing our information processing behaviors drastically mainly because it utilizes hypertext. Hypertext is "an open, user-selectable form of text where readers can move instantly from where they are reading to any other part of the text simply by pointing and clicking on a hot spot or hot button" [2, p. 91]. This unprecedented text form requires text processing which is different from conventional text processing. It should have great implications on literacy education in the 21st century.

WHAT IS THE INTERNET AND THE WORLD WIDE WEB?

As of September 2002, 605.60 million people are estimated to have Internet access worldwide according to a survey [3], and the number is still expanding. According to the Internet Society (ISOC):

> The Internet is a global network of networks enabling computes of all kinds to directly and transparently communicate and share services throughout much of the world. Because the Internet is an enormously valuable, enabling capability for so many people and organizations, it also constitutes a shared global resource of information, knowledge, and means of collaboration, and cooperation among countless diverse communities [4].

The most common applications of the Internet are for communication, files and software transfer, and information gathering. The Internet provides ways to communicate by using e-mail, electronic bulletin boards, or video teleconferences. Files and software can be transferred from computer to computer and from person to person on the Internet. By using the Web, unlimited sources of information can be accessed easily. According to Jonassen et al., the World Wide Web is "the sum of all documents stored using a multimedia format and made accessible via the Internet" [2, p. 23].

Web pages are made of hypertext, "an electronic form of text presentation that supports the linking of nodes or chunks of text in any order" [5, p. 5]. Because of the linking function, presentation of information on the Internet is no longer linear but multi-layered, not only vertically but also horizontally. Bolter calls the World Wide Web "global hypertext" [6], indicating that these hypertexts are connected globally. In its early days, the pages consisted of only written text. However, nowadays they are made up of a variety of different media forms such as graphics, audio, photos, video, animation, and written text. Web pages accommodate multimedia in digital format. Hypertext's linking function makes it easy to store and search for information. Writers can categorize and organize information efficiently by using this function. Writers can create a hierarchy of information in terms of levels of importance and levels of abstraction within their site by using the multi-layeredness. They can also connect related information across different sites by using the linking function. Readers can select and read only the subset of information that matches their needs. Vast amounts of information are stored on the Web, and each piece of information is accessible to readers who desire it. Moreover, there are tools to help searching and exploration. "Search engines" help readers find Web sites that contain key words specified by the reader. All readers have to do is enter key words into an on-screen dialogue box, and the computer will provide them with a list of sites which contain the words. Readers can explore sites which seem relevant or interesting and check out the content. "Menu-based search services" divide information on the Web into subject areas and provide well-organized and comprehensive menus to choose from. Readers can just keep clicking on words of interest and narrow down the search. Functions like these make information searching fast and efficient. Some Web pages contain underlined texts or images which appear in a different color. These are hot buttons and link the page to another display window; i.e., to a different part of the same page, to a different page of the same site, or to a totally different Web site. Some Web pages are linked to the writer's e-mail address or provide discussion forums where people can share opinions with others.

MECHANISM OF THE WORLD WIDE WEB

Accommodating Multimedia

Information on the World Wide Web consists of not only written text but a variety of media sources such as graphic images, photographs, audio, animations, or video clips. One of the advantages of information presentation on the Web is its capability of presenting various media sources simultaneously. With the advancement of computers and authoring tools, it is no longer difficult to create Web pages with various audio-visual effects. The media on the Web pages are in digital format and easy to control. By accommodating multiple media sources, Web pages can be more attractive and may motivate readers to process texts more. For example, Levie and Lentz' review of research suggests that illustrations attached to texts can attract and direct readers' attention, enhance enjoyment, and affect emotions and attitudes [7, pp. 218-220]. Nowadays, we are surrounded by various audio-visual products. Therefore, for decades we have been accustomed to acquiring information from various media forms, not only from written text. Appearance may be as important as the content in information presentation on the Web, so that the site or the page is selected and processed further.

Certain kinds of information can be conveyed better in other forms than written form. For example, Norton maintains that graphics are superior to written texts to communicate complex ideas because graphics can communicate them with more clarity, precision, and efficiency [8]. Kinzer and Risko assert that video recording is superior to written text to let the viewers experience authentic scenes, refocus, revisit, and look at a video segment in new ways for new purposes [9]. Especially when the video system is controlled by a computer, the viewers can quickly and accurately revisit appropriate scenes.

Williams asserts that the capability of the Internet to integrate verbal and visual components will promote deeper learning by saying that "the added complexity, then produces a more thorough engagement with rhetorical, critical, and technological skills, and approximates the linked, multimedia structure of problem solving more effectively than either verbal or visual compositions alone do" [10, p. 132].

Thus, the capability of housing multiple media sources is beneficial to make Web pages more attractive, to help readers comprehend information, and to promote deeper learning.

Linking Function

The pages on the Web utilize hypertext, which supports linking different parts of a page, different pages of a site, or even different sites with each other. This linking function does both good and harm.

It permits readers to access the most relevant information instantaneously. A well-structured set of Web pages provides both macro- and micro-structures of information effectively. Hierarchy of importance of information can be expressed either through the layout of a page or through the multi-layered characteristics of hypertext. Readers can choose the level of depth they want and zoom in and out of a piece of information. Readers can also learn interrelationship of different pieces of information or ideas by studying how a page is laid out and how pages are linked to each other.

Hypertext provides "an infinitely re-centerable system whose provisional point of focus depends upon the reader" [11, pp. 11-12]. This system forces readers to be mentally more active and monitor their navigation and comprehension. "The reader must remember her location in the network, make decisions about where to go next, and keep track of pages previously visited" [12, p. 17], while creating a coherent text representation. This environment can promote more self-regulation and meta-cognition on the part of the reader.

However, the linking function encourages flexible text processing and may create a complicated learning environment. The complexity of the environment will cost great cognitive demands on the reader and can be harmful to some readers. As a result, some readers fail to create a coherent representation of information. There also exist a great many Web sites which are poorly-structured or badly-intended, whose surface structures do not represent the underlying structures. Some readers can be confused or misled by these sites. Some writers use the linking function to allow the reader not only to "jump" within their Web sites, but to a different Web site. The association writers make can be arbitrary and subjective. The relationship between linked pages can be implicit and not clear to readers. Readers can get lost during their navigation and sometimes end up with a totally irrelevant site.

Interactivity

Web pages can be interactive by incorporating communication technologies. Because Web sites are connected globally, writers can post their products on their Web sites and share them with readers all over the world. Readers can respond to the writers easily if the pages are linked to the writers' e-mail addresses or if the pages provide discussion places. Writers learn how their writings were interpreted from the readers' responses. Writers can further exchange information and ideas with the readers using the communication technologies. By incorporating the responses, writers can even update their pages. Thus, the World Wide

Web provides excellent places to connect reading and writing, and to share and exchange ideas.

By connecting reading and writing, literacy skills may be enhanced. It is important to consider readers in writing. Novice writers tend to create what Flower calls "writer-based prose," which is structured according to the writer's memory or experience rather than according to the process the reader will go through in comprehending it [13, p. 83]. The opposite concept may be "reader-based prose." To produce this prose, a writer needs to change his/her perspective to that of the reader's. This change of perspectives is difficult for most people because they do not have the experience of playing the role of both reader and writer. Most of the time, they assume the receptive role of a reader. Usually, they read texts written by professional writers and they do not have to consider how well the writers' intentions are conveyed in written expressions. So when they write, not many people consider how much of their intentions are conveyed in used expressions or how their writing will be represented or interpreted by the readers. The ease of becoming a writer by participating in discussions on some Web sites or by creating their own Web site allows readers to "read as an author" [11, p. 41] and may help them consider the effects of written expressions. Thus, the Web environment offers valuable opportunities for people to experience the role of both reader and writer. This experience, in turn, may help them produce "reader-based prose" in regular writing.

Some Web sites create "cyber communities" and provide places to meet others. For example, a Web site called *Classroom Connect* provides a place for educators to meet other educators [14]. When one has some questions to ask or ideas to share, he/she can post his/her questions or ideas in the Teacher Discussion section. Because anyone can respond to the messages, various viewpoints and ideas can be exchanged there. There also is a discussion section for students in the site. Students can use the section to ask and discuss various topics such as "How could the Civil War have been avoided?" or "Rituals play a very important part in the spiritual life of Cubans. How is this different than the spiritual and religious beliefs in your society?" By learning various ways of viewing the world, students may broaden their own perspectives. The site also invites readers to join online projects. One can either find a project to join there or organize a project and post it there so that others can join. Today, I found a project called SARS Global Project posted by a Singapore educator. The school is organizing a project asking schools and students all over the world how SARS has affected their lives and education. Web sites like this provide readers opportunities to meet others who happen to have the same interest and will collaborate with them in a project. Thus, the Internet's interactivity can promote communication and collaboration with others. In exchanging information and ideas, people may learn that literacy is primarily a social act.

However, the interactivity can cause detrimental situations, too. From January 1, 2002 to December 31, 2002, the Internet Fraud Complaint Center (IFCC) received 75,063 complaints [1]. This total includes different fraudulent and non-fraudulent complaints, such as auction fraud, credit-debit card fraud, computer intrusions, unsolicited e-mail (SPAM), and child pornography. In this situation, one should be aware that information on his/her Web page or in communication exchange can be misused. One may receive SPAM mail to his/her e-mail address posted on his/her Web page. One may be invited to join a group holding ideological biases. As one can easily reach the writer of a Web page, he/she can be accessed easily by anyone through the Internet. People should remind themselves that crimes can take place on the Internet just as in the real world. People can be anonymous in the communication on the Internet. In this anonymity, people can be irresponsible or harmful to others. Some believe strangers they get acquainted with only through the Internet and provide personal information to them or meet them in person and fall victim of criminal cases. We need to protect ourselves so that we will not be involved in such situations.

CHARACTERISTICS OF THE WORLD WIDE WEB READING PROCESSES

Handling a Vast Amount of Information

Alexander and Jetton characterize contemporary living as "information flood," where "the creation and flow of information is endless and unmanageable" [15, p. 286]. This is the situation we find on the Web. A vast amount of information is there, which appears at first glance to provide us with more information than was available before. However, it is not necessarily the case. Information access can be slower or less efficient than before and as a result we may get less information.

Some tools help readers' information searching and information access. The tools assume that readers have specific goals to attain or specific problems to solve. If the assumption is not met, information searching is very difficult. Existence of a vast amount of information makes it difficult to distinguish important from unimportant or relevant from irrelevant information. Readers should know how to ignore irrelevant or unimportant information. The goals readers may have will serve as criteria to ignore irrelevant or unimportant information. Without them, readers will be overwhelmed by the amount of information presented on the World Wide Web.

More importantly, the meaning of literacy may change in this environment. In the past, information access was limited and having more information or having ways to access more information was advantageous. In the age of the Internet, when we can access a vast amount of information easily, it is more important to be able to identify important problems to solve, choose good information, and use the information effectively to solve the problems as Leu discussed below:

> In the Information age or post-information age in which we live, literacy is essential to enable individuals, groups, and societies to access the best information in the shortest time to identify and solve the most important problems and then communicate this information to others. Accessing information, evaluating information, solving problems, and communicating solutions are essential to success in this new era [16, p. 746].

We should remember that existence of a great deal of information does not in itself guarantee that we can access more information "we need." The task of distinguishing important from unimportant information has become more challenging. In this environment, how to use information is more important than how much information one has.

Handling Multiple Sources of Information

As Mikulecky and Kirkley pointed out, we need to be able to read various types of reading materials at work [17]. However, they wrote, most reading materials used at schools are either narrative prose from novels and anthologies or expository prose from textbooks. Thus, students are not prepared to handle the vast range of text types encountered at work. One advantage of using the Web is that it can expand the range of reading materials and help students prepare for handling them. Various types of reading materials can be found on the Web, such as individuals' and organizations' homepages, commercial advertisements, online news service, directories, etc. Each requires different reading skills and strategies. For example, when reading a newspaper, we scan headlines and only read the articles we are interested in intensively. Directories are used just to get the information you are searching for. More and more commercial advertisements use audio-visual effects for more attractive pages. This necessitates that readers understand messages conveyed in a variety of forms.

Another advantage of handling multiple sources is that you can encounter various perspectives and interpretations. For example, Hanaoka demonstrated her usage of newspaper Web sites in her English as a Foreign Language (EFL) classroom to show various perspectives, interpretations, and expressions when the 9-11 attack occurred [18]. She showed how different papers used different headlines, photos, descriptions to tell the story by comparing articles from different online news sites. Like this, online news services present a variety of viewpoints and interpretations of events and can be good materials to promote critical reading. Garner and Gillingham illustrated how "competing perspectives and conflicting facts are presented openly and abundantly on the Internet" by showing Texaco's case [19, p. 228]. When they were searching for a set of Web sites related to endangered species, they located a list of eight steps that children might take to save endangered species [20]. One step includes getting everyone in the family to avoid buying products from Texaco, which is boycotted for rainforest destruction. However, when they visited Texaco's home page [21], they found that the vision and values statement presented a corporate image of environmental sensitivity and responsibility. Garner and Gillingham warned us not to believe what is described in text because "persons and events described in text are never described without some intrusion from the teller" [19, p. 229]. Messages always operate in terms of their economic, political, and social intentions. Information on the Web demonstrates a variety of perspectives and interpretations and can warn us to read texts critically.

Handling multiple sources on the Internet is also advantageous to promote higher order thinking skills. An important goal of text processing is to generate a coherent representation. Because different Web sites were created with different intentions and purposes, there is no organizing principle there. Readers are forced to create a coherent mental representation of some information or an issue on their own. Readers can no longer be content with understanding the meaning of each text. They are asked to evaluate the reliability and the relevance to their goals and select information. Integrating multiple sources and creating a coherent mental representation advances our deep thinking skill. This skill is especially useful in considering complex social problems because most social problems are ill-defined and require us to explore and integrate multiple perspectives and interpretations and create a coherent mental representation.

Losing Context of Information

Grice and Ridgway warn us to be aware of the possibility of misinterpreting material out of context in reading on the World Wide Web as a tradeoff to locate information quickly [22]. According to them, traditionally we have viewed information as a linear flow of thought and have come to expect that parts of this linear flow develop a context in which ideas are expressed and are to be understood. In this view there is an implicit assumption that readers will take time and make efforts to understand the context and interpret statements and facts within this context. Recently, however, many researchers have come to employ Constructivism views of text processing, which contends that the goal of text processing is meaning construction rather than knowledge acquisition [23]. Spivey, one of the Constructivists, emphasizes the importance of selective reading, critical reading, and integrating information according to the writer's own perspective. Spivey asserts that "when reading, the person would have some kind of perspective (directed toward the new text) guiding how he or she selects material for relevance, organizes it mentally, and connects it with what is already known" [24, p. 321]. This view can be operationalized well in the reading processes on the Web because readers can jump and seek out specific pieces of information and disregard other pieces effectively.

A trade-off of this convenience is that "we may not be aware of the context an author has established; we may pull out an isolated piece of information and place it in our own context without ever becoming aware of the context in which the author placed it" [22, pp. 36-37]. We have to be aware that we may misinterpret information by not paying attention to the context well enough. The Web page's capability of jumping to linked pages allows the readers to be less patient and move around easily. Readers may spend less time or effort in trying to understand the content or the writer's intention fully. Another effect is that readers may lose opportunities to take time and consider different perspectives or logics by guiding their navigation using only their viewpoint.

Other Constructivists such as Duffy and Cunningham stress the importance of the negotiation process to achieve understanding [23]. Unlike Spivey, they do not assume literacy as one-way communication. They assume multiple perspectives and encourage debate. They contend that one should negotiate meaning with others to achieve deeper understanding. The interactivity which is another characteristic of the Internet could support the negotiation process. In the negotiation processes, misunderstanding and misinterpretation could be corrected and different perspectives could be considered.

Exposed to Information with Levels of Credibility

Information on the World Wide Web has not been filtered because "there is no single governing body that controls what happens on it or to it" [2, p. 23]. The result is different levels of credibility. This is also true with printed books and articles. However, to publish a printed text, the content is usually screened by the editor or the publisher and thus the quality is guaranteed to a certain degree. The author usually belongs to some discourse community which sets rules and regulations to follow. These inconveniences of publication or regulations do not exit in Web page publication. In addition, the Internet permits readers unrestricted access to almost any sites, some of which are dubious and can be harmful to readers. Readers are exposed to Web pages that try to persuade them to hold specific political, religious, or ideological stances. Research carried out by online monitoring organizations reports that "the World Wide Web has quickly become a convenient and effective base for thousands engaged in hate propagation" [25, p. 300]. In this situation, readers need to be more critical and analytic so that they will not be misled. That is, readers should not only try to understand written messages, but also try to consider the reliability of information or soundness of opinions.

Geisler calls this "rhetorical reading" [26], which is required in academic reading and which divides experts and laypersons because of the difficulty of acquisition. In her research, she investigated science experts' reading processes and found that experts read texts more critically than laypersons, which means that experts do not easily believe what is written in texts but pay more attention to contexts for the text production. She writes that "scientists actively resist the codification that writers have made. Instead they try to reconstruct the contextual factors they consider indispensable for evaluating the merits of a scientific claim" [26, p. 20]. She cites Bazerman's research [27], which suggests that the scientists he observed were particularly attentive to methodological details. The scientists, she contends, "seemed to have deconstructed the apparently smooth virtual experience that the text laid out for them and attempted to construct in its place what they considered to be a more accurate representation of the writer's actual laboratory procedure" [26, pp. 22-23].

Geisler claims that this skill of "rhetorical reading" is developed as an individual's expertise develops and usually only emerges in later undergraduate or graduate school. This is because up to high school level students learn cultural lessons that "the text was to be treated as an explicit source of information and that text was to be treated as a direct representation of a maximally coherent reality" [26, p. 34]. Thus, students rarely perceive text as having multiple levels — i.e., surface level and deeper level in which the truth of the written information needs to be investigated. Only in later stages in learning do students learn to understand the deeper levels of text meaning. At this stage, Geisler wrote,

> texts are now seen to have authors, to make claims, to be acts that can
> be understood only within a temporal and interpersonal framework.

> Some issues are hot, some issues irrelevant, some issues settled. Some
> authors are credible; some discredited; some irrelevant. People write
> texts not simply to say things, but to do things: To persuade, to argue,
> to excuse [26, p. 87].

One problem with reading on the World Wide Web is that Web pages with various levels of credibility can be found. In addition, important clues to judge the credibility such as the identity of the author or the sources of information are often missing. Another problem is that because anyone can access basically any site, not all readers possess the "rhetorical reading" skill, which is developed only in the later stage of learning. Hence, even if the contextual information is provided, not all readers will pay attention to it or make use of it.

What Should We Teach to Our Students?

Considering the above-mentioned mechanism and characteristics of text processing on the World Wide Web, what should we instructors teach to our students? What implications does text processing on the Web have on literacy education in the twenty-first century? Though this new technology has great potential to promote learning, the potential needs to be realized. Therefore, instructors should work hard to ensure that the potential is realized by each student. In addition, instructors need to provide students with skills to protect themselves from harmful information. Specifically, to these ends, instructors should: 1) let students have clear goals and control their processing; 2) teach a range of reading skills and strategies and how to regulate them; 3) teach how to analyze multimedia; 4) provide instruction to read texts critically; 5) provide tasks in which students will engage in higher order thinking; 6) have students consider social aspects of literate activities; 7) teach students how to cooperate and collaborate with others; and 8) teach students independent study skills so that they can continue studying on their own.

Let Students have Clear Goals and Control Their Processing

Usually, when using the World Wide Web, readers are assumed to have specific goals or reasons. Search tools function effectively only when the assumption is met. Their goals will help them decide their own center of exploration and investigation. Their goals will serve as criteria to choose relevant from irrelevant and important from unimportant pages or sites. Readers' goals will help them choose appropriate reading skills and strategies to process the content of a chosen page. Additionally, text processing on the Web involves computer and navigation skills. The linking function used in the Web permits readers to shift between the global processing of finding relevant sites or pages and the local processing of understanding the content of a page. Readers' goals will help them to focus their attention on important information in this complicated learning environment.

Thus, goals play important roles in text processing on the Web, which involves a variety of processes, decisions, skills, and strategies. Without clear goals, readers can easily be confused or lost in the navigation. So that they will not be overwhelmed by the complexity of text processing on the Web, readers should have clear goals and control their text processing accordingly.

Taking the initiative in text processing may not be familiar to students in some cultures where they are assigned to the more receptive role of understanding given texts. These students should learn to be independent, to create their own questions to solve, and to regulate their processing on their own. Until they feel comfortable with all these, careful instruction should be provided.

Teach a Range of Reading Skills and Strategies and How to Regulate Them

In text processing on the World Wide Web, conventional text processing is embedded. In order to "access the best information in the shortest time" [16, p. 746], it is advantageous to have a range of reading skills and strategies and learn when, how, and why to use them.

From reading conventional texts, we have learned various reading skills and strategies. Among them are traditionally recognized reading behaviors such as skimming, scanning, and rereading. Skimming is employed to obtain a general sense of a text's content. Scanning is employed to locate specific words or information. Complicated information requires intensive reading and sometimes rereading. Learning strategies research has identified more than 100 language learning strategies [28, p. 11]. Findings from cognitive research have also been applied to reading instructions. For example, content schema and rhetorical schema were identified and found to be helpful for efficient text comprehension. While content schema is background knowledge of the content area of a text, rhetorical schema is background knowledge of the rhetorical structures of different types of texts [29].

Recently, meta-cognitive processes have been drawing reading researchers' attention [28, 30]. Meta-cognitive processes are "internal 'executive' processes that supervise and control cognitive processes" [31, p. 82]. Meta-cognition enables one to plan, monitor, and evaluate performance throughout the execution of a task and to select and integrate skills and strategies appropriately and efficiently.

Web processing is a complex process involving various computer skills, navigation skills, reading skills, multimedia analyzing skills, and so forth. To reduce the cognitive load, it is helpful for readers to learn various reading skills and strategies and learn to use meta-cognition to regulate them.

Teach How to Analyze Multimedia

Though we are surrounded by multiple media and get much information from them, we do not know how to analyze them and understand information from them effectively. Hobbs pointed out that students receive little or no training in the skills of analyzing or evaluating messages conveyed in multimedia [32, p. 7]. Literacy training at school often focuses only on written text comprehension. Considering that the primary goal of text processing is constructing a coherent representation of an issue, comprehending written text is only a part of the process. We also learn from visual images and sounds. We are exposed to information coming from multiple media sources such as television, radio, billboards, computer programs, and Web sites in our everyday lives. Our perceptions and attitudes toward the world are shaped not only by information from textbooks or class lessons but also by information coming from these various media sources. Therefore, students need to learn how to analyze or evaluate information communicated in these multiple media, which have their own rules of production and interpretation.

The Center for Media Literacy (CML) asserts that media messages are constructed using a creative language with its own rules [33, p. 11]. For example, scary music heightens fear, camera close-ups convey intimacy, and big headlines signal significance. They recommend that we make media messages on our own or learn music, dance, theater, and the visual arts in order to understand how media are put together. They also provide specific guiding questions to analyze media messages in the *CML MediaLit Kit™ Orientation Guide* [33]. Guidance from organizations such as CML will be helpful for instructors to teach how to analyze information conveyed in various media forms.

Especially because information on the Internet is in a variety of media forms, students should learn how to analyze information communicated in multiple media forms.

Provide Instruction to Read Texts Critically

Because credibility is not guaranteed in the information on the World Wide Web, we need to develop "rhetorical reading" skills, in Geisler's term [26]; that is, we should not only understand the content but consider the level of reliability or certainty. Some readers may learn to consider credibility of information just by being exposed to competing perspectives or conflicting facts. However, it is not always the case.

For example, Stahl, Hynd, Britton, McNish, and Bosquet's study showed that instruction is necessary for readers to profit from comparing and contrasting different sources [34]. In their study, they provided high school students multiple source documents with contradicting remarks and facts about a controversial incident in U.S. history: primary sources such as legislative bills or eyewitness accounts; secondary sources such as editorials; or tertiary sources such as textbooks. Their observations suggest that high school students were not able to profit from multiple texts without some specific instruction. Because not all readers will acquire "rhetorical reading" skill naturally by being exposed to sources with different levels of credibility, careful instruction should be provided to ensure that students will learn this important skill. Especially in cultures where being trusting and harmonious towards others carries more emphasis than being suspicious and analytic or where respecting authority carries more emphasis than respecting the truth, people are reluctant to be critical. They should learn that criticizing what is written by a writer does not mean to criticize the writer's personality or authority.

On the World Wide Web, one can find resources to help him/her evaluate the quality of Web pages. One can conduct a key word search of "website evaluation." Each site on the list offers criteria to evaluate Web sites. Many of them include criteria to evaluate reliability and credibility. For example, the checklist created by the Owens library at Northwest Missouri State University uses purpose, authority, reliability, and timeliness as the criteria [35]. Specifically, it asks relevance to the reader's goal, the author's background, existence of the contact information, adequacy of the evidence of claims and a bibliography, currency of the information, and so on. The checklist of the Teaching Library at the University of California, Berkeley includes a criterion of the reputation of the site such as who links to the site or if the page is rated well in a directory [36]. University libraries at Virginia Tech offer a comprehensive bibliography on evaluating Web information, including Internet resources, sample evaluation forms, example Web sites, print resources, useful listservs, and useful books [37]. These sites should help one learn criteria to evaluate Web sites.

Provide Tasks in Which Students Will Engage in Higher Order Thinking

Information processing on the World Wide Web can offer an ideal environment to promote higher order thinking skills by integrating multimedia and hypertext in digital format and by the worldwide network system. However, students will not acquire higher order thinking skills just by being exposed to the environment. Tierney warns us by saying that "sometimes the possibilities with software are limited by the orientation of the teacher or the predisposition of the students and how the media is integrated" [38, p. 22].

Then, specifically, what tasks or problems should be provided to students? Jonassen et al. introduce some activities in *Learning with Technology: A Constructivist Perspective* [2]. The examples include creating home pages, conducting scientific research, discussing complex social problems, and so on.

Creating home pages will facilitate knowledge exploration because many decisions have to be made such as what materials to include, what media to use, what gets linked to what. If it is a collaborative activity, more decision-makings are involved such as how to break down the work, who will do what, how the work of an individual will be integrated with the work of others.

Conducting scientific research, according to Jonassen et al., is "among the most complete intellectual activities" involving "defining research problems, seeking evidence using the Internet as well as observing their own studies, and then communicating their results via the Internet" [2, p. 27]. All of these activities require and promote higher order thinking skills.

Discussing complex social problems with others will advance deep thinking skills. By using the Internet's interactivity, students can communicate with people around the world easily. By discussing complex social problems with people who have different perspectives or opinions, students will think the issue more deeply. Jonassen et al. wrote, "When joining in conversations, individuals are required to articulate their point of view and to reflect on the perspectives provided by other participants as well as their own" [2, p. 41]. Because most social problems require students to consider multiple viewpoints in order to understand them, it is beneficial for students to discuss complex social problems with others.

Many activities and projects can also be found in Web sites such as *Classroom Connect* [14] and *The Global Schoolhouse* [39]. What is important is that students will address important topics or problems and regulate their exploration or research according to their goals. Instructors should monitor students' activities and make sure that they are really engaged in deep thinking.

Have Students Consider Social Aspects of Literate Activities

Students can encounter authentic reading materials on the World Wide Web. They can also meet and communicate with others using the communication technologies. This is ideal to have students consider the social aspects of reading and writing. As Texaco's case demonstrated, description always includes intrusion of the writer's intentions or biases [19, p. 228]. Additionally, people with different opinions or backgrounds perceive the same information differently. The same information can be interpreted differently depending on the political, economic, or social contexts. Students should learn to analyze how much truth is represented in a description or what a piece of information can mean in a specific context and consider what implications it can have on our lives.

This world is very complicated and consists of people with a variety of perspectives and opinions. Especially on the Internet, because there is no governing organization which controls what happens there, people can freely provide any information or express any opinions. A trade-off is that people can be exposed to dubious or harmful information. To ensure the freedom of expressing opinions, we should train ourselves to handle information and opinions wisely. Students should keep in mind that the world is made up of different viewpoints and conflicting opinions and "people write not simply to say things, but to do things" [26, p. 87]. Fostering "rhetorical reading" skill and the ability to critically analyze information in students is more important than trying to protect them from dubious or harmful information by screening information for them, which happened after the 9-11 attack when some Web sites were shut down by the U.S. government, Internet service providers, or the Web owners [40].

Students should also learn how to use the Internet appropriately as a responsible member of the society. They are not only a receiver of information but can also be a provider. They themselves can cause trouble or be harmful toward others. Therefore, instructors should teach them what to do and what not to do as a receiver and a provider of information. Many organizations create their Acceptable Use Policies (AUPs). One can find some of them on the Internet, too. AUP is "a written agreement in the form of guidelines, signed by students, their parents and their teachers, outlining the terms and conditions of Internet use—rules of online behavior and access privileges" [41]. AUPs specify acceptable and unacceptable use of the Internet and serve as guidelines for the Internet users. They also describe the consequence of violating the policies. Let students read the AUPs of their schools or districts and learn what to do and what not to do in using the Internet. Let them discuss why certain behaviors are encouraged and certain behaviors are prohibited as well. In doing so, let them learn how to behave as a responsible member of the society.

Teach Students How to Cooperate and Collaborate with Others

Today more business is operated with computers and the Internet because of the versatility and efficiency. More business communication within and between companies is taking place on the Internet. More personalized service to customers is available there. For organizations, effective use of information technologies is the key to success in this competitive global marketplace [16, p. 747].

The most important change these technologies will promote may be "decentralization"; specifically, decentralization of decision-making and decentralization of workplaces. According to Leu, decentralization of decision-making should be brought about due to the necessity of restructuring into "high-performance" workplaces in order to keep up with the global competition [16, p. 747]. It means "change from a centrally planned organization to one that relies increasingly on collaborative teams at all levels in order to assume initiative for planning ways to work more effectively" [16, p. 747]. This requires effective collaboration and communication skills "so the best decisions get made at every level in an organization and so that changes at one level are clearly communicated to other levels" [16, p. 747]. Decentralization of workplaces means that by using the technologies, people no longer have to gather at the same place, but can collaborate with others by assuming their share of responsibility. As the result, more flexible work-styles are possible for workers. In fact, one in five U.S. employees participate in some form of teleworking according to a survey conducted by the International Telework Association and Council (ITAC) [42]. For a successful collaboration, they should be able to perform their share of responsibility and communicate it to others. Though some parts of face-to-face communication may be replaced by online communication, communication and collaboration skills will be as important or more important in the twenty-first century workplaces.

The globalization of business practices and the advancement of technologies will also necessitate working in collaboration with people from diverse cultures. The Internet's globally distributed network and the interactivity make global collaboration and communication easy. However, in intercultural communication, misunderstandings are likely to take place because "people are not aware that their partners in communication are playing by a different set of sometimes-unstated rules" [43, p. 110].

First, there are language problems. Even when both sides use the same language, most of the time the language is a foreign language for one side and connotations of the translated words may be different from the connotations of the original language [43, p. 115]. When a Japanese says "it is difficult," most of the time it means that it is impossible and that he/she will not make any more efforts to solve the difficulty. Some foreigners may fail to understand this connotation. Second, misunderstandings can occur because of different social systems between cultures. Often, Japanese companies are criticized for taking too long for making decisions. This is because many Japanese companies take the *ringi*-system which means that a plan needs to be circulated and obtaining the sanction of executives before decided. Third, values according to which people make important decisions differ from culture to culture. A Japanese boss might expect his/her workers to sacrifice their family lives for their work, which might upset foreign workers who place more value on family lives. Thus, there are many causes of misunderstanding in intercultural communication. Therefore, to work with people from different cultures collaboratively and cooperatively, one should know that differences exist between cultures and misunderstandings are likely to happen. One should also learn to accept different ways of thinking and behaving as they are and try to find ways to minimize frictions and work harmoniously with them.

Thus, advancement of information technologies is changing business operations and students should learn how to cooperate and collaborate with others to prepare for it.

Teach Students Independent Study Skills So That They Can Continue Studying on Their Own

The definition of literacy changes with time depending on the assumed educational theory and technology. Traditionally, when discussing learning we have only focused on the transmitted information. However, the contemporary educational theory Constructivism views "learning as the activity in context" and asserts that "the entire gestalt is integral to what is learned" [23, p. 171]. Literacy no longer means just the skills of reading and writing. Some Constructivists such as Flower, Stein, Ackerman, Kantz, McCormick, and Peck view it as a goal-directed problem-solving activity and state that "it is a 'goal-directed, context-specific' behavior, which means that a literacy person is able to use reading and writing in a transactional sense to achieve some purpose in the world at hand" [44, p. 4]. Other Constructivists such as Duffy and Cunningham view it as a collective social-cultural construction process and wrote, "We regard all learning as social, dialogical process of construction by distributed, multi-dimensional selves using tools and signs within contexts created by the various communities with which they interact" [23, pp. 181-182].

The capability of modern technologies including hypertext and the Internet has further been changing the definition of literacy. Readers are expected to handle nonlinearity caused by the linking function of hypertext. Because information can be conveyed in a variety of media forms, some researchers suggest that meaning negotiation using multimedia should be included in the definition of literacy [32]. Because text processing often takes place on computer screens in our time, computer knowledge and skills are to be included in literacy. Currently computer literacy is taught as a different discipline. However, as more and more text processing takes place on computers, soon the boundary will disappear. The definition of literacy may have to be augmented by including the abilities to handle nonlinear text presentation, to manage multimedia, to operate computer systems and so on.

Thus, because the definition of literacy is changing in accordance with the change of our conception of learning and the advancement of technologies, even instructors do not know what literacy will mean in the future. Leu wrote, "For the first time in our history, we are unable to accurately anticipate the literacy requirements expected at the time of graduation for children who will enter school this year" [16, p. 760]. The only thing we are sure of is that students should continue learning for their entire lives in order to keep up with the change. Therefore, instructors should at least teach students how to study on their own so that they can continue learning for the rest of their lives.

CONCLUSION

The emergence of the Internet has changed our lives drastically. Especially, hypertext and the World Wide Web, which is called "global hypertext," have changed our reading processes and our conception of literacy significantly. Hypertext consists of verbal or graphic units which are linked to each other. Texts are no longer structured linearly, but can be multi-layered and can incorporate a variety of media forms. Communication can be interactive and connect reading and writing or even listening and speaking. Text processing on the Web is considerably different from conventional text processing. On the Internet, we are handling vast amounts of information, various types of information, and information with varying levels of credibility. We are expected to be more strategic in information handling and be more critical in content comprehension. The Web has great potential to promote our learning. However, it also has possibilities to confuse us or expose us to danger or harm.

In this age when much communication and information access is carried out on computer screens and online, instructors should make sure that students can manage their information processing using the new technologies. Technology is advancing very rapidly and students should keep up with the advancement in order to function effectively in modern society. To be able to do so, students should develop self-study skills. Because hypertext and the Internet are capable of creating ideal learning environments to promote higher order thinking, instructors should make sure that they are truly engaged in appropriate tasks to promote such thinking. Using the Internet in itself is not difficult. Anyone may be able to netsurf for fun or use the network for a game. However, as Leu warns us, students who expect to encounter a game in a hypermedia environment may not be motivated to explore the context to acquire important knowledge, and as the result these students are less likely to learn important information [16, p. 752]. Instruction is necessary so that students will learn to use the Internet for learning or for deep thinking. Instructors should also equip students with criteria to judge the quality of information so that they will not be misled. The Internet provides networked open space for anyone to participate and promote communication. However, because there is no screening or mediating system there, students should learn how to protect themselves from dubious or harmful information.

ACKNOWLEDGMENT

I express my sincere gratitude to Dr. Charles H. Sides for inviting me to join this book project and for providing me with valuable editorial suggestions.

REFERENCES

1. National White Collar Crime Center and the Federal Bureau of Investigation, *IFCC 2002 Internet Fraud Report: January 1, 2002–December 31, 2002.* Accessed online May 17, 2003 at:
   http://www1.ifccfbi.gov/strategy/2002_IFCCReport.pdf
2. D. H. Jonassen, K. L. Peck, and B. G. Wilson, *Learning with Technology: A Constructivist Perspective,* Prentice Hall, Upper Saddle River, New Jersey, 1999.
3. Jupitermedia Corporation, *Nua Internet How Many Online.* Accessed online June 23, 2003 at:
   http://www.nua.com/surveys/now_many_online/index.html
4. Internet Society (ISOC), *All about the Internet.* Accessed online April 23, 2003 at: http://www.isoc.org/internet
5. H. van Oostendorp and S. de Mul, Introduction: Cognitive Aspects of Electronic Text Processing, in *Cognitive Aspects of Electronic Text Processing,* H. van Oostendorp and S. de Mul (eds.), Ablex Publishing Corporation, Norwood, New Jersey, pp. 1-6, 1996.

6. J. D. Bolter, Hypertext and the Question of Visual Literacy, in *Handbook of Literacy and Technology: Transformations in a Post-Typographic World*, D. Reinking, M. C. McKenna, L. D. Labbo, and R. D. Kieffer (eds.), Lawrence Erlbaum Associates, Mahwah, New Jersey, pp. 1-2, 1998.

7. W. H. Levie and R. Lentz, Effects of Text Illustrations: A Review of Research, *Educational Communication and Technology*, 30:4, pp. 195-232, 1982.

8. R. Norton, Commentary: Graphic Excellence for the Technical Communicator, *Journal of Technical Writing and Communication*, 23:1, pp. 1-6, 1993.

9. C. K. Kinzer and V. J. Risko, Multimedia and Enhanced Learning: Transforming Preservice Education, in *Handbook of Literacy and Technology: Transformations in a Post-Typographic World*, D. Reinking, M. C. McKenna, L. D. Labbo, and R. D. Kieffer (eds.), Lawrence Erlbaum Associates, Mahwah, New Jersey, pp. 185-202, 1998.

10. S. D. Williams, Part 2: Toward an Integrated Composition Pedagogy in Hypertext, *Computers and Composition*, 18, pp. 123-135, 2001.

11. G. P. Landow, *Hypertext: The Convergence of Contemporary Critical Theory and Technology*, The Johns Hopkins University Press, Baltimore, Maryland, 1992.

12. J. Rouet and J. J. Levonen, Studying and Learning with Hypertext: Empirical Studies and their Implications, in A *Hypertext and Cognition*, J. Rouet, J. J. Levonen, A. Dillon, and R. J. Spiro (eds.), Lawrence Erlbaum Associates, Mahwah, New Jersey, pp. 9-23, 1996.

13. C. Bereiter and M. Scardamalia, *The Psychology of Written Composition*, Lawrence Erlbaum Associates, Hillsdale, New Jersey, 1987.

14. *Classroom Connect*. Accessed online June 11, 2003 at: http://www.classroom.com/login/home.jhtml

15. P. A. Alexander and T. L. Jetton, Learning from Text: A Multidimensional and Developmental Perspective, in *Handbook of Reading Research Volume III*, M. L. Kamil, P. B. Mosenthal, P. D. Pearson, and R. Barr (eds.), Lawrence Erlbaum Associates, Mahwah, New Jersey, pp. 285-310, 2000.

16. D. J. Leu, Literacy and Technology: Deictic Consequences for Literacy Education in an Information Age, in *Handbook of Reading Research Volume III*, M. L. Kamil, P. B. Mosenthal, P. D. Pearson, and R. Barr (eds.), Lawrence Erlbaum Associates, Mahwah, New Jersey, pp. 743-770, 2000.

17. L. Mikulecky and J. R. Kirkley, Changing Workplaces, Changing Classes: The New Role of Technology in Workplace Literacy, in *Handbook of Literacy and Technology: Transformations in a Post-Typographic World*, D. Reinking, M. C. McKenna, L. D. Labbo, and R. D. Kieffer (eds.), Lawrence Erlbaum Associates, Mahwah, New Jersey, pp. 303-320, 1998.

18. T. D. Hanaoka, *Critical Literacy in Foreign Language Reading Classrooms*, paper presented at Research, Innovation & Collaboration in L2 Literacy: Foreign Language Literacy Special Interest Group Forum, JALT 2001, Kitakyushu, Japan, November 2001.

19. R. Garner and M. G. Gillingham, The Internet in the Classroom: Is It the End of Transmission-Oriented Pedagogy? in *Handbook of Literacy and Technology: Transformations in a Post-Typographic World*, D. Reinking, M. C. McKenna,

L. D. Labbo, and R. D. Kieffer (eds.), Lawrence Erlbaum Associates, Mahwah, New Jersey, pp. 221-233, 1998.

20. Rainforest Action Network, January 6, 1997. Available online at: http://www.ran.org/ran

21. Texaco, Inc., Texaco Online, January 6, 1997. Available online at: http://www.texaco.com

22. R. A. Grice and L. S. Ridgway, Presenting Technical Information in Hypermedia Format: Benefits and Pitfalls, *Technical Communication Quarterly*, 4:1, pp. 35-61, 1995.

23. T. M. Duffy and D. J. Cunningham, Constructivism: Implications for the Design and Delivery of Instruction, in *Handbook of Research for Educational Communications and Technology*, D. H. Jonassen (ed.), Macmillan Library Reference, New York, pp. 170-198, 1996.

24. N. N. Spivey, Written Discourse: A Constructivist Perspective, in *Constructivism in Education*, L. P. Steffe and J. Gale (eds.), Lawrence Erlbaum Associates, Hillsdale, New Jersey, pp. 313-329, 1995.

25. K. Eichhorn, Re-in/citing Linguistic Injuries: Speech Acts, Cyberhate, and the Spatial and Temporal Character of Networked Environments, *Computers and Composition*, 18, pp. 293-304, 2001.

26. C. Geisler, *Academic Literacy and the Nature of Expertise: Reading, Writing, and Knowing in Academic Philosophy*, Lawrence Erlbaum Associates, Hillsdale, New Jersey, 1994.

27. C. Bazerman, *Shaping Written Knowledge: The Genre and Activity of the Experimental Article in Science*, University of Wisconsin Press, Madison, Wisconsin, 1988.

28. A. U. Chamot, S. Barnhardt, P. B. El-Dinary, and J. Robbins, *The Learning Strategies Handbook*, Addison Wesley Longman, White Plains, New York, 1999.

29. P. L. Carrell, Some Issues in Studying the Role of Schemata, or Background Knowledge, in Second Language Comprehension, *Reading in a Foreign Language*, 1:2, pp. 81-92, 1983.

30. P. L. Carrell, L. Gajdusek, and T. Wise, Metacognition and EFL/ESL Reading, *Instructional Science*, 26, pp. 97-112, 1998.

31. A. F. Gourgey, Metacognition in Basic Skills Instruction, *Instructional Science*, 26, pp. 81-96, 1998.

32. R. Hobbs, Literacy for the Information Age, in *Handbook of Research on Teaching Literacy through the Communicative and Visual Arts*, J. Flood, S. B. Heath, and D. Lapp (eds.), Macmillan Library Reference, New York, 1997.

33. Center for Media Literacy (CML), *MediaLit KIT™ Orientation Guide*, June 6, 2003. Available online at: http://www.medialit.org

34. S. A. Stahl, C. R. Hynd, B. K. Britton, M. M. McNish, and D. Bosquet, What Happens When Students Read Multiple Source Documents in History? *Reading Research Quarterly*, 31:4, pp. 430-456, 1996.

35. C. Ury and L. Mardis, *Evaluating Websites: Part of the Research Process*, The Owens Library at Northwest Missouri State University, May 17, 2003. Available online at: http://www.nwmissouri.edu/library/courses/evaluation/edeval.htm

36. J. Baker, *Web Page Evaluation Worksheet*, The Teaching Library, University of California, Berkeley, May 17, 2003. Available online at: http://www.lib.berkeley.edu/TeachingLib/Guides/internet/EvalForm.pdf
37. University Libraries at Virginia Tech, Bibliography on Evaluating Internet Resources, May 17, 2003. Available online at: http://www.lib.vt.edu/research/evaluate/evalbiblio.html
38. R. J. Tierney, Learning with Multiple Symbol Systems: Possibilities, Realities, Paradigm Shifts and Developmental Considerations, in *Handbook of Research on Teaching Literacy through the Communicative and Visual Arts*, Macmillan Library Reference, New York, pp. 286-298, 1997.
39. Global SchoolNet, *The Global Schoolhouse*, June 3, 2003. Available online at: http://www.gsh.org
40. Electronic Frontier Foundation, Chilling Effects of Anti-Terrorism, April 29, 2003. Available online at: http://www.eff.org/Privacy/Surveillance/Terrorism_militias/antiterrorism_chill.html
41. Virginia Department of Education, *Acceptable Internet Use Policies – A Handbook*, Virginia Department of Education, May 17, 2003. Available online at: http://www.pen.k12.va.us/go/VDOE/Technology/AUP/home.shtml
42. International Telework Association and Council (ITAC), *Number of Teleworkers Increases by 17 percent, National Survey Shows 1 in 5 Americans are Teleworking*, May 19, 2003. Available online at: http://www.telecommutect.com/content/itacsurvey01.htm
43. W. W. Neher and D. H. Waite, *The Business and Professional Communicator*, Allyn and Bacon, Needham Heights, Massachusetts, 1993.
44. L. Flower, V. Stein, J. Ackerman, M. J. Kantz, K. McCormick, and W. C. Peck, *Reading to Write: Exploring a Cognitive and Social Process*, Oxford University Press, New York, 1990.

CHAPTER 6

Communal "Intelligence" and the Disarming of Dangerous Information

Robert Carr

That ideas should freely spread from one to another over the globe, for the moral and mutual instruction of man, and improvement of his condition, seems to have been peculiarly and benevolently designed by nature, when she made them, like fire, expansible over all space, without lessening their density at any point, and like the air in which we breathe, move, and have our physical being, incapable of confinement or exclusive appropriation.
— Thomas Jefferson, "No Patents on Ideas" [1]

The characteristics of democracy are as follows: all men should sit in judgment . . . the assembly should be supreme over all causes or at any rate the most important, for the people then draw all cases to themselves.
— Aristotle, Politics 1317b26–34 [2]

Charles Sides opens this collection by asking whether there is ever a time when information is too accurate or too available, and by extension too dangerous. Interestingly, though this question continues to haunt us in the aftermath of September 11, 2001, I believe our national conversation has remained conspicuously quiet in addressing it. Why? To begin with, as Sides also suggests, to entertain it directly with any seriousness requires that this question be accompanied by its root: Is there ever a time when free speech should be compromised, constrained, or reconceived? By cutting to the core of our most cherished rights and beliefs, even opening such explicit public discussion would be threatening and perhaps anathema. It would be to call into question one of our most defining foundational principles. In the absence of such discussion, however, the nagging question remains, where I believe it is being quietly, implicitly, and contextually assuaged through the implementation and use of our rapidly evolving communication technologies; the mundane communication practices that comprise the "networks" of our personal, communal, and national lives; and the incipient transparency in public environments that results as communication technologies from surveillance equipment to cellular phones gradually become ubiquitous. Freedom of speech per se remains untouchable in the public arena, but the public sphere wherein it is alive and well is itself rapidly changing. In an effort to tease out the implications of this shift, the following discussion takes up the evolving interrelationship between our communication technologies and their use at the convergence of our increasingly interwoven virtual and physical environments.

In *The Transparent Society*, published in 1998, David Brin paints an eerily prescient hypothetical: "As a mental experiment, let's go along with FBI director Freeh and try to envisage what might have happened if those bombers had actually succeeded in toppling both towers of New York's World Trade Center, killing tens of thousands" [3, p. 207]. Brin goes on to use this then scenario as a springboard to express what has now become a serious reality for many Americans in the aftermath of the 9/11 tragedy, namely that the Federal Government's war on terrorism often seems to pit civil defense against civil liberties. Though I believe our national discourse refuses to include freedom of speech in this quandary, Senator Dianne Feinstein's declaration, "When technology allows for bomb-making material over computers to millions of people in a matter of seconds, I believe that some restrictions on free speech are appropriate" [3, p. 208], suggests that the availability of potentially dangerous information was and is a very real problem.

In response to the Federal Government's approach to the war on terrorism more generally, over 130 communities have adopted resolutions protesting the erosion of civil liberties through the Patriot Act and other federal legislation. Laura W. Murphy, Director of the American Civil Liberties Union's (ACLU) Washington Legislative Office, suggests that many Americans weigh in against both terrorism *and* what is widely perceived as a federal assault on civil liberties that is ostensibly designed to confront it: "In my conversation with people from across the political spectrum, I hear one refrain over and over: If we give up our freedoms in the name of national security, we will have lost the war on terrorism" [4, p. 1]. From statements on National Public Radio and the comments of numerous students in my classrooms, I have repeatedly heard variations of this opinion since the tragedy of 9/11. And yet, while we refuse to compromise our freedom of speech, or yield civil liberties more generally on a conscious level, we have quietly, and to a degree unknowingly, already given up much or our privacy in public spaces. Whether due to the need for increased safety and security, the conveniences and pleasures enjoyed through use of our evolving communications technologies, or sheer somnambulance, our public spaces are quickly becoming shared and open in novel ways as the erosion of privacy gives way to transparency. And though we may be largely unaware of doing so, we implicitly support the increasingly transparent public environments that we ourselves create through our implementation and use of communication technologies.

Our loss of public privacy, however, in no way diminishes our steadfast demand for uncompromised free speech. This is almost certainly in part because this right helps constitute the bedrock of our democracy, but as the opening excerpt from Jefferson poetically elaborates, and which Stewart Brand punctuates with simple authority in the truism "Information wants to be free" [5, p. 7], it is arguably also the result of humans' intrinsic desire to collectively share (i.e., to communicate), of our increasingly pervasive mediums such as cyberspace, and even of messages themselves. This is the reasoning behind John Perry Barlow's aphorism: "Trying to stop the spread of a really robust piece of information is about as easy as keeping killer bees south of the border" [5, p. 7]. Within the context of our densely networked contemporary world, by dint of sheer connectivity as well as by nature, free speech trumps any efforts, legal or otherwise, to constrain it.

For each of these reasons, it makes sense that our handling of dangerous information appears to be far less about legally censoring or editing it than it is watch-guarding the agents who might abuse it, the materials and technologies, from airplanes to anthrax, that turn it from text into tragic reality, and the public spaces where such disasters might be prepared and ultimately enacted. This is supported by some striking statistics. For instance, though it lags Europe in the prevalence of surveillance technology, public anti-terrorist fears now drive the yearly installation of some two million closed circuit television cameras in the United States [6]. According to The Electronic Privacy Information Center, Britain alone has installed over 1.5 million such cameras in response to terrorist bombings, capturing the average Londoner more than three hundred times a day. As these cameras become smaller and less expensive, they also grow more sophisticated: many cameras already pan and tilt 360 degrees, carry zoom lenses that can read a cigarette package at 100 meters, and come equipped with infrared sensors, motion detectors, bullet-proof casing, and even small wipers to preserve clear vision in inclement weather. Across Great

Britain, police departments credit surveillance for the often remarkable successes in crime reduction, including declines of 75% in Airdrie, Scotland, 68% in Glasgow, Scotland, and 57% in Northampton, England. These results are consistent with the 50% reduction in crime across downtown Baltimore after it was saturated with 200 cameras [7].

Though these numbers might hearken to longstanding concerns over the emergence of an Orwellian Big Brother, the transparency that emerges as CCTV, cellular phones, WIFI, the portable Internet, and other nascent technologies such as wearable computers become interconnected is less centralized, or top-down, than it is integral to the physical world and our lived experience within it. At once vertical *and* horizontal, it informs central agencies and communities, nationalities and neighborhoods, often in a synergistic collaboration. From the Tacoma Hilltop Action Coalition, which won a federal grant to string cameras like Christmas lights as part of its neighborhood watch [7], to the government subsidized CATCH program that uses two-way radio communication in the West Midlands of the United Kingdom [8, p. 6], our virtual environments and the communications that dance across them coexist with our physical lived space; increasingly, we inhabit both, which affords us a small town national perspective whereby everybody's (public) business becomes known by, well, everybody.

In contrast to the claim that virtual technologies heighten anonymity and thereby tend to undermine community, which Sherry Turkle and Stephen Doheny-Farina make in *Life on the Screen* [9] and *The Wired Neighborhood* [10], respectively, it may well be that as such technologies become increasingly embedded in physical environments they often tend to complement face-to-face communications instead. By enriching rather than diminishing the matrix of communications that comprise community, such communication technologies and their use might enhance neighborhood safety and security.

As this ensuing discussion examines the implications of our current and prospective use of such technologies for public safety with an eye toward addressing such questions, it interprets and forecasts in both its method and findings, and therefore does not pretend to offer final answers to them, or the thorny original question raised by Sides. It does, however, develop some general answers by observing the communication environments and practices we bring to bear as we cope with a world where dangerous information abounds. As we continue, I will elaborate upon claims I have already raised about the intrusion of communication technologies into our physical world, which sets the stage for considering the role, in terms of safety and security, such technologies play in our communities. Specifically, I return to the question of whether communities enriched by communications technologies enjoy a transparent social fabric wherein public exposure renders potentially dangerous information comparatively harmless. Extending this train of thought, I consider the potential synergy of free speech and communal transparency in combining to enhance public safety and security. Insofar as freedom of speech and public transparency both provide open forums for shared discovery, do they conjointly produce a positive sum gain whereby the openness of information may be safely and securely considered in the public forum of the *polis*? Though admittedly idealistic, such a democratic notion could conceivably preserve free speech as it promotes and preserves public safety and security. Are there ways to turn this rosy notion into a pragmatic reality?

Whitfield Diffie's prognostication that "Electronic communication will be the fabric of tomorrow's society . . ." [3, p. 249] seems alive and well. The implied communion of real and ether-real communication that it assumes appears to be coming to fruition in myriad ways, with potentially far-reaching implications for public safety. The implementation of biometric technologies like face recognition and CCTV, for instance, have accelerated considerably since 9/11 [6]. In March 2002, Motorola and Visionics, the company that created the Super Bowl facial recognition system, announced their intention to market mobile telephones that include real-time facial recognition capabilities to law enforcement personnel [11]. Citizens, of course, already enjoy a host of mobile devices that connect them to a vast array of information technologies in the environment as well as one another. Assaying this rapidly changing status quo, Howard Rheingold forecasts that within a decade most citizens in industrial nations will carry or perhaps wear a device that enables them to link objects, places, and people to online content and processes: ". . . point at a book in a store and see what the *Times* and your neighborhood reading group have to say about it. Click on a restaurant and warn your friends that the service has deteriorated" [12, p. xii]. Use of such devices, connected with microchips embedded across smart cars, homes, and neighborhoods, as well as the mobile devices of others', would likely hold great potential for gaining new forms of grassroots social power.

Our community networks already demonstrate considerable coordination of our virtual, social, and physical environments. The more than 1.6 billion instant messages that are currently sent in real time each day, which include text, video, and photos, have become an intrinsic part of users' social fabric. With mobile Internet connections now built into cellular phones, we see more and more of what Rheingold has labeled "texting," namely the bursts of short messages sent by "texters" who carry an always-on connection to the Internet (and one another) through their fingertips wherever they go [12, p. xiii]. Such electronic communication unfolds in real time, enabling the collaboratively orchestrated group behavior across physical environments for which Kevin Kelly has coined the phrase "hive mind" [13, p. 12], which Rheingold attributes to the phenomenon of "smart mobs" [12, p. 28], and which Steven Johnson considers a form of emergent collective intelligence [14, p. 74]. In Kelly's words, "Global opinion polling in real time 24 hours a day, seven days a week, ubiquitous telephones, asynchronous e-mail, 500 TV channels, video on demand: all these add up to the matrix for a glorious network culture, a remarkable hivelike being" [13, p. 28]. Obviously, our "network" culture has continued to evolve at fiber optic speed toward ubiquitous connectivity since these words were published in 1994. Variously analogizing the organized macro-behavior of beehives, ant colonies, and the human brain to wired human communities, Kelly, Rheingold, and Johnson conclude that a "bionic hivelike supermind" [13, p. 13] arises through our electronic communications with far reaching social implications. Rather than replacing face-to-face human contact, telephony, surveillance, and other forms of virtual communication may extend the sphere of interaction and inhabitation to create a higher order of communal intelligence as the virtual and physical intertwine, or so believe these visionary thinkers. After studying the community network in Blacksburg, Virginia, Andrew Cohill has reached similar albeit more down to earth conclusions:

> It is no accident that the words *community* and *communication* have the same root. A community forms because a group of people with shared interests want to create a place in which they can share ideas, commerce, and common values . . . I believe that a community network has the potential not only to provide a new kind of community but also to strengthen the existing community. . . . A community network does not automatically solve difficult social and community problems, but a community of people using a network to communicate may find it a powerful tool to organize people with similar interests [15, p. 318].

Like Cohill, Rheingold is far more interested in the impact of new communication technologies on our social practices than in the technologies themselves. The deeper significance for Rheingold lies in the increasing richness of communications, and therefore communities, that our integrated technological and social infrastructures make possible [12, p. xii]. In his recent book *Emergence: The Connected Lives of Ants, Brains, Cities, and Software*, Steven Johnson affirms this capability in his description of the vast communities of concrete and technology that comprise our contemporary cities: ". . . cities can generate emergent intelligence, a macrobehavior spawned by a million micromotives" [14, p. 113].

It comes as no surprise, then, that in the aftermath of September 11, 2001, engineers, security consultants, and authorities on counter-terrorism have continued to weave the threads of our urban technological fabric, which include instruments that can detect harmful chemicals in a reservoir, send critical data about a damaged building's structural integrity to rescue workers, and even map escape routes or streamline the flow of electricity in a crisis. These high-tech networks, combined with simulation tools, enhanced communications channels, and safer building designs, go a long way toward creating an "intelligent city" wherein danger can be detected and emergency responses directed [16], but they grow even more powerful as they are conjoined with the technologically enhanced neighborhood watches across America. Though many of us do not support the federal government's apparent assault on our civil rights under the guise of its war on terrorism, we do feel an intense patriotic duty to ferret out terrorists (and anyone else) who would make use of dangerous information such as bomb making recipes, or misuse impor-tant information such as flight manuals in highly dangerous ways. In this sense, our sustained effort to disclose terrorists enjoys a centralized and grassroots cooperation that is enhanced by communication technologies at all levels.

At the neighborhood level, the elemental human need for safety is quietly assuaged through the local interactions of neighbors sharing the public space of the sidewalk, as Jane Jacobs describes in *The Death and Life of Great American Cities*: "Wherever the old city is working success-fully, is a marvelous order for maintaining the safety of the streets and the freedom of the city. It is a complex order. Its essence is intimacy of sidewalk use, bringing with it a constant succession of eyes" [17, p. 35]. In this seminal work, Jacobs argues compellingly that this fluid and typically improvised network of neighbors and strangers who converse upon the mundane technology of the sidewalk creates a sense of community, and with it a kind of collective awareness that goes a long way toward solving the problem of making a neighborhood safe. As with Cohill and Rheingold, among others, there is nothing about the physical existence of sidewalks per se that matters to Jacobs. Rather, what is significant is that they serve as the primary channel for the information flow among city residents.

The informal, accidental, and extemporaneous nature of such naturally occurring exchanges along the concrete network of the sidewalk may become more organized, engaged, and intrusive with the intro-duction of digital communications technologies. Quintessential examples of this include the November 30, 1999 protest of the meeting of the World Trade Organization, where squads of demonstrators used mobile telephones, Web sites, laptops, and handheld computers to win the

"Battle of Seattle," and President Estrada's fall from power on January 20, 2001, where more than one million Manila residents, mobilized and coordinated by waves of text messages, gathered at the site of the 1986 "People Power" peaceful demonstrations that had toppled the Marcos regime.

As roaming technologies (e.g., Bluetooth) that connect mobile devices and people in a computation-pervaded environment become more pervasive, our personages, technologies and the physical world are likely to become more intimately interwoven, and therefore mutually revealing. When such technologies also serve to connect the broad umbrella of law enforcement with community support, the resulting watchdog web combines broad coverage with penetration at the street level. In Project COPP (Communities on Phone Patrol), for instance, the Rosemont Community Watch received some 50,000 pre-programmed wireless phones and corresponding airtime to use in their collaboration with the police and sheriffs. This network constituted a distinct kind of social organization, at once democratic and centralized, aimed at a common goal [18, p. 311].

Like sidewalks, such wireless networks serve as meeting places to share neighborhood life, but the mobility and reach of their pathways also enable the coordination of collective behavior in new ways that intensify public transparency and with it safety [19, p. 104]. Neighborhood encounters are no longer left to chance; groups may be strategically contacted and enlisted through public messages and conferences; individual and group exchanges may be orchestrated on the fly across the dynamic flux of time, place, and situation; and in general the network of eyes and ears begins to function through coordination rather than the chaos of chance meetings. This integration of individual voices from across the community pools communal knowledge, rendering each neighbor a knowledgeable agent thereby. Through the cooperation afforded by their communication technologies, citizens are able to proactively maintain the security and safety of their respective neighborhoods. The attributes of such neighborhood activists are reminiscent of Karl Popper's praise in *The Open Society and Its Enemies* for those who transformed themselves into independent, cooperative, and indomitable citizens during the oppressive cold war era.

This portrayal of neighborhood communication matrices enhanced by electronic communications is obviously communitarian and democratic in its affirmation that technologically empowered citizens may participate directly in the orchestrations of their neighborhoods, and by extension their civilization. Shared participation creates a two-way visibility across communities that exposes illicit behavior and deters through mutual accountability. Reputation plays a crucial role in such communities, regardless of whether they exist online, in the physical world, or a combination thereof.

Online, reputation systems consisting of the aggregate opinions of users frequently serve as a basis for the trust that enables transactions and markets to flourish [12, p. xix]. From auctioning on eBay, brokering of consumer advice on Epinions, and selling on Amazon, among myriad other such environments, it is the shared public knowledge *about* the exchanges of millions of consumers that to a large degree (self) manages individual behavior. Ebay, for instance, uses a reputation system based on self-regulating feedback to conduct billions of dollars worth of transactions for people living all over the world who don't even know each other. Its auctions, rated buyers-and-sellers ratings lists, user feedback, cyber-communities formed around specific categories such as Stamp Collecting or Consumer Electronics, regional filters, and lists of new offerings from people you've done business with before, all expose patterns of individual and group behavior to users much the way a city neighborhood becomes transparent through its grapevine. As with the public safety grown of sidewalk kibitzing, the eBay population of over 30 million consumers polices itself with remarkable efficiency. Johnson notes that the early skeptics who believed online auctions could never go mainstream because the electronic medium would make it easy for scam artists to sell bogus merchandise were dead wrong: "Those critics wildly underestimated the extent to which software can create self-regulating systems, systems that separate the scoundrels from the honest dealers. Every seller on eBay has a public history of past deals; scam one buyer with a fake or broken item, and your reputation can be ruined forever" [15, p. 222].

Other online sites that have also enjoyed comparable success come of their own forms of self-regulated governance. Epinions's reputation system enables people to rate reviewers and to rate other raters through "webs of trust," and then pays contributors of the most popular online reviews of books, movies, appliances, restaurants, and thousands of other items. The most trusted reviewers are read by more people and therefore make more money. Similarly, Slashdot and other self-organized online forums enable participants to rate the postings of other participants in discussions, which causes the best writing to grow in prominence while the most objectionable postings diminish. Amazon's online recommendation system tells customers about books and records bought by people whose tastes are similar to their own, and in an implicit recommendation system Google.com, the foremost Internet search engine, lists first those Web sites that have the most links pointing to them first.

Of course, this catalog of success stories from cyberspace raises the important question of whether reputation systems are useful for book-buying and online auctions but ultimately incapable of addressing social dilemmas such neighborhood safety and national security. According to Rheingold, wireless communication technologies will soon extend the reach of such reputation systems from the desktop into the social world:

> As the cost of communication, coordination, and social accounting services drop, these devices make possible new ways for people to self-organize mutual aid. It is now technologically possible, for example, to create a service that would enable you to say to your handheld device: "I'm on my way to the office. Who is on my route and is looking for a ride in my direction right now—and who among them is recommended by my most trusted friends" [12, p. xx]?

While admittedly rather biased, Steve Mann, a professor at the University of Toronto who is considered the first online cyborg, extrapolates outward from Rheingold by envisioning a near future where citizens conduct their daily lives wearing sensor-equipped networked computers. Mann forecasts communities of such citizens monitoring, warning, and aiding each other across virtual safety nets as populations become collective surveillants [20, p. 1]. Whether or not this particular vision becomes a social reality, the expansion and increasing connectivity of our digital wireless technologies support social networks that will allow citizens to cooperatively monitor one another through mutual consent. Reminiscent of the sidewalk surveillance that Jacobs found so important to neighborhood safety, this wireless infrastructure may become an inexpensive means of mutual social control that supports safe, secure communities.

From her research on self-governing communities, sociologist Elinor Ostrom concluded in *Governing the Commons: The Evolution of Institutions for Collective Action* that such a means of creating mutual awareness of individual and group behaviors is fundamentally important to each community's successful self-governance [21]. Reaffirming Ostrom's findings in his own research on communal self-governance, Marc A. Smith observed that the shared awareness of coworkers around common coffeepot chores, for instance, or of neighbors around caring for common spaces, is often reached through casual interaction and the monitoring that occurs through it. By contrast, Smith found that when such social networks are lacking most neighborhoods become more dangerous and shabby [22, p. 157].

The implicit argument here, which has thus far been a subtext across this discussion, is that the success of communication networks, and with them communities more generally, actually depends upon open communication channels and the freedom of speech therein; enjoying a community wide conversation accompanied by the mutual support that engenders safe, secure, and generally healthy community may well depend upon a genuinely open forum for expression. As a corollary, it is at least arguable that potentially dangerous information aired in public becomes neutralized before the public eye by virtue of its display. Such sharing across a transparent community, or indeed an entire society, yields knowledge about the sharers, but it also provides a beneficial kind of meta-knowledge about who knows what, where knowledge comes from and where it goes, and how it is applied. This public exposure, which occurs within and between broad technologically supported networks of communication across communities of all flavors, at once arises through and exposes public rituals of social interaction, thereby returning a deeper knowledge of their actual unfolding back into the community. In *Rational Ritual: Culture, Coordination, and Common Knowledge,* Michael Suk-Young Chwe affirms, "A public ritual is not just about the transmission of meaning from a central source to each member of an audience; it is also about letting audience members know what other audience members know what other audience members know" [23, p. 7].

A small group clusters to converse on a street corner; several neighbors chew the fat through a conference call; an ever-growing pool of students share dorm life via Instant Messaging; guards at the capital building coordinate their patrol by radio; and downtown shop owners share a wireless network with the police. The endlessly burgeoning array of communication networks and their often surprising interconnectedness continually grow more expansive, more immediate, and indeed more integral to both our personal experiences and our physical environments. As our locations and roles as communicants within them variously define us (and I can almost hear William Gibson interject here that the triangulated locations of our social networks do largely define us), and as we simultaneously become more active and exposed as participants within them, we shape as we are shaped by this compendium of communication channels that in a very real sense *are* our communities. Adam Smith, the great student of the dynamics of social systems, speaks to this interrelationship between social accountability, community, identity, and behavior:

> While a man remains in a country village his conduct may be attended to, and he may be obliged to attend to it himself. . . . But as soon as he comes to a great city, he is sunk in obscurity and darkness. His conduct is observed and attended to by nobody, and he is therefore likely to neglect it himself, and to abandon himself to every low profligacy and vice [24, p. 945].

This is the driving theory behind CATCH, which Martin Wright examines in *Community Safety Through Communication*. Specifically, Wright finds that through their participation in neighborhood watch schemes, particularly those that enjoy a partnership with the government and the police, citizens and retailers feel a kind "participative reassurance" that is both personally and communally empowering [8, p. 8]. Significantly, this sense of community is itself enabled by communication technology, in this case combined CCTV and two way radio systems: "The [CATCH] report whilst identifying the benefits through sharing information between retailers and the police and alerting CCTV operators to incidents, also reported upon the 'great co-operation' and 'team spirit' that a radio link system can create" [8, p. 11].

This and other examples of community cooperation shared already enjoy considerable success in dealing with issues of community safety that transcend the ability of any individual to solve. Importantly, while the external threat of potential danger undoubtedly helps motivate the collaboration between citizens that results in a safe neighborhood, this is only possible in densely-knit communities where most people are directly connected through a community network [25, p. 227]. For Jacobs, this intimate communication matrix comprising city neighborhoods embodies a kind of living organism: "Vital cities have marvelous innate abilities for understanding, communicating, contriving and inventing what is required to combat their difficulties" [17, p. 447]. In Jacobs' metaphor, the collective communicative activity of a city streams through its technological neural system, coalescing citizens into a proactive community.

Rheingold believes these interrelationships enjoy a positive feedback loop, whereby the "breathless" growth of our communication technologies actually "nourishes" a concomitant growth in our social networks, and, by extension, community [12, p. 57]. Robert Putnam's discussion of telephone usage in *Bowling Alone: The Collapse and Revival of American Community* reinforces this:

> People make most of their telephone calls within the neighborhood in which they live . . . the telephone is used to maintain personal relationships now severed by space. . . . Thus somewhat paradoxically, the telephone seems to have had the effect of reinforcing, not transforming or replacing, existing personal networks [26, p. 168].

Later, he extends this conclusion to cyberspace, noting that ". . . the early evidence on Internet usage strongly suggest that computer-mediated communication will turn out to complement, not replace, face-to-face communities . . ." [26, p. 180]. According to Putnam, the sheer density of our social interactions over these and other mediums is accompanied by an intimacy that "reduces opportunism and malfeasance" [26, p. 21].

In the opening of this chapter I stated that most of us remain largely unaware that this density of communications also continuously shrinks our public privacy. Put slightly differently, the loss of public privacy is a quiet byproduct of the increasing communal intimacy and its natural transparency. As this dialectical trend continues, we hasten its evolution by continuing to develop and implement new communication technologies, often with the express purpose of orchestrating our collective thought. Like the sidewalks in Jacobs' *The Death and Life of Great American Cities*, which enabled the complex order of the city, these technologies are significant insofar as they enable local interactions to collectively create a larger global order.

Since 9/11, though there is little question this trend has continued at a rapid pace, perhaps further fueled by the tragedy, our communication technologies and the accompanying social practices of cooperation they enable are still in an "embryonic" stage [12, p. 215]. As new technologies arise and then penetrate our lives, our maturing communication networks are likely to grow ever more interwoven, heightening our shared awareness of all that unfolds in public thereby. Such transparency may imbue us with a collective awareness, and with it the communal intelligence that has recently begun to receive renewed attention in the academic and popular press. In *Emergence*, Johnson returns to the ant farm for a useful and apt analogy:

> You can restate it as "Local information can lead to global wisdom." The primary mechanism of swarm logic is the interaction between neighboring ants in the field: ants stumbling across each other, or each other's pheromone trails, while patrolling the area around the nest. Adding ants to the overall system will generate more interactions between neighbors and will consequently enable the colony itself to solve problems and regulate itself more effectively. Without neighboring ants stumbling across one another, colonies would be just a senseless assemblage of individual organisms—a swarm without logic [14, p. 79].

Much like Jacobs' city neighborhood, ant colonies solve problems by drawing on masses of individuals in a bottom-up rather than top-down system to produce a collective performance that is as productive as it is globally intelligent. As our own numbers and density continue to grow, and as our connectivity, from face-to-face to wireless, likewise grows more intimate, pervasive, and interconnected, we are ever more likely to enter a phase transition, or paradigm shift, whereby our communication practices transform our own collective performance. In *Linked: The New*

Science of Networks, Albert-Laszlo Barabasi describes this phenomena as somewhat analogous to the moment when water freezes, only within the context of network theory when a critical number of linkages is reached a network of individuals quite dramatically changes into a community. Prior to this phase transition, numerous "isolated cluster[s] of nodes" communicate amongst themselves, but beyond it a single "cluster" emerges, weaving one and all [27, p. 18].

Perhaps we are already on the cusp of such a natural phase transition, catalyzed by the evolving capabilities of our rapidly evolving (and spreading) communication technologies and our increasingly savvy collective use of them. If such is the case, an emerging transparency would be a natural attribute of our social practices, as would be the neutralization of dangerous information through its exposure before our collective observation. From our communal eye, a communion of a thousand perspectives technologically woven into an eclectic but pervasive vision, whose social physiology is in some ways similar to the compound orb of a praying mantis as it pivots 180 degrees to absorb the full spectrum of events before it, we (would) watch the origins and treatment of such dangerous information with a continuously disarming focus. Disinfected through this communal exposure, once threatening materials might now be discussed, managed, and preserved as *mere* information, rather than applied and animated in another horrific tragedy.

Fortunately, we are also as qualitatively different from the praying mantis as we are the invading colonies of deadly insects in *Starship Troopers,* robots in *The Terminator,* and cyborgs in *The Matrix,* which represent the distinctive collective intelligences of insects, fantastic robots, and futuristic software agents, respectively. As humans, we enjoy our own culturally and technologically influenced evolving individual and collective intelligences, which are imbued with varying degrees of (meta)consciousness, individualism, morality, heterogeneity, and improvisation, both individual and collaborative. Although these attributes may initially appear to be at odds with collective intelligence, particularly if we use the hive rather than the network or community (or both) as our model, each enriches and defines our distinctly human collective intelligence. Once again, Jacobs' description of sidewalk usage as a means for maintaining safe urban neighborhoods provides a wonderful means for understanding our human brand of collective intelligence within the model of the network, in this case one that is concrete:

> Under the seeming disorder of the old city, wherever the old city is working successfully, is a marvelous order for maintaining the safety of the streets and the freedom of the city. It is a complex order. Its essence is intricacy of sidewalk use, bringing with it a constant

succession of eyes. This order is all composed of movement and change, and although it is life, not art, we may fancifully call it the art form of the city and liken it to the dance—not the simple-minded precision dance with everyone kicking up at the same time, twirling in unison and bowing off *en masse*, but to an intricate ballet in which the individual dancers and ensembles all have distinctive parts which miraculously reinforce each other and compose an orderly whole. The ballet of the good city sidewalk never repeats itself from place to place, and in any one place is always replete with new improvisations [17, p. 50].

Whether we return to Jacobs' urban neighborhood, or adopt the model William Mitchell elaborates in his recently released *M++* of the dense technological connectivity that is rapidly turning us into a global community, the communication channels and practices therein which grow collective intelligence neither preclude nor even discourage the attributes listed above. Indeed, these fundamentally human characteristics are what make our collective intelligence less like ants, or slime mold for that matter, and more like the prescient vision H. G. Wells' develops in his 1938 book *World Brain:*

> . . . a World Brain which will replace our multitude of uncoordinated ganglia. . . . We do not want dictators, we do not want oligarchic parties or class rule, we want a widespread world intelligence conscious of itself [24, p. xvi]. . . . It can have at once, the concentration of a craniate animal and the diffused vitality of an amoeba [28, p. 87].

Throughout this text, Wells envisions a dense communal brain organized from the bottom up across the whole of humanity rather than a narrower dictatorial mind that rules from on high. In so doing, he conceives a single mind that is anything but single-minded. It is dynamic, diffuse, self-conscious, and, by virtue of its grassroots nature, a broad-based and symbiotic network that is implicitly dialogic, cooperative, and self-aware. This admittedly utopian perspective is marked by free and open exchange of information between citizens that is multi-vocal but united, like any healthy neighborhood, through essential structures, principles, and protocols; if this is a hive, it is an eclectic one to be sure.

Wells' and Jacobs' early and mid-twentieth century forecasts resonate nicely with George B. Dyson's analysis of our early twenty-first century collective intelligence in *Darwin among the Machines: The Evolution of Global Intelligence:* "And now, in the coalescence of electronics and biology, we are forming a complex collective organism composed of individual intelligences" [29, p. 13]. Like Wells and Dyson, Mitchell conceives humanity as a collective of individuals coalesced through ever more densely networked communications into a grand common consciousness; by implication, communication, public space, and consciousness, both personal and public, become integral. As Mitchell self-consciously reflects, "I construct, and I am constructed, in a mutually recursive process that continually engages my fluid, permeable boundaries and my endlessly ramifying networks. I am a spatially extended cyborg" [30, p. 39]. In slightly less abstract terms, Mitchell's similar observations of his relationship to the surrounding urban environment suggest that our communication technologies have continued to render us intimates with and within public space:

> My reach extends indefinitely and interacts with the similarly extended reaches of others to produce a global system of transfer, actuation, sensing, and control. My biological body meshes with the city; the city itself has become not only the domain of my networked cognitive system, but also — and crucially — the spatially and material embodiment of that system [30, p. 19].

This excerpt naturally relocates Jacobs' earlier description of networking upon the technology of the sidewalk at the present day intersection of our increasingly coexistent personal, digital, and physical realms. Wells, Jacobs, Mitchell, Dyson, and virtually every other expert cited herein share this understanding that networks, be they oral, neural, or electronic, have become the archetypal structures for our collective intelligence, and that the connectivity afforded by them to a large degree defines not only our contemporary experience but our engagement with public space itself [27].

The connectivity achieved through our networked world, which Mitchell likens to team play on the basketball court or soccer field [30, p. 61], produces dynamic and highly extemporaneous individual and collective performances reminiscent of Jacobs' observation of interlocutors' communicative dances across the sidewalks of safe neighborhoods. Our broadly observant and highly responsive networked public already uses real time visual, textual, and auditory communication to continuously coordinate and adjust their responses to evolving situational exigency so as to recursively transform the very situations they are in the process of observing. As an intelligent form of self defense, this increasingly rich, intimate, and one day pervasive feedback loop grows the collective consciousness of a grand social organism capable of swarming to and then smiting perceived danger in its midst as a coordinated response to anything that would threaten its healthy community.

Complementing the more centralized federal effort, which has traditionally been much better at concentrating on a known external enemy, this communal approach may ultimately prove more responsive to our deep collective fear that further terrorist malignancies might metastasize in our midst [31]. Within particular neighborhoods, and even small towns, it is pretty straightforward to see how such connectivity works—friends, enemies, and unfamiliars are immediately recognizable, and it is important to protect one's reputation. However, in the context of extended metropolitan areas, or even globally for that matter, is this possible? After all, Plato and Aristotle both observed that the social glue weakens and then fails when citizens become strangers, which by implication places fundamental limitations on the scope of healthy, self-conscious, and internally safeguarded communities [2, line 1326b; 32, line 737e].

In a world limited to face-to-face communication, this scope was necessarily small, as it was spatially contained by its oral and visual mediums of exchange within physical proximity. Messages could travel, albeit very slowly, so physical proximity defined the scope of close social relationships, and with them community. With new and rapidly evolving communication technologies that connect us across space in real time, neither proximity nor sheer numbers need delimit the size or reach of a community. As our networks continue to expand, our own networked inter-dependencies and extended social aggregates are bound to grow as a product of their use.

Hence the rapidly changing social landscape, which evolves qualitatively as a result of quantitative leaps in the sheer numbers of users engaged through ever more powerful and pervasive communication technologies. As Mitchell notes, "We are all tied together by our networks—both materially and morally—like climbers on a rope" [30, p. 208]. Diverse, dialogic, and encompassing, this networked world may raise fewer concerns about univocal homogeneity or loss of free will per se than it does the fundamental changes in privacy that inevitably accompany its ubiquitous connectivity. For instance, what will be the personal and communal costs of such openness, and will the resultant dividends in safety be worth any price we pay for the pervasive surveillance that such connectivity supports? Will we thrive on the reciprocity afforded by this densely networked world, or, feeling ensnared by the "rope" Mitchell describes, continuously rebel against public transparency by incorporating novel antisocial practices into our social fabric that enable a stealthy escape to anonymity? If we listen to history and human nature, the answer will almost certainly be "both."

REFERENCES

1. T. Jefferson, *No Patents on Ideas: Letter to Isaac McPherson,* August 13, 1813. Electronic Text Center, University of Virginia Library. Available online at: http://etext.virginia.edu/toc/modeng/public/JefLett.html
2. Aristotle, *Politics. The Basic Works of Aristotle,* R. McKeon (trans.), Random House, New York, 1941.
3. D. Brin, *The Transparent Society: Will Technology Force Us to Choose Between Privacy and Freedom?* Perseus Books, Reading, Massachusetts, 1998.
4. T. Gantert, Civil Defense vs. Civil Liberties: Government Says Expanded Powers Needed in Fight Against Terrorism; Critics Say They Have Gone Too Far, *Ann Arbor News,* front page, Sunday, July 6, 2003.
5. J. P. Barlow, The Economy of Ideas, *Wired,* pp. 1-13, March 1994.
6. A. Laurin, *2002 Global Security Prospects,* Axis Communications, January 2002. Availabe online at: http://www.axis.com/documentation/whitepaper/videoglobal_market_prospect
7. B. Taylor, The Screening of America: Crime, Cops, and Cameras, *Reasononline,* May 1997. Available online at: http://reason.com/9705/col.bjtaylor.shtml
8. M. Wright, Community Safety Through Communication: Reducing Crime and Fear with Radio Links, dissertation, Leicester University, 1999. Available online at: http://www.iscpp.net/ISCPPweb/Martin%20Wright%20MSc%20Dissertation.pdf
9. S. Turkle, *Life on the Screen: Identity in the Age of the Internet,* Simon & Schuster, New York, 1995.
10. S. Doheny-Farina, *The Wired Neighborhood,* Yale University Press, New Haven, 1996.
11. R. Naraine, Face Recognition, Via Cell-Phones, *Symobile,* March 27, 2002. Available online at: http://www.symobile.com/comtex/content.cfm?transmit_id=2002086a9917
12. H. Rheingold, *Smart Mobs: The Next Social Revolution,* Perseus, Cambridge, Massachusetts, 2002.
13. K. Kelly, *Out of Control: The New Biology of Machines, Social Systems, and the Economic World,* Addison-Wesley, Reading, Massachusetts, 1994.
14. S. Johnson, *Emergence: The Connected Lives of Ants, Brains, Cities, and Software,* Scribner, New York, 2001.
15. A. Cohill and A. L. Kavanaugh (eds.), *Community Networks: Lessons from Blacksburg,* Artech House, Virginia. Norwood, Massachusetts, 1997.
16. W. Roush, Networking the Infrastructure, *Technology Review,* December 2001. Available online at: http://www.technologyreview.com/article/roush1201
17. J. Jacobs, *The Death and Life of Great American Cities,* Vintage, New York, 1961.
18. J. Arquilla and D. Ronfeldt (eds.), *Networks and Netwars: The Future of Terror, Crime, and Militancy,* Rand, Santa Monica, California, 2001.
19. A. M. Townsend, Life in the Real-Time City: Mobile Telephone and Urban Metabolism, *Journal of Urban Technology,* pp. 85-104, August 2000.

20. S. Mann, Smart Clothing: The Wearable Computer and WearCam, *Personal Technologies,* March 1997.
21. E. Ostrom, *Governing the Commons: The Evolution of Institutions for Collective Action,* Cambridge University Press, Cambridge, 1990.
22. M. A. Smith, Mapping Social Cyberspace: Measures and Maps of Usenet, A Computer Mediated Social Space, dissertation, University of California, Los Angeles, 2001.
23. M. S.-Y. Chwe, *Rational Ritual: Culture, Coordination, and Common Knowledge,* Princeton University Press, Princeton, 2001.
24. A. Smith, *Wealth of Nations.* Available online at: http://www.onlinepcnet.com
25. B. Wellman, Physical Place and CyberPlace: The Rise of Personalized Networking, *International Journal of Urban and Regional Research,* pp. 227-252, February 2001.
26. R. D. Putnam, *Bowling Alone: The Collapse and Revival of American Community,* Touchstone, New York, 2000.
27. A.-L. Barabasi, *Linked: The New Science of Networks,* Perseus, Cambridge, Massachusetts, 2002.
28. H. G. Wells, *World Brain,* Doubleday, New York, 1938.
29. G. B. Dyson, *Darwin among the Machines: The Evolution of Global Intelligence,* Perseus, Reading, Massachusetts, 1997.
30. W. J. Mitchell, *ME++: The Cyborg Self and the Networked City,* The MIT Press, Cambridge, Massachusetts, 2003.
31. T. Homer-Dixon, The Rise of Complex Terrorism, *Foreign Policy,* January/February 2002. Available online at:
http://www.globalpolicy.org/wtc/terrorism/2002/0115complex.htm
32. Plato, *The Dialogues of Plato,* B. Jowett (trans.), Oxford University Press, American Branch, New York, 1893.

CHAPTER 7

The Open Society and Its Enemies: A Reappraisal

Michael Ben-Chaim

Promises, covenants, and oaths, which are the bond of human society, can have no hold upon or sanctity for an atheist; for the taking away of God, even only in thought, dissolves all.

John Locke, *Letter on Toleration*, 1689

INTRODUCTION

The events of 9/11/2001 were horrific manifestations of intricate and ambiguous relationships between knowledge, power, and freedom in modern history. When the natural sciences became a dominant cultural force in Western societies during the early part of the twentieth century, their political implications were contested by two major philosophical schools. On the one hand, advocates of empiricism and positivism highlighted the liberating power of cognitively reliable knowledge over authoritarian ideologies, notably communism and fascism. The diffusion of scientific method and knowledge throughout the civil sphere, they claimed, enabled people for the first time in human history to become genuinely responsible for the content of their opinions and beliefs. On the other hand, critics of the cultural dominance of science professed that the project of making political agents responsible implied in effect the systematic attempt to subject human conduct to methodical inspection and control, and if necessary, deterrence and punishment.

Apparent contrasts between these two philosophical viewpoints notwithstanding, both were highly focused on the public sphere in Western

135

industrialized societies. Both were predominantly concerned with the political relationship between government and individual agents in societies in which culture became relatively homogeneous, especially as a result of the wholesale diffusion of scientific and technological literacy. The terror of 9/11, however, was conceived in a radically different context. Social life in the Middle East has long been characterized by blatant inequalities in access to education and information, and the opportunities and privileges they render available. These inequalities were engendered by, and entrenched, cultural identities fragmented by different authoritative definitions of the common good.

Access to modern technical information and means of communication was of course a highly significant condition for making the Al Qaeda terrorist network possible. If modern scientific and technological literacy were more evenly diffused in the Middle East, the terror of 9/11 perhaps would not have been contemplated. The assumption underlying the following analysis is that the terror of 9/11 was a morally contorted reflection of continuous endeavors to integrate common goods that sustain Western industrialized societies with those sustaining Muslim culture. In this context, the analysis in what follows aims to reappraise some of the prevailing assumptions in Western society concerning the relationship between knowledge, freedom, and power.

THE INTENTION OF TERROR

Perpetrators of terror often consider themselves as political activists. Not unlike members of the military forces of nation-states, their working assumption is that they are part of a larger society which they choose to represent by defending its values and interests against an external threat. As a political strategy, terror is often based on the assumption that the powers that threaten the common goods that sustain society are too great to be defeated by conventional military tactics. The message of terror is that the superiority of these powers does not render them immune from defeat.

Since terrorist groups operate in an environment that is dominated by powerful enemy forces, their military undertakings are extremely risky. They know that they will suffer certain defeat whenever and wherever they expose themselves to their enemy. Their operations must be extremely secretive, and yet inflict the utmost harm. Unlike the legitimate representatives of nation-states, they do not enjoy the capacity to adopt and administrate policies of relative civil or peaceful deterrence prior to resorting to military action. For these reasons, terror carves out a realm of extreme violence, and is often associated with ideas and ideals that are sufficiently radical to motivate and justify its agents.

It is important to distinguish between the ideology of political terror on the one hand, and the threat that is imposed on the society which terrorist groups claim to defend on the other. The ideology addresses the threat, but conveys it in an idiom that concomitantly reflects the culture of political radicalism and extreme violence. Understanding the threat may not shed much light on the workings of terror. It is nevertheless a critical aspect of the endeavor to abate the violence of terrorism and counter-terrorism by addressing the conflict between threatened and threatening societies in a peaceful way.

THE SPECTER OF OPEN SOCIETY

Since the nineteenth century, Muslim societies in the Middle East have been subjected to unprecedented pressures and strains of reform as a result of their growing exposure to intensive expansions of Western industrial society. The challenge of reform was by no means foreign to Islam. Not unlike the Judo-Christian traditions with which it was always historically associated, Islamic tradition was predicated in part on changing conceptions of religious faith as a force of moral and cultural regeneration. The impact of industrial society was nevertheless unique, from this historical perspective, in that it was consistently conveyed by a new mode of thought that radically challenged Islam as a resilient and lasting repository of common goods.

What were the distinctive characteristics of this novel mode of thought? First, it represented science and democracy as the twin pillars of modern industrial society. Second, it portrayed science and democracy as universal common goods which could benefit all human beings irrespective of the specificity of their cultural identity. It was primarily the second characteristic of this novel mode of thought that undermined the credibility of Islam as repository of common goods.

From a logical viewpoint, the articles of Islam are *not* inconsistent with the tenets of industrialization. Indeed, Muslim scholars traditionally endorsed scientific learning as cultural pursuit. The alleged universality of modern science and democracy implied that adherence to Islamic faith did not necessarily prevent individual Muslims from taking part in, and benefiting from, their cultivation. It nevertheless portrayed the religion of Islam as neither a necessary nor important factor in establishing the institutions of modern science and democracy. Moreover, the cultural tradition could undermine endeavors to convene these institutions upon genuinely universal principles. Modernity addressed Muslims as human agents rather than as believers, thus forcing upon them hitherto barely conceivable moral and cultural distinctions.

Ideas of science and democracy as universal common goods are often considered as the distinctive legacy of eighteenth-century European enlightenment. As will be clarified in the next section, these ideas were further developed during the late nineteenth and twentieth centuries, within the framework of the positivist discourse on scientific method and its moral and political implications. Positivist scholars sought a rational explication of the credibility of scientific research and its products, and their efforts led to the development of more rigorous principles of demarcation between the universal value of scientific knowledge and the specific societal or psychological values of other belief-systems. In the early part of the twentieth century, the philosopher Karl Popper proposed a novel explication of these principles of demarcation, which later formed the foundation for his philosophical doctrine of the "open society." During the post-WWII era, Popper's doctrine was widely considered as one of the most successful philosophical attempts to link the scientific method with the underlying principles of liberal democracies.

The philosophical doctrine of the open society was initially conceived and debated in a scholarly context that centered upon fundamental problems in the history of western philosophy, notably the problem of knowledge, the search for truth, and the relationship between thought, language, and the physical world. The doctrine therefore did not specifically concern the cultural implications of the impact of Western industrial society on agrarian societies in the Muslim world or in other parts of the world. Popper and his early disciples did not apparently consider undermining the legitimacy of non-Western cultural traditions as an intended consequence of the philosophical defense of the open society.

It would be extremely misleading, therefore, to consider the philosophical doctrine of the open society as a pernicious endeavor to discredit Islamic religion, or even as a scholarly critique of its underlying philosophical principles. The relationship between the open society and Islam was primarily forged by political and economic factors, rather than within the world of scholarship, and was not necessarily intended by any specific agent or party to become, or be perceived as, a bone of contention between the Muslim world and any of the Western governments and businesses empowered by modern industrial culture.

The open society was nevertheless a principal ideological factor *preventing* Western governments and businesses from linking their vested interests in the Arab world with local Islamic perceptions of the common good. The open society concomitantly became an ideological force *discouraging* Arab nationalist movements and nation-state governments from considering traditions and institutions of Islamic faith as valuable tools of reform. The philosophical doctrine of the open society explains why the most influential agents of modernization in the Arab world did not appraise Islam as an important ally. The open society offered a model of a future society in which the universal goods of science and democracy would enormously benefit Muslim people at the expense, however, of depreciating their present common goods.

The discrepancy between the realities of Muslim society and the ideals of open society was bound to be perceived at least by some Muslims as a threat imposed by foreign forces upon the integrity of their personal identity and upon the binding forces of their families and communities. This threat could have been overlooked by the majority of Muslims if the agents of modernization could demonstrate how a Muslim society would be transformed into an open society. The results of experiments with modernity, however, were extremely disappointing for many Muslims in the Arab world. Throughout the twentieth century, they were passively witness to expanding state bureaucracies that promised, but failed to deliver, the goods of modern science and democracy. They were concurrently exposed to the rhetoric of secular forces that weakened their own faith in the good of Islam. They became more and more familiar with a Janus-faced modernity, conveyed by agencies of foreign governments and private businesses that were empowered by modern public goods only to serve foreign interests.

The religion of Islam did not, and arguably could not, offer its people effective means to come to terms with the predicaments of modernity. It nevertheless afforded perhaps the only available frame of reference for envisioning alternative reforms that could at least be trusted as genuinely serving *their* common good. Unfortunately—though perhaps not unexpectedly—some of these reforms portrayed the open society as the vicious enemy of Muslim society, and encouraged people to retaliate against it, to become its self-appointed enemies. It is not surprising that innocent U.S. citizens became the target of the enemies of the open society. With the collapse of European imperialism, U.S. governments and businesses became the most vigorous foreign power in the Arab world, and therefore the most widely recognized ambassadors of the open society. And aggression against expressions of innocence has always been one of terror's preferable tactics.

THE OPEN SOCIETY AND ITS PITFALLS

The open society is one of the most original and influential endeavors in recent history to construct a general political philosophy on the premises of a theory of knowledge. By and large, political philosophers have regarded the problem of elucidating the ideal government as their principal intellectual concern. This common approach may not be the most effective in solving political problems. First, a theory of government may include propositions which are not cognitively reliable. The theory may seem to be politically valuable; yet its credibility hinges on scrutinizing its claim to knowledge (of political history, the nature of human beings, the properties of social interaction, or any other matter relevant to political action). Another problem with the common approach pertains to implementing the supposedly ideal government. Whatever this ideal may be, it will be practically pursued by human agents who are likely to form some erroneous judgments even in their best effort to bring the ideal into life. Hence, solutions to political (or for that matter, moral, economic, or social) problems ought first to demonstrate an effective method of coping with the general problem of judgmental error. Prioritizing the problem of knowledge is the fundamental insight of the open society.

The open society thus offers a philosophical perspective on humankind as *homo sapiens*. It encapsulates, at its core, what may be construed as a secular version of the religious notion of original sin, depicted in a cognitive idiom. According to this version, human beings are so incorrigibly fallible when it comes to gaining knowledge of themselves and their surrounding world, that confession of methodical scepticism and ignorance always ought to be considered as the initial step in any human pursuit. The relevance of this premise to political life is straight forward: rather than contemplating the ideal government, political agents ought to be first and foremost committed to following the method of critical discourse in order to minimize the damage caused by inevitable misjudgments of any person in any government. As Popper noted in allusion to utilitarianism, "instead of the greatest happiness for the greatest number, one should demand, more modestly, the least amount of avoidable suffering for all; and further, that unavoidable suffering — such as hunger in times of unavoidable shortage of food — should be distributed as equally as possible" [1, Vol. I, pp. 284-285].

The presupposition that our moral and political aspirations ought to be checked by intellectual modesty is borne by reflections on the history and philosophy of modern natural science — apparently the most successful example of human learning known so far. In recent decades, studies have conclusively demonstrated that major methodological and theoretical innovations in the history of western science did not simply spring from the creative minds of individual researchers. Rather, these innovations always stemmed from the interplay between individuals and complex constellations of cultural components of learning as a collective endeavor. It is apparently undeniable, however, that a critical factor in the progress of science was quite simply the recognition that even the most widely held assumptions and theories about the natural world are, and can be shown to be, significantly inadequate. History baldly teaches that scientists have demonstrated their creativity by showing time and again that the search for truth never ends in finding the truth. The progress of science thus reaffirms its own fallibility, and therefore the fallibility of humankind.

Logical reflection on the scope and limits of human judgment leads to a similar conclusion. The credibility of our judgments hinges on the evidence that can be brought in their support. Yet this evidence is indefinite, and can be searched and collated in practically numerous different ways. For these reasons, it is not possible to demonstrate that a particular judgment is absolutely correct or true. These very same reasons explain, however, why any judgment is potentially false. For we do have the capacity to identify some evidence that is inconsistent with any specific judgment, and thereby to demonstrate that it is to a certain extent wrong, or at least partly false. The tools of logical inference are insufficient for verifying a judgment, though they are very useful for demonstrating its fallacy [2].

Thus, the history of natural science and the logical asymmetry between verification and falsification both affirm the epistemic fallibility of humankind. The implication of the fallibilist theory of knowledge upon which the open society is founded is twofold. First, claims to knowledge are devoid of authority, since there are no compelling reasons to accept any of them. These claims are at best cognitively reliable and practically useful conjectures, and we are always free to decline the invitation to embrace them. In rejecting the authority of a particular view or theory we do not necessarily underestimate its value. Rather, we simply affirm the methodological dictum that it is inevitably fallible. Second, since all conjectures are potentially erroneous, the endeavor to understand how erroneous they are appears to be the only viable way to advance our knowledge. The discovery of an alternative conjecture conveys new information about the world, and concomitantly reveals the drawbacks of prevailing conjectures.

The open society is therefore a model society of antiauthoritarian entrepreneurs who set out to transcend the bounds set by tradition or convention. Not surprisingly, it has become particularly influential among highly mobile communities of industrialized societies in which cultural change has become a prominent feature of everyday life. Cultural changes are hardly ever purely accumulative, and often involve the displacement of one form of behavior by another. A philosophy that depicts criticism as the engine of change is, therefore, especially akin to the ethos of modern life. Furthermore, the open society provides powerful philosophical justification for the decline of religion in Western industrialized societies. For, though it neither undermines the value of faith nor implies that religious faith must give way to scientific knowledge, it claims that articles of faith ought to be construed as conjectures devoid of authority.

The principal political implication of the open society is the radical liberalization and democratization of the public sphere. Its vision of liberal democracy is premised on the assumption that reason and experience enable every mature human being to actively partake in the critical assessment of beliefs. Although some people are always more learned than others in certain areas, they are all equally fallible, and therefore, none can claim authority over other people's judgments.

In recent decades, serious attempts have been made to apply this liberal democratic vision to the study of science itself. Although some advocates of the open society, including Popper, have claimed that criticism engenders the genuine progress of scientific knowledge, other scholars insisted that epistemological fallibilism implies that the scientific community cannot be credited with applying objective criteria to the comparative evaluation of theories. Since there are no compelling reasons to accept a particular theory, theory-choice inevitably follows pragmatic considerations that may vary from one individual researcher to another.

The scientific community is arguably more culturally homogeneous than the wider society; yet individual scientists differ from one another in their education and training, research agendas, and institutional affiliations. The transaction of knowledge within the scientific community is conducted between researchers whose interests in a particular theory, method, or instrument are not unanimous. Scientists are free to chose the components of their research projects in accordance with their particular interests, as well as to revise their interests to adapt their careers to their ever-changing work environment. Thus, scientists pursue their common interest in the advancement of knowledge in what is in effect an "agonistic field" of self-interested maneuvers calculated to maximize the benefits of each and every transacting party. In the open society, knowledge is a nominal common good since none of the members of this society is able to demonstrate that accepting a particular conjecture is in the best interest of everyone else. Knowledge is a commodity sold and bought by free agents [3-5].

The philosophical constitution of the open society inevitably leads to epistemological relativism. This form of relativism does not imply that theory-choice is arbitrary. Individual agents may find good reasons to accept a particular conjecture, but they nevertheless recognize that their reasons are not necessary shared by others. Logical inference and experience do not provide sufficient means to substantiate the obligation to accept belief. Moreover, since the open society is *premised* on a fallibilist theory of knowledge and on an epistemically fallible conception of human kind, the epistemological relativism which it implies leads, in turn, to moral relativism.

Once we consider the theory of knowledge as providing overriding guidelines in all our deliberations, we are bound to construe any proposition as implying a specific claim to knowledge. Since all claims to knowledge are fallible, it follows that no proposition conveys a legitimate obligation. We may choose to adhere to a particular moral proposition; yet the theory of knowledge that overrides our decision asserts that we have no obligation to do so. Consider, for example, the proposition that physicians are obliged to ameliorate their patient's well-being. We may construe this proposition as specifying a rule of conduct physicians ought to respect; yet we may alternatively construe it as a knowledge claim about the obligation of physicians. The former interpretation appeals to our self-conception as moral agents. The latter appeals to our self-conception as knowing agents. We may feel or believe that the rule obliging physicians to devote themselves to their patient's health is sacred. Our fallibilist theory of knowledge advises us, however, that a judgment concerning the obligation of physicians is derived from conjectures that are not necessarily true, are inherently inconclusive, and need not be accepted. Our commitment to the open society obliges us to reject the authority of human judgments, even though our moral sensibilities may motivate us to acknowledge their sanctity.

The physician's obligation to his or her patient illustrates an important characteristic of moral principles, which is that they appeal to our intellect as moral agents. While it is obviously impossible to follow a moral principle without understanding it, its meaning is supposed to include reference to its obligatory status. We can only understand its moral import and the obligation it contains when we examine it as moral beings. As a philosophical doctrine, the open society drives a wedge between our cognitive self and our moral self, and offers a model of human deliberation in which cognition always takes priority over morality. Coupled with the notion of epistemological fallibility, this rigid hierarchy of values leads to the conclusion that moral principles are but non-authoritative conjectures.

As a political philosophy predicated on a theory of knowledge, the open society appears to be self-refuting. It purports to elucidate a model of the search for knowledge and its public transaction; yet, by undermining the authority of any ideal of conduct, the model fails to adequately clarify its own normative status. With its emphasis on the cardinal role of criticism in human learning, the fallibilist theory of knowledge has provided important insights into the history of science, though its overall value as a tool for historical reconstruction of scientific change has been severely challenged [6]. The open society purports to stipulate rules of intellectual conduct; yet it cannot coherently command authority and ascertain the conjectural status of all claims to knowledge at the same time.

It appears, more broadly, that a theory of knowledge may play an important role in clarifying moral or political issues as long as it does not claim the status of an independent arbitrator on such issues. There are notable affinities, in this respect, between Popper's philosophy of science and other attempts to derive general rules of conduct from philosophical reflections on scientific knowledge. Logical positivists, for example, have propounded a meaning criterion according to which a meaningful proposition was either analytic or empirically testable; but the criterion itself has been proposed as neither an analytic statement nor an empirically testable one. What could render the criterion not only a meaningful but also an authoritative rule for legislating proper intellectual conduct, despite its incoherence, was the culturally entrenched faith in the logical structure of the empirical basis of scientific knowledge [7, pp. 184-191].

The problematic status of modern theories of knowledge does not only pertain to their technical aspects. More broadly, perhaps, it involves a particular conception of the development of modern culture, which, primarily through the writings of Max Weber, has been commonly associated with the notion of the scientific disenchantment of the world. As Weber stated in his celebrated article, "Science as a Vocation," the world is disenchanted when "one need no longer have recourse to magical means in order to master or implore the spirits," for such mysterious powers are no longer recognized as part of the world whose nature is now genuinely grasped by the tools of scientific research. In their stead, "technical means and calculations perform the service" [8, p. 139]. Modern science is the prime generator of the rationally organized society. Rationality is thus posited as the sovereign ideal of human conduct, especially the conduct of human understanding.

However, the grounds for assigning reason such a prominent position in human life is unaccountable. The appeal to reason to justify the sovereignty of reason is itself logically vacuous, while any other consideration in the light of which the thesis may be justified undermines the alleged sovereignty of reason. Despite the rational idiom of the scientific disenchantment of the world, it is the faith in the rationality of science which is supposed to undermine enchanted visions of the world. The world is disenchanted if, and as long as, one is enchanted with the rationality of science and the rationally structured domains of action modern science engenders.

Notwithstanding its incoherence, the allegedly authoritative status of modern theories of knowledge appears to be predicated on the following position: first, a dual nature of the human is assumed. On the one hand, we are by nature part of an environment which, in Weber's words, "organically" prescribes the "cycle of natural life" [8, p. 356]. On the other hand, humans are by nature rational, capable of purely rational actions which need not be constrained by practical considerations. Second, because our two aforementioned natures are totally separated, it is assumed that our rational nature can provide a means for emancipating ourselves from practical constraints and for considering our conduct from a purely rational view-point. According to Weber, culture, and especially the systematization of symbolic systems, are of intrinsically emancipating value. The process of emancipation is purely intellectual, yet it nevertheless molds perceptions of human existence and the world as a whole. Finally, it is our duty as rational beings to judge our conduct by purely rational standards, even at the expense of renouncing practically convenient beliefs. The open society, the positivist meaning criterion, and the vision of the disenchanted world convey different yet closely related ways of considering modern science as a means to discharge this duty, by stipulating science as the paradigm of the rational legislation of correct intellectual conduct.

In Weber's writings, the disenchantment of the world forms the central aspect in the narrative of the evolution of humanity. As he suggested in the introduction to *The Protestant Ethic and the Spirit of Capitalism*, Western culture has often taken the leading role in this process. Rational harmonious music, rational theology, rational economic behavior, and empirically validated knowledge of the natural world, comprise some of the major contributions of European civilization to universal, that is, objectively evaluated, history [9]. Ancient Greek philosophy introduced the notion of the dual nature of man, by stipulating a dichotomous distinction between two naturally potential virtues: the virtue of theoretical reasoning about abstract questions of science and philosophy, and the virtue of practical reasoning concerning one's desires and actions. In the history of Christianity, the theoretical attitude toward religious life, embodied in traditions of theological scholarship, engendered the rationalization of the Christian faith and the religious conduct of individual believers.

Yet, it was only in the seventeenth century, when theory was fully emancipated from the shackles of Christianity, that science could fully evolve as the only possible form of a rationally justified view of the world. From that moment of disenchantment, "the cosmos of natural causality and the [religiously] postulated cosmos of ethical, compensatory causality have stood in irreconcilable opposition" [8, pp. 139-142]. Weber's rhetoric leaves no doubt as to the asymmetrical nature of this opposition, as the reader is rather explicitly led to embrace the supposedly rationally compelling scientific representation of the universe and to reject the merely "postulated" ethical causality proffered by faith. In the bright light of science, different versions of the world appear illusory.

As noted earlier, the open society does not necessarily discredit religious versions of an enchanted universe. According to Popper, religious ideas may provide inspiration for scientists. Nevertheless, in the open society, the notion that religious institutions derive their authority from divine truths appears to be an illegitimate breach of the freedom to engage in the critical assessment of the value of conjectures. In this respect, the open society and the disenchanted society are indistinguishable: both assume that we must subordinate our self-conception as moral agents to our self-conception as rational thinkers. Moreover, both disenchanted and open societies construe rationality as substantiated and exemplified by modern natural science, and contrast the latter with traditional endeavors to anchor moral obligation and other beliefs in divine government.

It is not, then, surprising that the open society has become influential among the educated public in contemporary Western societies. The open society derives its cultural — if not its philosophical — meaning and appeal from the historical fact that in these societies the impact of science on the wider culture has steadily increased by inverse proportion to that of religious institutions at least since the eighteenth century. Moreover, in portraying scientific theories and public policies as conjectures competing for the support of informed and critical consumers, the open society reinforces common images of contemporary market economies.

However, Western industrialized societies have never been, and are unlikely to become, open societies. In various domains of public life, common and deeply entrenched patterns of conduct are incongruent with the philosophical implications of the open society. For example, researchers in natural science construe theories as tools for understanding the physical reality rather as merely pragmatically convenient conjectures. They consider empirical research primarily as a means to finding the truth rather than falsifying evidence. Although it is widely acknowledged that scientific theories are fallible, the authority of science is arguably wider than that of any other civic institution in the history of humankind. Scientific methods and theories are certainly more rooted in public education than Christian theology has ever been. The obligation to support science either through state agencies or philanthropy is, at least in principle, taken for granted. In this respect, it appears that the public regards the advancement of science as a moral ideal rather than a calculated outcome of a policy predicated on theory of knowledge. The prevalence of cultural and moral relativism in Western societies notwithstanding, moral issues such as the responsibility of physicians to their patients are commonly regarded as pertaining first and foremost to the obligation of persons as moral agents rather than to their views on the problem of knowledge.

Contrary to the fundamental dictum of the open society, individuals in Western societies do not subordinate their self-conceptions as moral agents to their self-conception as rational thinkers. Members of other societies should not, therefore, construe civil affairs in the industrialized world as founded upon, or leading to, the open society. However, it is precisely in the context of encounters between modern Western societies and other societies that the former do appear to be inspired by the model of open society. The Egyptian, Palestinian, Yemen, or Iraqi public is not familiar with, or even particularly aware of, the complex web of moral obligations within which most Americans pursue their every-day lives. The American it encounters in its homeland is often an impersonal representative of a foreign and powerful body of shareholders oblivious to the moral obligations that constitute the local culture. In a context marked by overwhelming inequalities between foreign powers and local traditions, the open society erodes moral constraints on the pursuit of foreign interests which thus appear oppressive rather than progressive.

Reflected in the evil darkness of the terror of 9/11, the open society appears to be a self-fulfilling prophesy. The prophecy is premised on a dichotomy between the critical thinking of rational and free persons on the one hand, and the authoritarian dogmas that constitute regimes of oppression on the other. This dichotomy poses a dilemma for those who seek to participate in the advancement of modern science and democracy but nevertheless regard authority as a social or political structure that is founded on, and embodies, obligatory moral ideals and principles. The open society implies, however, that they must choose between the commitment to modern values and the commitment to their authoritarian views. Yet they cannot make this choice because their authoritarian views form part of their moral identities. Failing to accept the rules set by the open society, they become its enemies, and consider, in turn, the open society as their enemy.

Thus, notwithstanding its well-intended claim to defend the freedom of all humanity against oppression, the open society's dichotomy between critical and authoritarian thinking delineates a battle field between contesting claims to modernization and its goods. This ideo-logical battle field centers, more specifically, on the failure to distin-guish oppressive powers from authoritarian conceptions of moral obligation. As noted earlier, this failure stems from assuming that all forms of authority are illegitimate inasmuch as they fail to recognize the epistemic fallibility of their claims. Paradoxically, the open society holds the sovereignty of its fallibilist theory of knowledge as a dogma which has become, in turn, a frame of reference for expressions of fear and hostility.

THE ILLUSION OF KNOWLEDGE AS POWER

In ascribing theory of knowledge priority over morality, the open society expresses an unwarranted confidence in knowledge as power. It assumes that genuine problems can be effectively solved by gaining objective knowledge of situations that give rise to these problems; yet it fails to address the subjective aspects in virtue of which problem-situations pose difficulties for agents in pursuit of particular objectives. Knowledge as instrumental power provides agents with ammunition that is bound to inflame situations in which interests are in conflict.

The Middle East has been a particularly fertile ground for the spread of the illusion of the ultimate efficacy of modern technology. In the early part of the nineteenth century, it was one of the poorest regions neighboring Europe. Modern technology was gradually transferred to the region during the nineteenth and twentieth centuries by European colonial agencies. This process gave rise, in turn, to local nationalist movements whose search for power was predicated on the assumption that modern technology provided political elites with the means to create and rule modern states.

During the twentieth century, however, it gradually became apparent that Middle Eastern nation-states—notably Syria, Iraq, Jordan, Egypt, and Libya—were modern primarily in virtue of their capacity to use technology to enforce political apparatuses on communities that barely enjoyed the fruits of technological progress. The growing gaps between state apparatuses and the populations which they allegedly represented, and were officially designed to serve, were bound to generate popular sentiments of mistrust and resentment. But the new regimes were sufficiently powerful to oppress these sentiments whenever they seemed to threaten their sovereignty, or alternatively, to manipulate them by turning them against real or imagined enemies in the international arena.

Quite predictably, the technology of oppression and manipulation was not always efficient. The gaps between relatively weak communities and relatively powerful regimes were gradually mediated by resistance groups that gained some access to sources of technological might. These groups were often led by individuals who had already gained experience of the knowledge-intensive enterprises as businessmen, engineers, physicians, or journalists. Perhaps the most notable among these leaders are Yasir Arafat and Osama bin Laden. Both were born to affluent families, acquired higher education, and joined their highly successful multinational family industries. Both advanced their political career by demonstrating that small clandestine organizations can acquire the technology to become highly significant players in the agonistic field of international politics.

The relations between the PLO under Arafat's leadership and the State of Israel is one of the most tragic illustrations of the debilitating illusion of knowledge as power, at least in the Middle East. Arafat built his leadership in part by commanding numerous attacks on Israel that gradually demonstrated that the latter, despite the indubitable superiority of its military technology, could not eradicate Palestinian resistance to its rule over Palestinian lands. As a result of these attacks, the vast majority of Israel's Jewish population have personally experienced the shattering blow of terror. But Israeli forces nevertheless demonstrated time and again that the cost of suffering Israeli citizens was borne by the Palestinian population as well. In 1993, the Israeli government, chaired by prime-minister Rabin, finally acknowledged the Palestinians' right to an independent state. However, since then the Palestinian population have experienced the worst economic crises as a result of the failure of Palestinian leadership to contain the culture of Palestinian terror which it had originally engineered. The growing vulnerability of Arafat's Palestine demonstrates, at the same time, that Israeli governments, despite their principal commendation of a peaceful solution to the Israeli-Palestinian conflict, have not yet found the alternative to policies of technological aggression that the Zionist movement had cultivated in Palestine throughout its struggle for political independence.

The destructive know-how that bin Laden and his comrades demonstrated on 9/11 is yet another tragic demonstration of the illusion of knowledge as power. Al Qaeda members who are suspected to have taken part in any terrorist activity are currently hunted by U.S. forces all over the world, and this apparently will be their fate throughout the foreseeable future. They now must learn to live a life reigned by severe limitations and disabilities. As a result of U.S. retaliation, the Taliban regime in Afghanistan, which had only recently been associated with liberating the country from the oppression of Soviet power, was destroyed. The Taliban and Al Qaeda have claimed to be the guardians of Muslim civilization; yet the war against Al Qaeda's terror inevitably has deleterious effects on hundreds of thousands of innocent Muslims. Al Qaeda has claimed to be inspired by the teachings of the Koran; yet millions of Americans who were perhaps willing to appreciate the book as a source of learning now, as a result of the terror of 9/11, regard it as a potential threat to the very possibility of civilized life.

It may seem that Al Qaeda has been severely weakened as a result of American power targeted against it. This is undoubtedly the case in some respects; for example, the destruction of Al Qaeda's training camps in Afghanistan by U.S. military forces. However, the terror of 9/11 and the ensuing U.S. policies in the international arena call into question the power of American technological superiority as well. Indeed, the involvement of American private businesses and government agencies in the Middle East since the Second World War is especially notable for demonstrating how short-sighted and exaggerated the reliance on the power of American know-how could be. For example, U.S. government and private businesses were the most powerful allies of the Shah regime in Iran until the Islamic revolution of 1978. As a result of this revolution, Iran turned into one the most powerful nations in which anti-American sentiments were infused into official ideology and public opinion.

REINSTATING THE PRIORITY OF MORALITY OVER EPISTEMOLOGY

The widespread confidence in technologically empowered capacities to manipulate at will natural and human resources, and to control entire communities and their natural environment, is a double-edged sword. To mitigate the aggression it incites, the production and public transaction of knowledge must be carried out within institutional settings premised on a perspective on knowledge as common good. This perspective can only be rendered coherent by reinstating the priority of a moral conception of the good over epistemological explications of human learning, and by considering the latter as serving the former.

The history of science and philosophy offers many different models that demonstrate how theory of knowledge can serve morality. The philosophical studies of John Locke are particularly relevant in this respect, since he has often been regarded among the founding fathers of modern empiricism and liberalism. A precursor of the advocates of the open society, Locke professed in arguably unprecedented clarity that human rights, and especially the right to resist political oppression, could be best secured by institutions that engendered and protected the intellectual autonomy of individual agents. As he noted in his *An Essay Concerning Human Understanding*, first published in 1690, "they who are blind, will always be led by those that see, or else fall into the Ditch: and he is certainly the most subjected, the most enslaved, who is so in his understanding" [10, p. 711]. Locke was an ardent critic of the widespread notion that moral precepts were innate, and baldly rejected the age old Christian view of conscience as a reliable guide of moral conduct. Reformulating the Aristotelian dictum that knowledge originated in experience, Locke demonstrated that empirical knowledge was inherently fallible and stressed the importance of considering epistemological fallibilism as a bulwark against dogmatism.

Though his celebrated *Essay* centered upon intellectual conduct, Locke addressed problems concerning the search and public transaction of information within a general anthropological perspective on the relationship between the individual and his or her physical and social environment. The universe is not a mere object of knowledge. It is first and foremost an ordered universe that structures and regiments all forms of life, including the lives of all human beings. It constitutes a system of rules that sets constraints on, and offer opportunities for, maintaining and promoting our well-being. Human beings are endowed with intelligence which they apply to understanding these rules; yet the problem of knowledge originated in the sheer necessity to respect them. As Locke pointed out in the Introduction to his *Essay*, "our business here is not to know all things, but those which concern our Conduct. If we can find out those Measures, whereby a rational Creature put in that State, which Man is in, in this World, may, and ought to govern his opinions, and Actions depending thereon, we need not be troubled, that some other things escape our Knowledge" [10, p. 46].

Rather than disenchanting the world, cognitive labor partakes in the process of investing interest and discovering value in the world by learning to identify, represent, and understand specific qualities of objects which may enhance, or, conversely, endanger, the well-being of human agents. Precisely for this reason, matters of fact are neither the mirror of an objective world, indifferent to human needs, nor the constructs of human— individual or collective—agency. Since perception is inherently involved in rendering the world into a habitable place, its crucial function is to discover the qualities of the world which are of value to the agent. The perceived world is always already an environment of desirable activities, of preferable states of affair. From this perspective, the problem of knowledge originates in the ineradicable problem-situation of our survival as human beings in an environment which we do not make and therefore have to learn to understand. Moreover, because understanding an object implies, in this context, appreciating what it affords, perception inherently involves the selective identification of specific valuable properties. The more we learn about the world, the greater is our capacity to refine our goals and objectives and to increase the scope of our actions. The world, accordingly, is increasingly invested with our interests.

The ecological concept of niche provides a useful metaphor of the function of learning. Population ecologists often define niche as the way a species population is specialized in relation to other species within a community in a specific environment or habitat. Considering problems as embedded in situations, learning is the means by which a problem-situation is transformed into a niche for competent problem-solving activities. The niche is assumed by researchers by virtue of those special skills and techniques which distinguish their specialized manner of defining and solving particular problems. The niche which is thus accomplished by learning is marked out by specific skills and specialized

practices on the one hand, and those qualities of a particular environment—the niche variables—the knowledge of which provides the
solution to particular problems on the other. Thus, the niche is neither
part of nature nor a human invention. Accordingly, a niche variable
neither denotes an objective state of affairs nor does it simply gloss a
human construct. Rather, it refers to matters of fact relevant to a specific
problem-situation and, simultaneously, defines a value in practical terms.

In accordance with the teachings of the Christian church, Locke
conceived the human condition of total dependence in a thoroughly
theocentric idiom [11-15]. He took it for granted that the physical and
spiritual well-being of human beings was predicated on the practical
availability of goods, the ultimate origin of which was God's dominion.
God was the "active" owner of the world by creating and governing it. He
had the sole, absolute, and inalienable right in everything that happened
in the world, but in virtue of his absolute goodness, he allowed inferior
creatures to have a share in this right. This divine right defined the
"passive" entitlement of human agents as beneficiaries of divine goods.
As Locke noted in his *Two Treatises of Government*, "for Men being all the
Workmanship of one Omnipotent, and infinitely wise Maker . . . [are] sent
into the World by his order and about his business." Divine government
entailed that everyone "is bound to preserve himself"; yet it also entailed
that self-preservation formed part of an inclusive duty to preserve "the
rest of mankind." This duty requires that we refrain "from doing hurt to
one another," and places us, moreover, under the positive obligation to
promote the "preservation of Mankind" [16, pp. 288-290, 375-376].

From the viewpoint of the positivistic disenchantment of the world,
Locke's theocentric notion of the universe as God's dominion appears to
be an expression of his dogmatic adherence to the teachings of Christianity. Modern commentators have accordingly claimed that Locke's
theocentric morality was incongruent with an empiricist theory of
knowledge that confines cognitively credible assertions to empirically
testable conjectures. However, Locke did not consider faith in divine
government and its moral implications as conjectures whose validity
must be assessed in light of empirical evidence. Quite to the contrary, his
empiricist theory of knowledge was predicated on the assumption that
valuable information was ingrained in the order of things, and that, in
searching for this information in a methodologically appropriate manner,
human agents discharged a basic duty to God and fellow believers.

Though Locke and his contemporaries undoubtedly took at least some
articles of the Christian faith for granted, it is important to recognize that
Locke assumed that theology was relevant to anthropology in virtue
of the undeniable human condition of total dependence on an orderly
universe. The Christian faith has traditionally portrayed this condition in

particular ways, but it did not create it. Every human being depends on the environment for obtaining the goods necessary for sustaining and enriching his or her life, and every human being relies on other fellow human beings in coming to terms with this universal condition of dependence.

The condition of absolute dependence does not pertain to our lives as individual agents, but rather as members of the human species. Our capacity to take care of our own needs critically depends on the support of our own kin, as well as on means of survival developed by numerous other human beings, most of whom did not belong to our family, community, or polity. Because human beings must learn from fellow beings how to survive, their dependence on the physical world and their debt to other human agents form two closely related aspects of their existence. The ecological system of constraints and opportunities within which we pursue our own lives is therefore inseparable from a moral economic system of rights and duties that regulate our lives as members of the species. In this context, the moral dimension of our identity as human beings transcends the bounds of our cultural values as members of particular societies. The endeavor to understand our place in this world presupposes the desire for a truth that is inseparable from the good. This has traditionally been the presupposition of the Christian religion as well as many other belief systems, including science.

Current trends of globalization increase the scope of human interdependence and of the common dependence of human agents on a shared natural environment. The notion of the human species as a cultural category is therefore likely to become a more important frame of reference than it used to be in the past, relative to more particular categories of affiliation such as the nation, the ethnic group, or a particular faith or church. Knowledge has always been one of the principal spearheads of globalization, though it has been too often used to promote particular and divisive interests. It is currently widely acknowledged that scientific knowledge is one of the most important assets of humankind. Knowledge as common good should therefore be regarded as a critical means for founding global networks on principles of mutual respect and collaboration. Moreover, it should be regarded as commensurate with, and complementary to, the variety of beliefs in the common good of humankind.

REFERENCES

1. K. Popper, *The Open Society and Its Enemies* (2 vols.), Princeton University Press, Princeton, 1956.
2. K. Popper, *The Logic of Scientific Discovery*, Basic Books, New York, 1959.

3. H. M. Collins, *Changing Order: Replication and Induction in Scientific Practice*, Sage, London, 1985.

4. H. M. Collins and T. Pinch, *The Golem: What You Should Know About Science*, Cambridge University Press, Cambridge, 1998.

5. B. Latour, *Science in Action*, Open University Press, Milton Keynes, 1987.

6. I. Lakatos and A. Musgrave (eds.), *Criticism and the Growth of Knowledge*, Cambridge University Press, Cambridge, 1970.

7. H. Putnam, Philosophers and Human Understanding, in *Realism and Reason*, Cambridge University Press, Cambridge, pp. 184-204, 1985.

8. M. Weber, *From Max Weber: Essays in Sociology*, H. H. Gerth and C. Wright (eds.), Oxford University Press, New York, 1958.

9. M. Weber, *The Protestant Ethic and the Spirit of Capitalism*, T. Parsons (trans.), Charles Scribner's Sons, New York, 1958.

10. J. Locke, *An Essay Concerning Human Understanding*, P. H. Nidditch (ed.), Clarendon, Oxford, 1975.

11. R. Ashcraft, Faith and Knowledge in Locke's Philosophy, in *John Locke: Problems and Perspectives*, J. W. Yolton (ed.), Cambridge University Press, Cambridge, pp. 194-223, 1969.

12. J. Dunn, *The Political Thought of John Locke*, Cambridge University Press, Cambridge, 1969.

13. J. Dunn, Trust in the Politics of John Locke, in *Rethinking Modern Political Theory. Essays 1979-83*, Cambridge University Press, Cambridge, 1986.

14. M. Ben-Chaim, Locke's Ideology of "Common Sense," *Studies in History and Philosophy of Science, 31*, pp. 473-501, 2000.

15. M. Ben-Chaim, *Experimental Philosophy and the Birth of Empirical Science*, Ashgate, Aldershot, 2004.

16. J. Locke, *Two Treatises of Government*, P. Laslett (ed.), Cambridge University Press, Cambridge, 1965.

CHAPTER 8

9-11 Communicative Grammar

Dorota Zielinska

The events of 9-11 above all raised the issue of the advisability and feasibility of limiting freedom of information in order to minimize its potential misuse. Also, in view of the claim being made here that the information we possess influences the meaning purported by natural language, the events of September 2001, which reshaped our perception of the world around us, have changed the language we speak. The focus of this chapter is on the latter issue.

Communicative grammar presumes a bio-cognitive model of language that takes the perspective of the theory of models used in empirical sciences on language studies. From that perspective, communicative grammar aims at accounting for the biological instantiation of language and taking into account state-of-the-art formalization techniques, the assumptions of which result in stress being laid on the communicative aspect of language as a function of our view of the world. The final sections of this chapter outline the major ways the September events in New York reshaped, in particular, the Polish view of the surrounding reality.

THE IMPLICATIONS OF THE THEORY OF MODELS IN NATURAL SCIENCES FOR LINGUISTICS: COMMUNICATIVE GRAMMAR

This chapter outlines the foundations of a bio-cognitive informational model of language arrived at by applying the theory of models used in empirical sciences to language studies. From this perspective, the grammar of natural language must allow for the biological realization of language in the brain on the one hand, and consider the implications of available state-of-the-art formalization techniques, which could model the relationships between the relevant parameters, on the other. These restrictions result in a natural language grammar focusing on its communicative, informational aspect.

Models in the Natural Sciences:
Model, Reality, and Formalism

Contemporary science researches the world via models, i.e., by constructing models of a phenomenon and then testing these models against reality. Such tests typically reveal discrepancies between the data collected and model-derived predictions, which prompts researchers to fine tune the model in question. With time, the amount and quality of the data that can no longer be accommodated within the model through its fine tuning becomes so significant that a radically new model needs to be tried out. In Kuhn's words [1], a paradigm shift is needed for further progress to take place.

A model takes into account the characteristics of the phenomena studied which are intuitively regarded as relevant. At this stage, in addition to his own intuition, a scholar can be guided only by drawing an analogy between the phenomenon studied and another one with a successful model.

The more formalized a model is, the more advanced it is considered to be [2]. Traditionally, formalizing a model means finding for its parameters selected objects in a mathematical theory the relationships between whose elements are assumed to correspond to those between the respective model components. Formalizing a model allows for it to be rigidly tested, and maybe even more importantly, to be used to make predictions and discover new facts.

Most recent advances in empirical sciences and mathematics have revealed, however, yet another venue for researching reality. Some concepts in the theory of Quantum Mechanics, for instance, can only be investigated formally and only some of these correspond in some way to "our" classical concepts. Chaotic processes, in turn, calculated using computers, have led to concepts (such as that of a periodic attractor) and to results that could not have been envisaged by logical thinking alone. Thus, in the contemporary scientific paradigm, formalism not only imposes order onto data and allows to make predictions from data collected, but formalism may also precede concept formation and, thus, be directly used to research reality [3, 4].

One specific paradigm that has played an important role in investigating the cognitive capabilities of the brain is the AI (artificial intelligence) perspective, which assumes that if we can construct a replica of the brain, a device that behaves like the brain, it is likely that the brain acts this way too. This approach also fits in with the general picture of the theory of models used in the empirical sciences. Constructing an artificial brain requires both determining the relevant parameters of its object of investigation and defining mathematically expressible relations between them, whether all of those are to be modeled directly physically or, more practically, simulated on a computer.

The Constraints on Language Models Imposed by the Physical Characteristics of the Brain; and the Respective Mathematical Techniques Required

In the case of language studies, if we intend to construct a psychologically realistic model of language — that is, one which will eventually be grounded in the processes of the brain — the boundary conditions restricting viable language models are imposed by the brain structure and its functioning — i.e., by the biophysical parameters of the brain. (This is not the only approach to language studies that is possible. Another approach covered by the literature is to approximate language as a self-standing system with no regard for its biological functioning and to describe it mathematically as such. Such a perspective, however, which has produced many significant results [5, 6], involves an approximation that seems to have already been exploited to the full; the lack of progress in tackling figurative language (reconciling the openness of natural language with its predictably) as well as explaining the origin of basic encoding seems to indicate that this paradigm can no longer offer significant new results.)

Coming back to the bio-cognitive model of the brain, the first results concerning the linguistic functioning of the brain came from comparing the cognitive, and in particular the linguistic, capabilities of brain-damaged people with those of healthy ones. In recent years, brain mapping has proceeded in a more or less uninvasive way by using technologically sophisticated, sometimes multimillion dollar devices that monitor brain activity during specific, e.g., linguistic tasks. Studies have revealed some correlation between particular linguistic activities and areas primarily involved in these processes. Yet, to a lesser degree, many other areas have been observed as active during the performance of most linguistic tasks, too. Some correlation has been found between linguistic and general cognitive skills such as generating verbs and performing motor activities related to these verbs. Such a relationship between each general cognitive skill and its corresponding linguistic one is not, however, universal. For instance, there is no direct relationship between the ability to perform spatial tasks and using space when signing. Some signing people, with brain injuries disrupting the spatial aspect of their signing skills such as locating story characters consistently in space (which is the way signing languages identify them), have been found to perform well in purely spatial tests. Conversely, another type of brain injury allowed signing people who were unable to pass spatial tests to sign a consistent story. Thus, such experiments have demonstrated both a certain degree of the autonomy of the linguistic module and some correlation between the linguistic capabilities and general cognitive skills. In other words, the results collected are rather of a general, preliminary nature, indicative of phenomena, rather than offering specific linguistic solutions [7].

Another reason why the answers arrived at in brain mapping are non-specific are methodological constraints. Neurolinguistic studies face some serious methodological problems resulting from the limitations of the devices used on the one hand, and the subtraction paradigm on which they rely on the other. By a subtraction paradigm, we mean the assumption that the difference between the brain's activities during two successive tasks reflects the aspects distinguishing between these two tasks. Thus, ideally, we would like to compare two activities that differ as to the involvement of only one extra skill. Such a seemingly reasonable assumption, however, is extremely hard to achieve in practice for it is hard to envisage two activities differing with regard to one extra component only. Besides, the subtraction paradigm makes assumptions about parameters contributing to a given task, which can easily turn out to be premature.

Far more specific answers come from investigating the brain on the molecular level. A correlation has been established between the number of specific cells and the respective stimuli they respond to. A degree of randomness that has also been discovered in these processes indicates the potential role of Quantum Mechanical processes in the cognitive functioning of the brain. Cells responding to stimuli of a given type and strength by sending out a signal and modifying the current strength of synapses have been found to be the basic process taking place in the brain. Also, specific proteins influencing the time the synapses are opened have been identified. Moreover, entire communication tracks have been discovered. Even the first genes responsible for certain linguistic skills have been separated. Nevertheless, research has only begun and although new data are being accumulated with astounding speed, the information available, although highly reliable, is sparse and fragmentary, thereby once more imposing general limits rather than prompting specific linguistic solutions. Most importantly, from inspecting the physical structure of the brain on the cellular level, we learned that it consists of a very complex network of highly interconnected neuronal connections, unlike the orderly structure of modules in a linear computer. Mathematical methods selected for modeling linguistic processes must reflect this fact. The techniques that describe systems with similar characteristics and could be tried out here, ones with at least some history of application to linguistics or cognitive sciences, include analogical modeling, hidden Markov processes, simulated annealing, and neural networks.

Besides, since every piece of information must have some sort of physical embodiment—be it classical or quantum—biological systems with physical embodiment correspond to informational systems. (Information is never purely mathematical; the newly developing field of quantum information science puts information in a quantum context.) Conversely, a change in physical state corresponds to a change in information. This leads to the conclusion that a model of language based on its physical realization in the brain should focus on its informational role. Such a model should emphasize the information conveyed by language as its basic parameter rather than focusing merely on its representational aspect and building its informational characteristics merely as a function of the representational ones. Conversely, in view of what has been adumbrated so far, this latter representational parameter seems to be a derivative, the result of the group effects of comparison effected on world knowledge.

The most important general conclusions relevant for modeling the language drawn from researching the brain can be summed up in the following way:

a. The brain has a gross modularity with areas primarily activated during the performance of specific linguistic tasks, such as production vs. comprehension, lexical vs. structural tasks.

b. There is some but not a full correlation between certain linguistic and general cognitive skills. To some degree, language is based on general cognitive skills but it may also be based to some extent on modules of an exclusively linguistic character.

c. The complexity inherent in the brain's architecture and some initial successes in modeling selected of its cognitive capabilities, e.g., pattern recognition on neural networks indicates the role of collective effects on the brain functioning [8]. The relevance of chaotic processes in the brain modeling mentioned above, as well as the discovery of some inherent randomness in cell responses pointing to the relevance of QM for modeling brain cognitive processes, suggests that the venue for researching reality with formalisms and creating conceptually comprehensible aspects of the models mentioned above, should also be kept in mind when investigating language.

d. One of the basic characteristics of the brain established so far is its capability of effecting comparisons: a single cell fires in response to a given input or not; thus at the bottom of a language model there is classification, not description. Description seems to be a group effect very much in the way that temperature and volume are group effects resulting from the interaction of a large collection of individual atoms, none of which is characterized by the features of volume or temperature. Similarly, there is no place for basic encoding in the philosophical results offered; e.g., by Putnam [9], Brickhard and Campbell [10]. Brickhard and Campbell point to classification as an operation in terms of its uses for the system as the foundation for encoding. Thus, the result is a comparison in the sense of selecting, pointing out which group of objects a given one is like, without enumerating separately the specific factors which determined the choice.

e. The inability to ground basic encoding in the brain processes, along with a brain architecture consisting of a highly complex network of neural interconnections, motivates a relational rather than atomistic description of linguistic data. That approach defines basic objects by describing their interaction with other objects and not merely by enumerating their components. The issue of choosing between an atomistic and a relational approach to describing data featured prominently in the dispute between Leibniz and Newton over the best way of describing the physical world. Leibniz's proposition of taking a relational perspective, which could not, however, be tackled mathematically at that time, was motivated by precisely such a factor—the inability to define the characteristics of basic matter components. For practical reasons arising from Newton's ability to give a mathematical form to his philosophy, despite requiring, counter intuitively, the introduction of eternal space and an omniscient observer, carried the day. The fact that lexemes do not evoke merely their respective referents has especially been emphasized by cognitivists but was already acknowledged in a way by Tesniere and his concept of valence.

f. Complexity of the brain structure points to the importance of group effects. Even when introducing encoding as a stand in representation for practical purposes, a comparison does not need to be made in relation to a pattern. The very complexity of the neural interconnections leading to new processes suggests the opposite. It points out the need to use formalisms capable of capturing "ecological" effects. The following fallacy may serve as an illustration of group effects not predictable on the basis of the qualities of the constituting elements. "A square consists of four sides. Every side of a square is a line section; therefore, a square is a line section." Viable formalisms with a history of application in modeling cognitive processes include hidden Markov processes, neural networks, stochastic simulated annealing, genetic programming, and analogical modeling [8, 11-14].

g. Receiving an impulse by a neuron results in a permanent change in the physical state of a given synapse. Thus, what takes place in the brain is a comparison (a selection of impulses) on the one hand, and a change in its state on the other. Analyzing the changes of states corresponds to analyzing changes in information. Thus, in addition to including a selection mechanism in the language model, the concept of information change (creating a relevant information theory) must be central to the study of language.

Linguistic Motivation for the Model

In this section, we shall explicate the characteristics of linguistic data that we take to be of primary relevance. (Further on, in the last section, we shall outline a model which reflects the characteristics presented below.)

Openness of Natural Language

Natural language is an open system [15], i.e., meaning in natural language is not fixed; we can communicate new meaning using "old lexemes," or sets of lexemes. Thus, content expressible through natural language is not fixed in the sense of being a simple function of sentential/phrasal constituents with the constituent elements having constant (coded) value.

This is visible, first, in the practically unlimited amount of new content expressible through a single lexeme. For example, the value of the lexeme *red* is considerably different when accompanying the lexemes *eye, hair, dress,* and *sky,* respectively. Even numerals function this way. Compare the actual distance expressed with the numeral *ten* in *it is a 10 Kkm race* and in *I work 10 km from home.*

The openness of language is also revealed in linguistic compositionality, which in fact is partial even in seemingly compositional cases. For instance, in the phrase *red rose,* the red rose referred to has red petals only, which is not formally marked by the phrase employed.

Figurative language itself is obviously the most conspicuous example of the openness of natural language, in which case the same set of words may refer to a very different referent in separate contexts.

Yet another, less obvious case of the openness of natural language takes place when one part of the utterance in practice determines another one, which can be illustrated with the following.

Replying once to my son's request to go to a summer camp, I answered: *You may go to a summer camp in July,* by which I meant to indicate when his going to a camp was all right with me. On another occasion, I used the same grammatical occasion in a very different way. On that day, I entered my son's room and saw a mess on his desk. I yelled at him "what a mess," but after noticing that he was watching his favorite TV show, I added *You may clean your desk after "Goosebumps."*

Although I used the same grammatical construction — "You may + do + something + time" — on that occasion I meant to say that my son need not clean his desk right away. The communication could not be interpreted based merely on the encoded value of the sentence but had to be processed in relation to the background information: when a mother sees a mess she wants to have it cleaned up right away. Note, that the sentence discussed as an answer to: *What may I do after Goosebumps?* will not have the same sense.

Predictability of Natural Language

Yet, despite there being apparently no limit to what a given lexeme or a set of lexemes may serve to convey, natural language is predictable. For instance, given a variety of software to choose from, one will understand what a "video game" is even if he has not heard the term before. It seems that the same mechanisms allow children to acquire language without having the meaning of each newly encountered lexeme explained. Interestingly, we can even understand broken English, which testifies again to the fact that we can communicate without requiring a full correspondence between the coded meanings of constituent items and the whole linguistic construct. (Note that a computer program with even the slightest mistake will not be executed properly, or more likely not executed at all.)

Correlated Information

Yet another widely acknowledged observation characterizing natural language is that what is conveyed with lexemes is not limited to information about their respective references and their characteristics (propositions). What also gets conveyed (correlated) is the usage history including, e.g., the illocutionary force, or locative function. The illocutionary force (the act of promising, threatening, requesting, etc.) can be indicated without being explicitly coded: e.g., *Could you open a window?* is typically understood not as a question concerning the ability of the addressee to open the window but as a request to do so. This is done without explicitly saying *I am asking you to open the window.* Or, for instance, the locative information is conveyed with the lexeme *table,* employed as the answer to the question *where are the keys? — on the table.* The speaker treats the *table* as a location in the house. In this case the lexeme *table* also informs us of the high probability that the table being talked about is standing the right way up and probably on the floor of the room rather than out in the open air, and that it is surrounded by chairs.

Because the table provides a stable location, while a key does not, the sentence *The table is under the key* is not an acceptable answer to the question "where is the table?" On the other hand, one could say *The table is under the lamp.*

Thus, what a given lexeme communicates in the sense of the information being correlated with its usage is more than the physical characteristics of its referent. New lexical items appear in use, and it is only later that they get untangled to reveal their approximated "systemic meaning." The amount and type of information related to a given lexeme on a given occasion obviously varies, too; e.g., not every usage of the lexeme *table* will involve marking its potential locative function. In other words, to establish the lexical meaning, we have no other choice but to start from assessing its full communicative purport in particular utterances and only then attempt to extract some approximate systemic meaning.

Information Transfer

We assume that the basic function of language is to convey information. As will be argued below, information can be conveyed not only in quantum units — i.e., consisting of the full content of individual lexemes or their sets — but also with the subparts of the information correlated with the respective lexemes.

a. The primary way of conveying information in natural language is by means of analytic constructions (i.e., The rose / is red as opposed to the red / rose (has withered)).

b. Yet, as Awdiejew notices [16], synthetic constructions also serve to communicate, rather than being merely used to express presupposition. As Zielinska notices [17], such usage is especially common in marketing literature and press headings. For instance, at the back of the *Animal Atlas*, one of the sentences reads:

> This exciting guide to the world's wildlife contains over two hundred lifelike illustrations.

Obviously, the fact that the *Animal Atlas* is an exciting guide to the world's wildlife, is not presupposed here but readers are informed of it. In turn, one of the press titles that I came across after the events of 9/11 reads:

> A Polish Wife of a Terrorist

With that title, the audience was informed that a terrorist had a Polish wife. This fact must have come as more of a surprise than would have been presupposed in the case of a wife of a Muslim. Only in that latter case could we postulate that the title merely states what the article is about.

c. Typically, both in analytic and synthetic constructions, a separate group of lexemes (each group may be limited to one lexeme only) denotes the topic of a piece of information, and another one the comment, i.e., {what} and [what about] are singled out by separate groups of lexemes. (The same situation occurs in the language of mathematics, where a typical statement takes the form {[A] = a}.) We might say that the information transfer in such situations is quantitized.

As Zielinska notices [18], however, it turns out that this is not the only way of conveying information in natural language. It turns out that the {what is said} and [about what] need not be expressed by the respective content of a separate group of lexemes each. This is so because, as has already been pointed out, the information correlated with a single lexeme does more than inform us about its referent — it also evokes related information containing links to other items with which the given referent happened to interact, or co-occur with. We shall be referring to the full set of information, including related information, as the communicative-space of a given lexeme, or c-space for short. Every group of lexemes naturally evokes its respective c-space, too. Consequently, coupled with the formation requirements, the information introduced by a given lexeme or a construction into a sentence may, and usually is, partially predictable by the c-space of the remaining elements of the given sentence. For instance, let us consider the information brought in by the lexeme *boys* in the phrase:

the school for boys

The new information introduced by the lexeme *boys* into the phrase above does not exhaust all the information correlated with the lexeme *boys* when used in isolation. Since the construction *the school for* evokes "children," the lexeme boys says {male [young humans]} and only the subpart {male} constitutes new information that assesses [young humans] which is the topic of the piece of information discussed. In other phrases, the other informational subpart of the information correlated with the same lexeme may constitute the new information. For instance in

the boxing competition for boys

since the boxing competition is for male humans, the lexeme *boys* can be depicted as {young [male humans]} where only the subpart {young} apprizing [male humans] is new. The topic, [male humans], has been provided in part by the c-space of the phrase *the boxing competition for*. Thus the subpart of the lexical content along with the c-space can serve to define the information conveyed.

Note, the informational structure of a lexeme (and thus the informational content of an utterance) depends not only on the very words used in a linguistic construction, but also on the distribution of the New and the Given, which in speech is largely specified by intonation, for the distribution between the New and the Given determines the communicative space for the lexemes. The ones brought in as the given part typically need to be interpreted as lexemes in isolation while those constituting the New part must be interpreted in the c-space provided by the Old part. Therefore, if we say, e.g.,:

This is a **school** for boys.

with the lexeme *school* being treated as the NEW, which could be marked with the appropriate intonation, the lexeme *boys* is interpreted, one might say, as if it were in an empty c-space thus evoking the full information related to that lexeme whose core content is {young [male human]}. Yet, if we place the stress on the lexeme *boys* as in:

This is a school for **boys**.

The lexeme *boys* appears in the c-space of the item *school* and thus will be interpreted again as {male [young human]}.

Note also that, typically, we express verbally only information that has some informational value. We do not say about John, "John is sober today" if everyone knows that he is sober every day. The sentence quoted makes sense only if John is often drunk. Therefore, the sentence "John is sober today" communicates both its coded value and that "John's being sober is not a typical situation."

Scaling

The concept of scaling captures the observation that the value of a given lexeme used on a particular occasion depends on the scale made by other lexemes that could have been used to assess the {what} for the given [what about] — the relation of a given parameter of the given lexeme to the value of the same parameter in other appropriate lexemes that could be chosen in a given situation. For instance, the value of "good" in the phrase *he is a good student* depends on the actual terms a given speaker uses for such an appraisal. When spoken by a lenient teacher, it will indicate a different value than when pronounced by a strict one.

Note also that the value of the parameter considered need not be expressed with the same type of grammatical units. For instance, in the reply to *How fit is he?* we may express the degree of fitness not only with an adverb, e.g., as in *he is very fit,* but also with sentences like: *He is a ski instructor, he regularly practices jogging.* This considerably enlarges the scale of meaning expressible in natural language. For more information on scaling, see Zielinska [17].

Dynamicity of Natural Language

Natural language is dynamic. It has changed over time and will continue to change. Syntax and vocabulary have evolved and keep evolving; we observe a shift of meaning in the case of individual lexemes as well as the evolution of syntax. Language has evolved from the "sign=sentence message type" stage to, in practice, approximately the "sign=reference" stage. There are also differences in interpreting linguistic messages among individual language users; also, the linguistic command of same user changes with time.

The Model Construction

Taking into account the physical make up of the brain, the resultant viable mathematical formalisms, and the characteristics of the linguistic data that we set out to model, the following proposition for the foundations of natural language model can be put forward.

Selection

To ensure the openness of language, and in accordance with the brain studies results, we postulate selection as the basic mechanism underlying the functioning of natural language. Using language selectively means that the information conveyed with natural language comes from a selection of one of a number of pieces of predetermined (guessed, predicted) content with the help of the information correlated with respective lexical items. The result of selection amounts to stating that of the options that can be selected, the one actually chosen (the given referent, situation, etc.) more closely resembles that correlated with the lexeme used to select it with than any other option does. In this way, by employing the selective mode of language use, linguistic information need not be fully coded with those lexemes (and their sets) to be conveyed unambiguously. If the options can change independently from the coded value of linguistic expression, the selection process will account for the openness of the system.

To define the selection process, we need to identify the options and propose a mechanism of selection (i.e., for assessing resemblance). The options are created by two factors. First, as has been mentioned, the information correlated with an individual lexeme goes beyond the information in the main item correlated with it, but also includes that information which reflects past relationships between a given item and other items. Second, this space of options is adjusted by our knowledge of the specific situation involved, one coming also from non-linguistic sources. It is such an adjustment that makes the space of options independent from the coded value of lexemes.

To sum up, the openness of language can be modeled by introducing a selective mode of language use. Now, lexemes and their ordered sets will not only be used to code the information correlated with themselves, but also as operators selecting options from a given space. If the space proposed changes independently from the information correlated with lexemes, so will the content selected with them. We propose that the space be created by information correlated with lexical items and augmented by our current knowledge of the world along with information obtained in a non-linguistic manner in a way to be specified later. Thus, the space changes independently from the information coming from the correlation with lexemes.

As has been argued, effecting comparison (i.e., selecting) is the main operation reflected by the functioning of the brain. To build on the dynamicity of language and to comply with the biological constraints reflecting the complexity of the brain architecture, we propose that such a comparison not be effected in relation to a pattern but a set of tokens, e.g., as described by the mechanism of analogical modeling introduced in Skousen [14].

Analogical modeling, in a nutshell, judges a given item to belong to one of the available sets of items by calculating in a practice, mathematical way the distance measured from each element of each set. As a result, the procedure provides an answer in percentage terms with regard to the similarity of the element considered (X) in relation to each of the sets. Consequently, an element that is located closer to the prototypical elements of set A than to those of set B may be classified as belonging to set B rather than set A if that element is surrounded by a larger number of even unprototypical elements belonging to set B than to set A. For instance, see Figure 1.

Conversely, analogical modeling can be used to assess which of the items considered resembles best a given set of items (correlated with a specific lexeme).

Thus, an analogical-operational model of language allows one to treat lexemes as operators acting on the knowledge of the world, where every

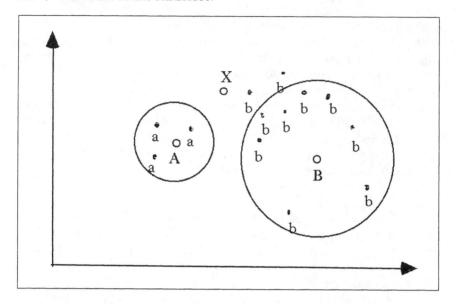

Figure 1. Distribution of tokens of types a and b in the space
of their characteristics m and n. Capital letters mark the most
prototypical elements of a given category. X is the element
to be categorized either a or b.

lexeme is correlated with a set of its past uses. The statistically averaged
"use(s)" may be treated as corresponding to coded meaning(s). Depending on the type of averaging, we will end up with Aristotelian definitions,
or if we average close enough items only, and take for an answer most
central occurrences, the result will be prototypes.

To sum up, in an analogical-operational model, lexemes code or effect
comparison. The effect of the comparison operation is the statement that a
given "object" a_x is more like a_1, a_2, ..., a_n than like y_1, y_2, ..., y_n. Such
a process actually takes place in the brain. A given impulse leads with
a certain degree of probability to one of a number of possible responses.
Analogical modeling is a way of capturing such a comparison.

Each usage of a lexeme results in its being correlated with a particular
piece of information. If we allow the oldest uses to be deleted after
a prescribed amount of time, as if forgetting old data, this gives us a
natural mechanism of a shift in meaning. A "gangling effect" [14] on the
other hand, a mathematical effect inherent in the statistical mechanism
employed, makes a number of similar objects close to a given one influence its behavior more strongly than the sum of each of these impacts.
This leads to regularization in the choices made thus in relation to the

emergence of morpho-syntax (the imposing of meaning on specific types of grammatical compounds consisting of lexemes or morphemes).

Because the result of a comparison is an option, which also depends on our current knowledge of the world, a knowledge which comes both through linguistic and non-linguistic means, and not merely from past information correlated with respective lexemes, the openness of the system is ensured. A non-linguistically derived change in our knowledge of the world directly modifies our options, and thus influences the future results of comparison (due to modifications in the items a given one will be compared to), thereby changing the information hitherto conveyed by the language.

Note that analogical modeling is not the only plausible solution for modeling comparison. Other statistical techniques that may bring in some interesting group effects should also be tried out for the purposes of describing the selection process and only final empirical verification will be able to select the best mechanism. At the moment, i.e., when defining the foundations of the model, analogical modeling serves as a good example of the mechanism instantiating the operation of the selection needed, one which makes it possible to model the openness of the system and at the same time ensure compositionality, as well as establish a connection between the systemic (i.e., averaged) and the particular.

Constructing the Space of Options:
Communicative Space (C-Space)

To select, we first need items to select from. We suggest introducing a relational space of options instead of limiting ourselves to an atomic description of referents as objects of comparison. As has already been explained, this has both cognitive/linguistic and philosophical justification. First, as has already been stressed, a given lexeme generates not only information that describes its referent, but also information that describes the situation in which its referent functions, e.g., other referents alongside which it co-occurs as well as the interactions it enters into with those co-occurring referents. Second, the existence of such relational communicative space is corroborated by a philosophical need for a relational rather than a purely atomic description of the most basic components of meaning that cannot be defined by enumerating their parts. Relational perspective solutions have come to be known as solutions to analogical problems in modern physics, where gauge fields have been introduced to solve similar problems involved in describing foundational components. (For instance, Weyl proposed a gauge field to account for the impossibility to define objectively, and not merely conventionally, negative as opposed to positive charges, while von t'Hooft constructed a gauge field theory for a set of three elements, doing for quarks what Weyl did for charges. Quarks are the building blocks of neutrons and protons, which come in three "colors.")

Coming back to linguistics, for instance, the lexeme *dog* could be presented relationally as a set of individual occurrences or, alternately (in the first approximation, i.e., disregarding the potential interdependence of features) as

dog ::= {(a_1 • big, a_2 • small, ..), (b_1 • brown, b_2 • black, b_3 • white, ..), ..., (m_1 • barks, m_2 • growls, ..), (n_1 • runs, n_2 • walks, ..), (u_1 • eats [meat • u_{11}, fish • u_{12}], u_2 • devours[....], ...), ... w_1 • bites [a dog • w_1, a man • w_2, a child • w_3]).....,(y_1 • in a kennel, y_2 • in the field, ...), ... (is accompanied by [])....

where a_1, .., b_1, ..., y_1, ... express the relative probabilities of a particular type of occurrence and the sum of the probabilities $a_1^2 + \ldots z_1^2$ equals one.

At this point, it is hard to tell how easily a communicative space resulting from a combination of lexical items could be composed out of these respective c-spaces of the constituting lexemes. In any case, the communicative space for ordered sets of lexemes also needs to be described. For instance, the communicative space of ("My car . . . petrol") evokes the c-space of options in practice limited to those including lexemes covering the semantic content expressible with the lexeme "uses." Thus, we may understand the figurative sentence "My car <u>drinks</u> petrol" with the lexeme *drink* assessing the verb "uses" induced by the c-space of "my car . . . petrol." Next, from the relational description of the lexeme "use" we obtain such parameters as the amount of what is used, the speed of using it, etc. Given which of these parameters could be assessed with the parameters specifying the c-space of the lexeme "drinks" and the informative significance of each of these, after having compared those of their values that could be conveyed with other lexical items (scaling), we infer that the speaker most probably intended the lexeme *drinks* to assess the way the car uses gasoline: he intended to say that his car uses gasoline too fast and thus too much of it.

When creating c-space, we also need to decide how to extend the c-space derived from past uses with information derived from a non-linguistic context, e.g., information that we perceive visually in a specific situation or know with regard to specific participants, a knowledge which is situation-specific and not the result of statistical experience. (This phenomenon has already been partially analyzed, e.g., under the concepts of actualization [16], anchoring [19], or enriching [20].

Information Transfer and the Role of C-Space

C-space essential not only to instantiate the mechanism of selection, but, as was said in a previous section, also as a means of extracting new information from that provided by a given lexeme or linguistic construct in a given c-space, i.e., it can serve as an additional way of separating the {what} from the [what about], in addition to this being achieved with synthetic or analytic constructions. A situation in which c-space serves to separate the {what} from the [what about] was illustrated above, e.g., with the phrase *a boxing competition for boys* when discussing the aspects of natural language we intend to model.

The informational value of a given piece of information introduced with a given lexeme or a bigger linguistic unit may, in turn, be used as criteria for deciding which particular information conveyed is intended as the communicate (cf. the theory of relevance, where informativeness points out the intended implication). Eventually, the theory of information needed for the model of natural language will not be limited solely to the issue of predictability, but must also reflect the relevance/significance of a given item of information for a human.

Conclusions

Given the constraints implied by the theory of models used in empirical sciences, I have proposed a number of foundational assumptions for a model of language that can be instantiated in the brain. I have also adumbrated selected characteristics of a model based on such assumptions.

The Foundational Assumptions for a Bio-Cognitive Model of Language

To sum up, in view of the constraints mentioned above, the following foundational assumptions for a bio-cognitive grammar emerge.

The primary goal of a linguistic model from the perspective outlined so far will be to establish what "new" (and significant) information language communicates — in other words what a given lexeme/sentence or other linguistic construct informs us of; what new information it introduces to a given sentence/text/or situation.

Establishing the information brought in by a selected lexeme (or an ordered set of lexemes) in a given communicative space requires specifying what is being assessed, the [what about], as well as the {what} is said about that [what about]. The {what} and the [what about] can be designated by separate lexemes (or their sets) each as has been studied by means of functional analysis, or can both be contained in the information correlated with the same lexeme (or a set of lexemes). In each case the information can be coded or selected out of the communicative space. What needs to be done to establish the information conveyed by a given lexeme or a set of lexemes in the latter case is:

1. Establish the communicative space for individual lexemes and then for ordered sets of lexemes within a relational framework. (A practical approximation of such a communicative space for lexemes has been developed by Awdiejew [16], who at that stage disregards the probabilities of options. He proposes describing predicates, and relating any other speech part to a respective predicate. Yet, to reduce the amount of the information provided by the c-space, some sort of information theory would be useful, one focusing on limiting/ordering the space correlated with lexemes and their sets.
2. Find the mechanism for selecting from options pointed out by the communicative space (including the non-linguistic context), when there is no direct (coded, i.e., highly correlated) correspondence between lexically correlated pieces of information and those corresponding to the options, e.g., using analogical modeling.
3. Describe the mechanism for establishing the information brought in by a selected lexeme (or an ordered set of lexemes) in a given communicative space by comparing the communicative space of that selected lexeme with the communicative space induced by the remaining part of the linguistic construction in which that given lexeme appears, including a non-linguistic context. Including a non-linguistic (non-coded) context means including specific situation parameters, information, (objects), perceived non-linguistically.
4. Take into account the fact that only non-trivial information is verbalized.

Selected Characteristics of the Model Built on the Assumptions Outlined Above

The model of natural language proposed will have the following characteristics:

- It will account for the openness of natural language by allowing it to point out new content with a limited set of lexical values, e.g., point out "a computer game" from computer software by finding that type of software to have more in common with games like chess, poker, etc., than other types of software. Yet, without presupposing that we are supposed to choose from among software types, the lexemes *computer* and *game* do not encode the desired interpretation when encountered for the first time.

- It will account for the evolution of meaning (of categories). By erasing old uses from the analogical set, and thus mimicking the process of forgetting, we will make a selection in relation to a changing set of tokens which may lead to other choices than those that would have resulted from using an original set of tokens in the comparison process.

- It will imitate the evolution of syntax. A "ganging effect" is a mathematical effect of the analogical formalism introduced by Skousen, which makes the contribution of items with the same outcome depend on their number in a way that at first depends linearly on their number, but after exceeding a certain percentage of all items their joined contribution increases much faster than linearly, favoring the items with the given predominant behavior thus leading to regularization; in other words to the emergence of a morpho-syntax.

- It will explain figurative speech in the following way. First, the metaphorically-used construction serves to select the [what about] from options provided by the communicative space of the remaining lexemes in a given utterance. Second, the information correlated with the construct used is compared to (as if projected onto) the content of lexemes that would be most likely to assess the [what about] selected, which provides the {what}.

- As was the case with selecting [the what] in the case of figurative speech, selection explains the ability to understand broken language (e.g., by selecting from viable options provided by the c-space).

- The model will explain the process of language acquisition by accounting for the making of better linguistic choices over time as a result of a set of past uses containing a steadily increasing percentage of "right choices." The older choices, more often not the correct ones, are forgotten and substituted with choices which are more frequently the right ones. Thus, the percentage of right choices in the set of past uses increases, increasing the probability of the right analogical choice being made in the future, etc.

- The model will account for the phenomena of scaling. Establishing the options induced by the communicative space and forming a scale of the relative values of linguistic constructions which could assess the options in a given situation redefines the values of these linguistic constructs in comparison with their values in isolation.

- By assuming the relational description of lexical meaning plus selection, the model will incorporate in a homogenous way such parameters into the concept of meaning, as the illocutionary force, the function of helping to locate, and other information reflecting the usage of a given lexeme or linguistic construct.

A POLISH PERSPECTIVE

As has been pointed out earlier in this chapter, what we select from (i.e., the communicative space built out of our general and specific knowledge of the world) as well as what we select with (i.e., the information correlated with individual lexemes), determines the information that is selected with a given linguistic construct of natural language on a given occasion. Our knowledge of the world determines our options and these in turn constitute tokens used in the process of comparison on future occasions thus influencing the subsequent outcome of that process.

The options to select from change for several reasons. First, new situations are encountered, which can be described using extra parameters. Second, since the information related to a lexeme reflects its correlations not only with its direct referent, but also with co-occurring facts and situations, with each use of a given lexeme some new facts become correlated with it and the weights reflecting the relative significance of specific, correlated facts become adjusted to reflect the relative significance of each of them for the speaker.

To sum up, changes in our knowledge of the world directly affect the options we may select from (the existing state of world knowledge), as well as the results of comparing (classifying), in effect changing the information conveyed by natural language. In other words, the communicative impact of natural language depends on our knowledge/ perception of the world, including the associations between facts, both of which have been significantly changed by the events of 9-11.

The events of 9-11 not only introduced a new situation, a new option, but also influenced a significant amount of the vocabulary by relating to the act of terrorism areas of life never before associated with it, thus changing the informational field of these lexemes. Consequently, the events of 9-11 changed the meaning of an important fraction of the daily vocabulary used by practically everyone in the world, including the Poles.

What happened on the 11th of September shook the Poles as it did all other nations. The extent and unpredictability of the tragedy overwhelmed all of us. That same evening, in a spontaneous gesture, a burning candle appeared in every Pole's window, very much the way it happened when the Polish commemorated the dramatic events of Marital Law in Poland in December 1981. At that time, placing burning candles in windows was all that most of us could do to protest the situation, as well as to express our compassion for those who had died or were in prison.

The tragic events of September 2001 in the United States, like the events in the Moscow theater Dubrovka in October of the following year, have brought to the surface the issue of personal safety in view of people's freedom of access to information, including bomb-making manuals. In other words, should we introduce constraints on the freedom of information, if that were at all feasible? On the one hand, we seem to acknowledge the need to impose limits on access to some data such as health records, matters of national security, and now possibly the technical details of bomb construction. On the other hand, any limitation on access to information inevitably gives rise to corruption and soon becomes not only ineffective, but begins to have a negative impact on the majority of society. In this part of the chapter, using the example of the situation in contemporary Poland, I shall argue that a better way of ensuring safety than limiting access to information is to try and ensure that such freedom can be exercised in a legal way that is just.

Poland is not only a post 9-11, but also a "post Berlin wall" society, and its situation after September 11th cannot be understood properly without having some background knowledge of its most recent history. Until 1989, life in post-war Poland was, in a way, idyllically simple, for the communist regime divided society into two clearly separate groups, one holding Communist Party membership cards, the other consisting of people without such IDs. This division accordingly introduced very clear and transparent rules in life. For instance, if you wanted to become a company director, entitled to receiving certain benefits, you should become a communist party member first, which among other things, entailed stopping going to church. (At this point, a few words should be added about the role of church membership in Poland, which was unlike that in any other country. More than anywhere else, the Polish church has for centuries been closely linked with the national aspirations of its members; support for the church has been tantamount to the fight for freedom from oppressors. In 1772, Poland was partially partitioned by its stronger neighbors (Russia, Austria, and Prussia) for the first time, eventually disappearing from the map of Europe for well over a century in the final partition in 1795. During these years of occupation, it was in the Catholic church that the Polish patriotic spirit survived. When, after a brief period of freedom between the First and the Second World Wars, the whole of Poland ended up under Russian occupation, the church naturally resumed its freedom-harboring function again. For this reason, it was persecuted and kept under surveillance. Therefore, in post-war Poland going or not going to church was tantamount respectively to expressing or renouncing ambitions of living in a free Poland.)

Becoming a party member was also the easiest way of achieving the final rank of full professor at a university. If you were not a party member, sometimes you could still become a university professor but at the least you needed to gain the seal of approval from a district Communist Party Secretary (the local boss). To this end, you had to avoid expressing any opinions contradicting those of the Party and obviously avoid having anything to do with the underground opposition.

In those days, the vast majority of Poles, excluding high party officials, lived in one-bedroom, state-owned apartments in residential housing estates, and the right to rent such an apartment very cheaply was done by effectively deducting rent from their wages. A surgeon, a lawyer, a civil engineer, just as a factory worker, were paid about $20 or $30 a month in cash respectively. Each additionally had the right to free medical services, cheap apartment rent (for approximately $2 a week), and free education for their children. In addition to education from kindergarten to university, all clubs for children were in practice free, too, including horseback riding, tennis, ceramics classes, or anything else children might like to do. In fact, these activities were free in a sense only, for these were underpaid parents who jointly provided for them through reduced wages. Under the communist regime, Poland also enjoyed zero unemployment (work was actually compulsory in those days, and the authorities would put an individual in jail for not having a job!), we all traveled throughout the communist block in practically identical cars, Warszawas, Trabants, and Wartburgs, or somewhat later in Fiat 126s or 125s.

We got used to getting by on the little we had, and in exchange we had a clear picture of who was bad, who was neutral, and who was good. To the majority of society, the bad were the party members. The neutrals were the majority of obedient non-party members who did not believe in taking chances by opposing communism, and who lived practically at the same level as lower party members. Finally, the good were the minority of people with a strong desire for a free, independent Poland. Depending on their degree of involvement in opposition movements, they could lose their lives, be imprisoned or "merely" be denied lucrative, managerial position in any walk of life.

Thus, life with "the Berlin wall around us" was pleasantly black and white in moral terms and made those who were not party members, and even more so those involved in opposing the ruling party, feel good about themselves. By ensuring a minimum standard of living for everyone, Poland's Moscow-backed communist party kept the nation from rebelling.

Yet, step by step, the economic system practiced in communism went bankrupt and was soon unable to provide the minimum needed to prevent social unrest. This, combined with the pressure for national freedom and boosted by the election of Karol Wojtyla as Pope, led to the birth of the Solidarity Trade Union. This workers' union, with its strong nationalist aspirations, eventually numbered 10 million people in a country of 40 million, and thus about 90% of the workforce. Naturally, in addition to the good and the neutrals, its sheer size must have ensured that it was infested with collaborators and secret police members.

Although it had agreed to the creation of Solidarity in August 1980, the communist regime tried to regain its former status by imposing Marshal Law in December 1981. However, it failed to win back the position it had once enjoyed. In response, the communists devised a devilish plan. As a result, the communist officials, instead of being kicked out of the government, signed an astounding agreement with the Solidarity leaders, which effectively allowed the communist hierarchy to recast the old communist personal structure in terms of democracy and capitalism. At first glance, this agreement between Solidarity and the communists, signed in Magdalenka near Warsaw and called the "Round Table agreement," gave the impression of a victory for Solidarity, and of being the best possible compromise. At that time, only the most sagacious saw the clandestine deals for what they were—that it was only due to the high ranking solidarity officials with close clandestine connections with the communists that the latter retained the position of co-leader in the country. In fact, the "Round Table agreement" was signed between communists. Consequently, the issue fought for most furiously by subsequent governments (except one) which originated at the Round Table, was that of making sure that communist collaborators could not be exposed and thus prevented from participating in government and benefiting from the national economy. This situation was different from what happened, e.g., in the Czech Republic, or Lithuania, where vetting, a procedure designed to expose collaborators of the former regime, did take place. The only Polish "post Berlin wall" government that attempted to reveal collaborators paid for its efforts by being promptly dissolved by parliament.

Consequently, the transformation from communism to capitalism and democracy in Poland has been accompanied by unimaginable corruption. Poland's national industry has been destroyed, the most efficient factories and plants having been one by one deliberately brought to the point of bankruptcy and then sold for peanuts. The beneficiaries of such moves are former communist directors, who, in the case of smaller factories, have become owners of the factories they once managed as communist party deputies. (There is a joke that while in the communist era it was a common crime to steal a piece of fabric from a factory, nowadays factories themselves get stolen). Former directors of big plants, as well as other prominent politicians, rewarded themselves by assigning themselves positions on the Executive Boards of Directors of companies retained by the government as joint owners. Astounding wages are paid to people from the new system with no professional background. Occasionally, someone is sacrificed, and Polish TV covers corruption trials implicating high ranking politicians the way American TV followed the O. J. Simpson trial. Corruption is one of the most popular topics of press articles, too. Yet, merely talking about it does not curb it in any way.

Former personal connections have fossilized in almost all walks of life. For instance, just as was the case during the communist regime, when a university opening is announced (which, in a literal translation, is still called a "contest"), what is meant is "a position opened for Mr. Smith." One even refers to the opening as "a contest for Mr. Smith" and no other candidate is expected to apply. Communist-era professors now nominate their successes and keep the number of new professorships under a tight lead. This has clear benefits. New private universities need professors on their faculty lists to be allowed to operate. Thus, some of them resort to paying wages to professors simply for keeping their names on the payroll. The professor revealed by the popular Polish newspaper *Gazeta Wyborcza* as holding the record in this light held professorships at 17 institutions of higher learning.

However, it is not only the multimillion dollar FOZ-gates or Lewin-gates that Polish society has lived through vicariously via TV. Groups and individuals suffer from corruption on an everyday basis both as minority groups and as individuals.

One example of a minority group who are victims of the corrupt system are the tenants of private pre-war town houses. A law passed recently bestowed upon citizens the right to buy out the apartment in which they live for about 3% of its market value, provided it is located in buildings built after the Second World War and thus built by the communist regime, or in older buildings if the owner is not to be found. No respective compensation has been offered to people with apartments located in pre-war buildings whose private pre-war owners have regained owner-ship of those buildings. To understand the injustice and why the word "compensation" is in order, some relevant background information must be adumbrated.

As has already been said, Poland was occupied for over a hundred years prior to the end of the First World War (1918). During that time, the bravest Poles who fought the occupants had their lands, palaces, and town houses confiscated. Those estates not overtaken by the aggressors before the outbreak of the First World War, were either confiscated by the communists after the Second World War, or the owners of buildings with more than one apartment had tenants assigned to the remaining apartments against their will and the will of the tenants. These tenants paid government-controlled rent and were selected to live in such houses at random (those who lived in such houses considered themselves unlucky to not get apartments located in new apartment buildings). As was already mentioned earlier, with salaries at that time amounting to USD 20-30 a month, the right to cheap housing was effectively part of a citizen's wages. Money not paid in cash was used to finance, among other things, national industry and all housing projects.

Thus, the tenants who, when the Berlin Wall crumbled, got the right to buy their own apartments for about 3% of their market value, in effect were paid back those wages still owed to them. No similar offer was made to the unlucky ones who lived in pre-war houses and were never paid the wages that would allow them now to buy an apartment on the free market these days.

In some old towns like Cracow, this problem affects about 3% of the entire population, mainly elderly widows living downtown (this amounts to about 25,000 tenants in Cracow) who live in what turned out to be privately-owned houses. Unfortunately, the Polish government, unlike, for example in Lithuania, felt responsible only for the debts and crimes of the previous communist government toward the rich and the influential, e.g., owners of pre-war town houses. The Polish government not only returned these buildings to their previous owners, but did so with no regard for the tenants, allowing owners to impose free rent within four years of the law coming into force. The government did not, however, feel any responsibility for the debts of the communist government owed to the tenants of such houses, whose wages, which were never paid in full, were used not only to maintain and upgrade these very buildings, but also to build all other new government-owned apartment buildings for so many years. In effect, while the communist government stole the houses from their original owners (today, the present government) to pay back the debts of the communist regime, stole them again—this time from the tenants. The government "returned" the buildings, asking their current tenants to foot the bill. The verdict was to please the strongest, the group which is likely to benefit the government, at the expense of the weakest. (The tenants of pre-war buildings have appealed against the decision of the Polish court to the European Court in Strasbourg, yet not many of them will live to see the verdict.)

If the current government cannot pay the debts owed to all those cheated by the communists, at least it should not pay some of those debts using the money of others. A just solution to the problem could be for both landlords and tenants to pay the debts in half (e.g., by maintaining a controlled rent till the end of the lives of current tenants over 60 and 10 years for the remaining ones), or even better to sell government-owned buildings and distribute the money among all the tenants who were assigned their apartments in any type of housing without being asked.

It should also be added that among those who have had their ownership of pre-war town houses restored, there are speculators who bought their houses for peanuts during the Second World War from widows whose husbands died in combat during that conflict (as, for example, in the case of my grandmother whose husband was killed by the Russians at Katyń along with about 15,000 other Polish officers), and who, having lost their incomes and needing to support their children, had to sell their houses at unfair prices. Present day house owners also include some common cheats who have used fabricated documents to prove their ownership (quite a number of such cases have recently been revealed by the media), and unscrupulous profiteers who bought the houses along with the people living in them a few years ago for a fraction of the market value of an empty town house, counting on the government's allowing them to raise rents at will and thus in effect to evict current tenants. Their hopes proved well-grounded.

The owners of private town houses in Poland were allowed to impose a free rent in Poland with four transitional years, while in much richer France the transitional period of controlled rent lasted 50 years. Additionally, current free rents in Poland in relation to average incomes exceed levels imposed by European Union law, but most of these people will die homeless before their case will ever be heard in the Strasbourg Court.

Corruption is also felt on a daily basis by individuals. For instance, for the past four years my neighbors, who turned out to have connections with the past establishment, have prevented me from inhabiting my newly built one-family house. When I bought the plot of land from a real estate agent, I did not suspect that the majority of my neighbors had come into possession of their plots of lands by buying them very cheaply from the city, which acquired the land by dispossessing the previous owners during the communist regime. The privilege of buying that land was given to high administrative clerks in Cracow's municipal offices. To make matters worse, it turned out that one of my neighbors was a Senator, a former Minister of Justice in one of the post "Round Table" governments. The Senator and my neighbors did not wish to have the views from their windows disturbed by the erection of new houses. For four years I kept coming up against a dozen of administrative and judicial "mistakes" preventing me from completing the construction of my house and then from moving into it. For instance, the head geologist of the Voievodship of Cracow issued a half-page statement declaring my plot of land unsuitable for building purposes for geological reasons without ever doing a single field test. His opinion was long considered by various clerks to be more important than two studies, about 60 pages long each, based on excavations carried out by teams of independent experts. Only when I went to court did the supervisor of the head geologist, the departmental head, issue the statement that the opinion concerned the "macro region and not the specific plot of land." Although he did it even before the first court hearing, he also made sure that this opinion never actually reached the court itself but kept circling among offices. The judge, in justifying his ruling temporarily stopping the construction of my house, referred to the opinion of the head geologist. I did not know about the existence of that opinion at the time of the court hearing either; I came across it only three months after the court ruling. Interestingly, the chief geologist of Cracow does not even hold a Ph.D. degree, although Cracow is regarded as the academic center of Poland and boasts the best geological department in the country.

Incidentally, these problems (literally hundreds of them) all started to melt away significantly when the senator failed to get re-elected. Apparently, in view of his advanced age, the chances of his re-election in four years and thus of ever getting back on the political scene are slim.

To cut a long story short, Polish law is being designed to favor the strong. Predominantly dishonest politicians mind their private business only, selling national industry for their private benefit. Politics and business are completely fused. Former communist party-nominated factory directors have in practice been given the factories they used to manage; university professors with communist pedigrees now nominate their successors and protégés; people from the old system still call the shots. Interestingly, Polish army officers educated in Moscow are now building the country's new NATO army. At the same time, there is no legal way for minorities or individuals not implicated in the system to claim their rights because of running up against corruption. Democracy and capitalism in Poland have merely solidified old personal connections and, despite offering much greater access to information, they deprive citizens of the possibility of acting on the information they now have. (Ubiquitous corruption in the so-called transitional economies, has been pointed out as a serious problem, e.g., by Transparency International, the Batory Foundation, and Brussels UE officials.)

On the other hand, the corruption-induced injustice suffered by the majority of Poles these days seems a minor grievance compared to the plight of, for example, Chechens, Palestinians, Kurds, as well as many other minorities and individuals in the world, who also have no legal way of safeguarding their rights. We all condemn terrorism, no question about it, but can we blame the mistreated with no legal way of defending themselves for refusing to support an unjust status quo in the only way they can without blaming ourselves at the same time? So far the

182 / FREEDOM OF INFORMATION

well-to-do beneficiaries of the democratic-system-as-it-is have been defending it furiously with laws which increasingly strengthen their power. The attack of 9-11 has shown that the defenders of such justice cannot feel safe. It is high time we realized that in this age of globalization, not only the terrorists themselves but also all citizens of civilized nations not striving for a more just economic and political system are to blame. We need a system that will allow people to act on the information they have in a law-abiding manner and in accordance with laws that are far more just than those we have at present.

REFERENCES

1. S. T. Kuhn, *The Structure of Scientific Revolution*, The University of Chicago Press, Chicago, 1968.
2. J. Pogonowski, *Matemtyczny Model Alalizy Lingwistycznej* [Mathematical Model of Linguistic Analysis], Adam Mickiewicz University Working Papers, Poznań, 1988.
3. T. Grabinska, *Teoria, Model, Rzeczywistosc* [Theory, Model, Reality], Wydawnictwo Politechniki Wrocławskiej, Wroclaw, 1993.
4. R. Omnes, *Quantum Philosophy: Understanding and Interpreting Contemporary Science*, Princeton University Press, Princeton, New Jersey, 1994.
5. N. Chomsky, *Aspects of the Theory of Syntax*, MIT Press, Cambridge, Massachusetts, 1957.
6. R. Montague, English as a Formal Language, in *Linguaggi nella Societa e nella Technica*, B. Visentini et al. (eds.), Edizioni di Communita, Milan, pp. 184-224, 1970 (reprinted in R. Montague, *Formal Philosphy, Selected Papers*, R. H. Thomason (ed.), Yale University Press, Hartford, Connecticut).
7. R. Crafton, Mapping Language Function in the Brain: A Review of the Recent Literature, *Journal of Technical Writing and Communication*, 30:3, pp. 199-221, 2000.
8. D. Amit, *Modeling Brain Function: The World of Attractor Neural Networks*, Cambridge University Press, Cambridge, 1989.
9. H. Putnam, Mind, Language, and Reality, *Philosophical Papers*, Vol. 2, Cambridge University Press, Cambridge, 1975.
10. M. Brickhard and R. Campbell, Some Foundational Questions Concerning Language Studies, *Journal of Pragmatics*, 17, pp. 472-486, 1992.
11. E. Charniak, *Statistical Language Learning*, Bradford, Cambridge, Massachusetts, 1993.
12. G. Sampson, A Stochastic Approach to Parsing, *Proceedings of the 11th International Conference on Computational Linguistics COLING '86*, pp. 151-156, 1986.
13. U. Furuhashi, *Fuzzy Logic, Neural Networks, and Evolutionary Computation*, Springer, Berlin, 1996.
14. R. Skousen, *Analogical Modeling of Language*, Kluver Academic Publishers, Dortdrecht, Netherlands, 1989.

15. V. V. Nalimov, *Probabilistyczny Model Jezyka* (Polish translation), PWN, Warszawa, 1976.
16. A. Awdiejew, Standardy Semantyczne w gramatyce komunikacyjnej, in *Gramatyka Komunikacyjna*, PWN, Warszawa, 1999.
17. D. Zielinska, A Note on Extended Functional Analysis, *The Journal of Pragmatics, 7,* pp. 841-843, 1997.
18. D. Zielinska, Functional Base and Profile, *Zeszyty Naukowe Uniwersytetu Jagiellonskiego,* Prace Jezykoznawcze, z.120, pp. 281-287, 2000.
19. R. W. Langacker, *Concept, Image, and Symbol: The Cognitive Basis of Grammar,* Mouton de Gruyter, The Hague, 1991.
20. D. Sperber and D. Wilson, *Relevance: Communication and Cognition,* Harvard University Press, Cambridge, Massachusetts, 1986.

CHAPTER 9

Accessible Information and International Business

David Dobrin

FREE FLOW, SURE. THAT'S THE DEFAULT

Scratch a typical business executive, and ask whether September 11 affected the free flow of information worldwide. The answer would be, "Huh?" Yes, there are laws, restrictions, concerns. There were before September 11. There are afterwards. But most information flow in business is utterly unaffected by them.

There are two clear reasons for this. First, it's just not a burning issue in most businesses. And second, even if it were a burning issue, most businesses still wouldn't be able to do much to restrict the flow.

Far from wanting to restrict the flow of information, most businesses want to improve it. In the corporate world, it is an article of faith that too much important information is locked up in what they quaintly call "silos." "If only we knew what we know," runs the plaint—to some extent, a legitimate one.

You hear the complaint most often when people talk about their IT systems. Most such systems are not exactly "open." It takes passwords, training, and a good deal of knowhow before you can get at the useful information that they do have. There is many a minion trolling the darker reaches of IT whose charge is "getting that information out" or "making information more accessible." But the consensus is that what they do isn't adequate.

In some corporations, the same complaint is also voiced about the corporation's expertise or its "corporate knowledge." In some corporations

185

where you hear this complaint, the problem is seen as so pressing, that whole departments have been created and charged with "knowledge management," and a Chief Knowledge Officer (I am not making this up), directs the effort.

Of course this is not the norm. In most corporations, neither getting information out nor keeping information in matters a whole lot. On the whole, there is more concern about the information in IT systems than there is about knowledge.

It may be fair, at this point, for you to wonder who I am, that I speak so breezily and confidently about these issues. Ever since I left the field of technical writing 14 years ago, I have been concerned with corporate IT systems: building them, helping people to use them, and evaluating them. In those 14 years, I have encountered an attempt to address concerns about information flowing overseas exactly once — and this was before September 11. (The company was doing work in computer technology that the government regarded as sensitive and had a large operation in an Asian country. I'll describe how they addressed the issue later in this piece.) By contrast, I am asked almost daily to help with integrating systems or creating processes for making systems information more accessible.

In my experience, most of this effort is futile. Most corporations are not able to put in anything more than pragmatic, common-sense controls on keeping information in. And neither IT departments nor Chief Knowledge Officers have had much luck satisfying the demand for more information. One reason that you don't see very many interesting attempts in either direction is that this sense of the futility of the effort is widespread.

So why are these efforts mostly futile? If it's hard to restrict information flow, shouldn't it be easy to encourage it? Or if it's hard to encourage the flow, why shouldn't it be easy to restrict it?

There are some simple answers to these questions, which I'll try to provide in the rest of this article. But before I do, I'd like to simplify my task by urging you to believe that in reality both problems are the same. Both problems are problems of controlling information. More precisely, the problem in each case is to pick out the information that is relevant to the people who want it and either make it more difficult to get it or less difficult. In both cases, the reason the effort founders is that there isn't any practical way of picking out the relevant information. If you know in advance what information people need, it's relatively simple to make sure that they do or don't get it. It's when you don't know that you've got the problem.

This should be a very, very familiar problem to this audience. Isn't the essence of technical writing the effort of getting the right information in the right way to the user? (I read some other definition somewhere, something about accommodating technology, but the critics have roundly disposed of that one.)

In technical writing, of course, the underlying theoretical framework for addressing this problem is rhetoric. There is a writer, a reader, and something the writer wants to accomplish with the reader. The writer takes advantage of what he or she knows about the reader, what they share in the way of language and knowledge of form, to do most of the work. The successful piece of rhetoric informs or persuades the reader without making them work harder than they want to.

As you'll see, most of the people I encounter in corporations who are charged with these missions would find this way of describing the problem profoundly uncongenial, even peculiar. "Get a writer to help with this? Don't be silly." But as you'll see, it might actually do them some good to learn something about rhetoric.

Controlling the Distribution of Structured Data

People concerned with exerting control over information flow in corporate situations make a strong distinction between structured and unstructured data. They feel they can exert much more control over structured data, because they can set up automatic rules that restrict access, and they can also draw out and distribute what they consider to be relevant information using computer processes. From their point of view, one of the advantages of this is that it is not (apparently) rhetorical. Systems do the work of controlling, and once it's in place, the control is automatic.

The person in charge of doing this at most corporations is the CIO, a person whose background and orientation tends to make him a little boneheaded about communication. (I'm talking about the average here; as always, there are people who are brilliant at it.)

I am most familiar with large corporate management systems, sometimes called ERP systems, which keep track of the money, materials, and people at corporations. To restrict information, these ERP systems usually have a fairly primitive set of security tools. Their strategy is usually to define roles that people have, such as AP (accounts payable) Clerk or Senior Executive or Owner of Budget in a department. Attached to the roles are rules about what information these people can or can't see and what information they can modify.

The packages usually come with a few pre-defined roles, but if you want greater granularity (say AP Clerk, US), you have to define those yourself, and you have to write the rules. So, if you want the AP clerk to be able to look only at suppliers in the US, you'd have to write a little program that filtered the display whenever he/she wanted to look at suppliers. This can get very complicated, very fast; it's very, very easy to cut the person off from vital information by writing the rules in the wrong way or by making some other mistake. (Someone, for instance, could mistakenly assign a key US supplier to the group of European suppliers, and then they'd be gone to the US AP Clerks.) The tendency, therefore, is to use these restriction rules only in a very broad way.

These rules, of course, only work for the system in question. If you've got multiple systems (and everybody does), each with its own role strategies and systems for segregating information, your management problem explodes.

To get around this, there are several strategies. One is to limit access to the systems themselves, but have the systems put out key information in report format. Then, you use the file system to manage access to the reports. This is less granular, but it does allow you to get some information (the right information?) to people without their having to learn the system.

The file system security is also easier to manage. Essentially, it says, "Here is a group of people who can open the file." It doesn't try to go into the file and determine which content is available. And (for the most part), it doesn't try to do anything more than say, "You can open it" or "You can't."

All this is pretty clumsy, and at best, it only provides the kind of security that a white picket fence gives to your prize primroses. It stops clumsy people from treading on the information, but that's about it. Anybody who has access can easily attach the file to an e-mail message and send it out to the entire world, or, if he/she is at all adept, put it on a Web page, so the world can come to it. Even if you don't have access, file systems can be relatively easy to break into, though if a CIO is on his/her toes, they can also be extremely secure.

What about getting the information out? Well, the assumption is that only people inside the group that has security access will want to look at this stuff. If someone else needs access, they ask somebody in the group. If, as many companies do, you use very large groups, because you don't want to close off information, then distribution of information is confronted with a new challenge. There's too much stuff in there. Most of the people in the group wouldn't know where to look even though they do have access.

There are a few technologies, such as portals, that do help out here. But since they basically treat even the structured information I'm talking about as unstructured information, I'll talk them later.

So what is it about structured information that makes it so different from unstructured information in the eyes of most of the people who are responsible for controlling information flow? What is structured data, anyway? Well, if you don't know, you're going to be surprised. Structured data is simply a string of characters that has one or more labels attached to it. Take the address of a customer. It's stored in what's called the Address field on a row of a Customer table, the row being identified by the customer number and customer name. The name of the field, table, and row are all labels that allow you to find that address.

So if you want to find the address of the customer, and you know the customer's name and some details of the programming language used to store this, you can write a little program to find out the address. From the point of view of control, the great advantage of structured information is that you can also write a program that attaches another label to that address field that says, "Only show this to people who are on this list," or, alternatively, send this information as part of a larger report to people who are on that list.

What is truly astonishing to me is that people in IT think this klugey system of labeling is a great way of controlling the flow of information. Believe me, it isn't. What we as technical communicators (or former technical communicators) do routinely, that is, determine what information is relevant to people who want it and present it to them in a way that satisfies their needs simply and easily—oh, my, another definition—is almost impossible for people who are armed only with some skill in programming languages and a list of labels.

No wonder most people think the information is locked up. It is. It's not locked up by the security rules, really. It's locked up by the system itself. The system, you see, does little to pick out the people who might need to know the information, little to highlight the information that's particularly relevant to them, little to tell them the quality of the information, little to answer any follow-up questions, all something that a writer can do a lot about. The system is really best used as a passive device, something that allows people who are skilled in the labels and the programming to ask questions using those tools. But the only people who can do that are the very few who are intimately involved with the data and the tools.

We now can see one reason why that mythical executive says, "Huh." The "vital" corporate information that is stored as structured data is already locked up so tight, de facto, that even the good guys can't get at it. So why worry about the bad guys.

In recent years, the CIO has been pushed by the software companies to buy some new kinds of tools to address this issue. If these tools were widespread and easy to use, they might actually begin to make the CIO worry about whether bad guys can get at some of this data. They include event visibility systems (where people are notified by e-mail when data takes on certain values), analytics systems (which display data in ways that make it easier to troll through it), and workbenches, which bring together information from disparate sources onto a desktop.

All these systems work by making it possible for people who are somewhat less familiar with the systems to get at some subset of the information that might be relevant to them without quite as much work as had been required. All of these, however, work with the core labeling system that I described above, so they are unlikely to make the CIO think of his problem differently and extremely unlikely to give structured information anything like real free flow. The information that people really want may be grabbed by way of their labels and may not be drowned by irrelevant information, but it's very much a hit or miss thing.

The lack of real acceptance in the marketplace of many of these tools suggests that most CIOS think it's miss, as much as hit.

Controlling the Flow of Unstructured Data

From the CIO point of view, unstructured data is simply sits in what are called "blobs" in file systems or databases. Since unstructured data does not have a system of labels identifying any portion of its contents, you can only restrict access to it through the security system, which prevents you from opening the blob unless you have permission and, typically, you can only provide access through syntactic search schemes. The best known of these is Google — yes, they sell a version to people inside corporations — and the faults and virtues of Google are well known.

So what do you do if you are a Chief Knowledge Officer, and you want to make sure that what is known in the company gets out to the people in the company who need it?

There are a number of software packages that can allow you to index all corporate documents (a la Google) and also to organize them in hierarchies (a la Yahoo). You can also make these tools available to external users, who are known and trusted enough to be given a password. Several of the software companies that I cover have set up big pools of documents like this. One even calls it a "knowledge garden."

In many cases, a technology called a portal uses these indexing and hierarchy tools as part of its system for giving access to people in the corporation. A portal is simply a nice-looking desktop Web page with windows in it that display Web pages. They will typically have a search window that searches the indexed documents or displays the hierarchy. Then you can Google into the document.

If you are concerned with restricting flow, you can prevent everyone but the people who are named on a list from getting access to the documents themselves.

Of course, what you get is just as overwhelming and unselective as what you get from public Google or Yahoo. For most corporate users, this mess of porridge is no good at all.

It isn't just that key word search is a very weak tool, that the number of duplicates and irrelevancies is huge, and that few people want to put much effort into something so apparently fruitless. It is also the quality of the documents. Many of them are, for some reason, extremely poorly written. And even the ones that are written well are often addressed to audiences who are not the reader.

There are a lot of things that could be done to make it more likely that what's in the blob suited the audience that was looking for it. One could structure the documents in a way that required them to state what level of audience they were meant for and then allow you to search based on that. They could make it much easier to select documents by date and author. They could, in other words, provide you with the kinds of tools that libraries and bibliographies provide you with. But people who create these tools or are responsible for improving the transfer of knowledge do not, in my experience, appreciate these rhetorical dimensions of the problem.

In my experience, Chief Knowledge Officers don't usually think document access is really all that important to their mission. They know that most people don't read, and they're sure from personal experience that most people can't write. So why waste time on document retrieval.

Their primary thrust depends largely on their theory of why knowledge distribution fails. Some CKOs think that the real problem is that people "hold the information in their heads," so they set up systems for "documenting" what is done. The theory seems to be that if you turn the unstructured document that is the indifferent, but voluntary product of the indifferent writer into a semi-structured document that is coerced from an unwilling writer, the amount of communication will improve.

What is startling about all this, when you see it in action, is how tone-deaf from a rhetorical point of view, these semi-structured documents are. They might have a required "summary" of the document that is supposed to be for executives, but nobody bothers to teach the writer what an executive summary ought or ought not to contain, so the end product is what you might expect. If they even said, "In this section, tell people who are paying for this project what they spent their money on," they would do better, but of course they don't.

Their solution to this problem is to keep on breaking the document up into more and more independent pieces and to assign rules for constructing each separate segment. But giving the documents more structure is still only assigning labels to the content; these strategies simply try to make unstructured data aspire to the condition of structured data. And having people write rules that apply generically is as effective as telling students that the rule for good writing is to write five paragraph argumentative essays.

The other strategy that people use is to allow the experts to keep the knowledge in their heads, but give other people more access to them. I think this is probably the most effective way of encouraging greater distribution of knowledge. Technologies that people use include various versions of chat rooms, allowing people to create and maintain their own Intranet Web sites, publishing descriptions of what people are working on, etc., etc.

Do CKOs recognize that technologies like these make it very difficult to restrict the free flow of information across a corporation? I think so. But again, I don't think they care very much. They, like the CIO, are in a situation where the current system restricts information so much that restricting it further is supererogatory. Here the reasons for the restriction are less clear to people and more fundamental. They include people's natural disinclination to write things down, their inability to appreciate the needs of the people they need to communicate with, their inarticulateness, and, let us admit it, people's natural distrust of any document even as long as this article, most of which are so leaden, pompous, and uninformative that they deter reading the way an electric fence deters a sheep.

Buried under a mountain of leaden and irrelevant corporate information, they are just trying to dig themselves out any way they can. They have my sympathies.

Huh?

But what about the bad guys? Is "Huh?" really a good reaction when there really are bad guys out there who really do want things that corporations are only too ready, it seems, to give them?

I think so. You see, relevant corporate information is just as creaky, incomprehensible, and irrelevant for them as it is for us. Yes, there are jewels in the corporate information mine, but the bad guys need the same giant sluice to pull them out that the good guys do.

Until people do write better and more inclusively, bringing the information that is most likely to be useful to a wide audience to the prominence that it should have, it is unlikely that this will change. Yes, I believe, that's right. We are protected by our own inability to write.

Many technical communication teachers that I know feel frustrated that they have had so little effect on so many students and (ironically) even more frustrated at how many other students never even passed through their hands. Perhaps these words will give them comfort. If they had been more effective, maybe they would have unwittingly been giving aid and comfort to the enemy.

Contributors

MICHAEL BEN-CHAIM specializes in history and social studies of science. His recent work is *Experimental Philosophy and the Birth of Empirical Science. Boyle, Locke, and Newton* (Ashgate Publishing, 2004). He has recently immigrated from Israel to the United States, and now teaches at the University of Massachusetts.

GEORGE BOHRER, JR., is professor and chair of the Communications Media department at Fitchburg State College, where he has taught communication law for 20 years. He has a Ph.D. in communication studies from the University of Massachusetts at Amherst. His research interests include communication law, political communication, and film studies.

ROBERT I. CARR, III, is an assistant professor in the Communications Media Department at Fitchburg State College, where he teaches professional communication and communication theory. His research interests include studies of the relationship between communication technologies and practices at the intersection of our physical and virtual realities, particularly as a means to gaining insight into our evolving collective intelligence.

DAVID DOBRIN is a recognized expert on ERP, supply chain, and collaboration applications. Before founding B2B Analysts, he was Chief Business Architect at Benchmarking Partners. While at Benchmarking Partners he helped companies develop coherent and workable application strategies, and also sat on the original CFAR committee, where he helped develop what became the CPFR standard. David learned about enterprise applications when he worked in R&D at QAD, Inc. and later implemented ERP applications all over the world. David's column on global issues "Passport" appears regularly in CIO.

JOHN CHETRO-SZIVOS is an assistant professor of Communications Media at Fitchburg State College in Fitchburg, Massachusetts. He has conducted research in the area of intercultural communication, and has served as a consultant or worked with managers and leaders throughout Europe, the Middle East, and Central America. He holds a

Doctorate degree in Communication and a Master's Degree in Business Administration.

JAMES POON TENG FATT is a lecturer in English and Communication at the Nanyang Technological University. He has conducted technical communication seminars for engineers and technical managers in East Asia and Singapore. He was also a consultant editor for the *Singapore Business Executives Journal* and an editorial member of the *ENDEC Journal of Enterprising Culture*. Furthermore, he is an editorial advisor for *SABRE Centre's Research Papers* and is currently a member of the review panel for the *International Entrepreneurship and Innovation Management (IJEIM)* special issue. Professor Poon is also a competent toastmaster and writer of many local and international journal articles.

CHARLES H. SIDES is a professor and directs the internship program for the Department of Communications Media at Fitchburg State College. A recognized scholar, he has published seven books and over two dozen articles concerning a wide range of technical and professional communication issues. He serves as executive editor of the *Journal of Technical Writing and Communication*, the leading international scholarly journal in its field, and editor of the prestigious *Baywood's Technical Communications Series*. An active consultant to defense, high-tech, and publications industries, he has worked with clients across the United States, as well as in the Middle East and Far East.

FUMIKO YOSHIMURA is an associate professor at Kyushu Institute of Information Sciences. She received her M.A. degree in linguistics from Ohio University. Her research interests and previous publications have been in the fields of: 1) reading and writing processes; 2) text comprehension; and 3) language teaching.

DOROTA ZIELINSKA, of the Jagiellonian University, Poland, is a linguist interested in the practice and theory of natural language communication. Since in addition to her language-related background she holds Master's degrees in Physics (she was involved in Fermi Lab experiments), her interest in language takes the perspective of the theory of models of empirical sciences. These interests, combined with degrees in technical and professional communication, provide a unique perspective on international communications.

Index